OFF

22

Bui

Building Libraries for the 21st Century

Building Libraries for the 21st Century

The Shape of Information

Edited by
T. D. WEBB

McFarland & Company, Inc., Publishers
Jefferson, North Carolina, and London

Library of Congress Cataloguing-in-Publication Data

Building libraries for the 21st century : the shape of information /
edited by T. D. Webb.
p.   cm.
Includes bibliographical references and index.
ISBN 0-7864-0665-8 (library binding : 50# and 70# alkaline papers) ∞
1. Library architecture — History — 20th century.   I. Webb, Terry.
II. Title: Building libraries for the twenty-first century.
Z679.B945   2000   022'.3'0904 — dc21   99-39093 CIP

British Library Cataloguing-in-Publication data are available

Manufactured in the United States of America

*McFarland & Company, Inc., Publishers
Box 611, Jefferson, North Carolina 28640
www.mcfarlandpub.com*

Acknowledgment

I am, of course, most indebted for the existence of this study to each and every contributor and translator, whose very admirable work was produced with no small sacrifice of their time and energy. I am just as grateful to Mr. Bin Zhang and Ms. Alva Kodama of Kapiolani Library for their technical assistance with the electronic texts. And without the encouragement of my wife, Mei Mee, and her translations and delightful company on travels related to this international project, it would not have been completed.

Contents

Preface

Welcome to the 21st century. We have actually been living in it for quite some time already. There have not been any sudden differences because the social, economic, and political movements that will carry the world in the new millennium have already been in motion for years.

Celebrating a new year, a new century, or a new millennium is a symbolic observance, a marking of time to measure progress and consider the possibilities of the future. Nothing necessarily closes or opens at the end of a calendar year. The real points of closure and departure in the passage of time are set by events, new ideas, fresh articulations of human needs, and innovative responses to them, whether they be philosophical, political, social, or technological.

The same is true for librarianship as well. Most of the libraries now in existence are 21st-century libraries. They will not disappear soon. But librarianship has been changing, and not simply because of new technologies. Ideas, perceptions, aspirations, and technologies weave themselves together in the larger fabric of civilization. And as librarianship has changed in response to society's new ideas and expectations, the new libraries being constructed to embody those changes are the prototypes that other libraries can study and learn from.

This book is about a few of those prototypes. But it is not a "how-to" designed to help librarians build new libraries. Its chapters do contain a wealth of insightful information about the library construction process, which itself becomes more complicated every day with the coming of new technologies. The process of designing and building new libraries is even further complicated by the perplexing lack of consensus in the library profession on what libraries in the digital age should look like, what services they should provide, and whether they will even exist. It is possible that the library profession has never been as divided and many-headed as it now appears to be. That no doubt is because few professions have been as profoundly affected by the changes in knowledge and information delivery as are we, the knowledge and information specialists. So profoundly are we affected that some within our own profession are stating that the technological advances will "advance" us right out of our livelihoods.

But I chose not to obtain contributions from advocates of wholly electronic, paperless libraries because I did not intend for this book to take the form of a debate. Instead, it is like a collection of position papers. The contributors are called on to clarify their positions, and justify the recent surge in library construction. Readers can then examine the accounts, and make their own evaluations.

So, instead of attempting to explain how to succeed in the bewildering process of designing and constructing a new library facility, this book presents the assembled construction experiences of the contributors as a lens through which one might see the directions that libraries and librarianship are likely to take at least for the foreseeable future, and perhaps well into the next decade and beyond.

To achieve this vision, the contributors were instructed to write whatever they wanted about their building experience. The resulting presentations cover everything from technology to management, architecture to library instruction, building materials to symbolism, and much more. Through this process of natural selection, I hoped to find a conformity of thinking among these builder-librarians that might be a guide to all of us as we enter what some think could be a New Enlightenment fostered by the new ways of information and knowledge handling.

I am deeply grateful to each of the contributors and translators, of course, for managing their time and energy so that we can read about their experiences. The project design I had in mind required that no constraints be placed on the contributors. And as the chapters show, they chose the features of their separate experiences that were the most important to them. This makes their words all the more instructive to us readers. The sought-for conformity of thought also emerges in several areas, despite the diversity of architectural forms it takes in the different locations.

With all the new libraries being built in the United States and around the world at the turn of the century, so many contributors could have been invited to participate that it was necessary to make a comparatively spare selection. I am solely responsible for the selection.

From the beginning of the project, I knew it was essential that the selection of libraries be international. For one thing, the technology that is transforming the means of information delivery and refashioning the agencies that conduct the delivery has already and quite suddenly achieved a global presence. In a way, the new technology with its global accessibility has become a great equalizer, and has reset clocks and calendars to zero. Measures of library greatness that served us well in the past, such as size and reputation, are not necessarily relevant to the new technology. With respect to the new information delivery methods, we all find ourselves in developing nations.

Moreover, I have found that librarians are eager to share ideas, discoveries, and ventures with each other internationally. This is surely a time to learn from each other. And also, the technology is opening local information and knowledge resources, users and missions to a global stage, while integrating international resources, services and expertise into the local scene.

I believed it was also necessary to include the perspective of the architects who designed some of these new libraries. Architects bring the idea of a library into reality by applying their considerable artistry, science, and ingenuity. But their own ideas, and especially their personal feelings about libraries, are just as significant in the building process as their technical skills, and are just as prominently displayed in the final product as are the intentions of librarians.

Because this is not a "how-to" book, it is interpretive rather than evaluative. For my part in the study, I attempt to draw out certain issues, matters, and threads of logic that relate to my own experience in library administration and construction, or that seem to me to open a view of the meaning underlying the building projects and their portents for librarianship. I realize that just now there is no shortage of other persons in the profession attempting to do the same thing. I only hope that the method I have chosen, and the information that I have assembled from these esteemed contributors, will provide some singular insight and enjoyment.

T.D. Webb
Summer 1999

Introduction: Functions and Forms

A few decades ago, George Kubler wrote an insightful and wonderful book entitled *The Shape of Time*. In it, he observed that every object made by a human, whether the object be art or tool, script or edifice, is created as a possible solution to a problem, need, or requirement, and that a thing thus made crystallizes the prevailing attitudes and abilities of the moment of its creation. As such, an object gives a shape to its time, in a sense, and when a group of objects with a common origin are taken together, "A visible portrait of the collective identity, whether tribe, class, or nation, comes into being. This self-image reflected in things is a guide and a point of reference to the group for the future" (9).

I believe Kubler's ideas to be reasonable, and the present book owes a great deal to him as it examines a set of objects — libraries — and tries to find in them a point of reference to guide a collective identity, in this case a profession, into the future. For despite calls for electronic, virtual, digital libraries without walls, librarians and architects are still busy building the walled variety, some of them more vast in size and mission than any library previously attempted. The explanation for this contradiction may lie simply in the fact that the amount of knowledge in electronic formats has not yet reached the critical mass necessary to carry learning forward without further reference to printed collections, and we are simply in the middle of a transition period. If this is true, some of the new libraries in this book may be the last extravagance of a disintegrating discipline, a grandiose expiration on the brink of a new century. Or it may be that as a diverse society we prefer the redundancy of varied information formats — print and electronic. Such luxury is not likely to endure for long, however. Or it may be that a library stands for something more than just a repository of information and knowledge, and epitomizes a higher aspiration that is fundamental to civilization and its persistence.

To apply Kubler's terms, the libraries being built now are attempts to solve problems that go beyond the mere technical requirements of construction. This book looks at some of these new libraries, but the book is not so much about their construction as it is about the thinking behind the construction. Around the world, among nations that are at different points along the technological spectrum, library construction is moving in similar directions and exhibits common bases in thought. The purpose of the book is to present these common thoughts as they manifest themselves in the new libraries of this decade, and articulate what they might portend for libraries and librarianship of the future.

Kubler said that on rare, unpredictable occasions, there appears a "prime object" (39) which, like a prime number, is not reducible beyond itself. That is, a prime object is not a derivation of other influences. Like masterpieces and scientific breakthroughs, prime objects are original entities. They are seminal inventions that provide a new and original solution to the problem at hand, and inspire replicas, reiterations, styles, and tempers for a considerable period after their appearance. Perhaps there is a prime object among the libraries represented in this collection, an innovation to guide us into the future of librarianship.

Architecture: Form Contra Function

Form, significance, function and style seem always to have been components of artistic expression. Form is no more than the shape of an object, but to be artistic, the shape must be pleasingly rendered. Significance is the meaning or symbolism of the art work, the element that tells the story or conveys a discursive message, perhaps one that arouses strong emotions in the viewer. Formalists, however, contend that a beautiful form alone, even without significance, can be sufficient to stimulate a special, "aesthetic" appreciation in the viewer, an empathy that is intuitive rather than discursive. Function is the social action that the art piece is intended to provoke or facilitate, although sometimes communicating the significance itself is the sole function. Style resides in the manner in which the compositional techniques of line, color, tone, lighting, subject matter, etc. are held constant amid other variations within a specific set of art works so as to become characteristic of the set. Style can be found on the level of an individual artist, a movement, a nation, or an entire era.

Architecture is a curious art, however, because while it exhibits all the artistic components, it must be more functional than other art forms have to be in order for them to be called art. In architecture, there normally is not the same separation of art from utility, of form from functionality, that has progressively developed in the other arts over the centuries. In architecture, as in engineering and other areas of practical design, it is said that form follows function, which to a formalist like myself can only sound like a contradiction in terms. It is the architect's peculiar artistry not to aspire to the purely aesthetic, the pure appreciation of form, but rather to make the functional also beautiful and appealing in form, almost after the fact.

In another sense, architecture could be considered the grandest of arts because of its monumental scale. The spaces to be contained and the massive building materials are aesthetic elements that allow for the greatest degree of expressive arrangement and treatment simply because of their hugeness. Distinctive trends, movements, styles, and even schools of architecture have arisen over such consciousness of the architect's large-scale materials.

Yet the need for functionality remains, like a kind of gravity, always pulling the architect back down toward practical concerns, preventing complete escape into the plasticity of pure form. For some structures, utility is so paramount that pleasing form has been almost entirely dismissed as unnecessary. And so service stations, movie theaters, supermarkets, firehouses, and many other commonplace buildings have come to a state of finality in their design. Hardly inspiring, they have been reduced to formulas. They embody the converse of the formalist position: preeminence of function and significance in a construction virtually devoid of pleasing form.

This is certainly not the case with libraries. Despite their exceedingly long history, no one has developed a universally acceptable formula for designing a library. And yet certain space elements are necessary in any library design — circulation areas, reading areas, stack areas, processing areas — and their spatial relationships to each other almost seem to be matters of common sense. Perhaps library design is really only a matter of interior space arrangement, and any shell of a building could become a very functionally effective library. The library at Kapiolani College, for instance, was assigned a predetermined external form, and the library at California State University, Monterey Bay was installed in the existing military buildings left over from the Fort Ord site. The new Phoenix Public Library, on the other hand, was specifically designed to be like a big box at the determined request of the city librarian. Not surprisingly, other new libraries in this book also conform to that shape. And according to David Kaser, "the most efficient shape for library operations … is almost always a simple rectangle" (300).

But without some engaging internal unity, or some decorative relief, we would find even highly functional or minimal architecture to be stark and barely tolerable. We crave visual interest. And indeed the Kapiolani Library, the Phoenix Public Library and the rest have their internal coherence and remarkable eye-catching treatments. Perhaps the origin of the architectural arts — and perhaps of all art — can be found in a human desire to escape visual tedium, or to infuse in human creation the diversity and visual interest inherent in nature.

Moreover, there seems to be a persistent need to express library significance that exceeds the desire for pure functionality in library design. Even in the contemporary era, there remains much more to library form than mere function.

Library Function and Form

The "function" that any architectural form is supposed to follow is determined, of course, by the activities to be performed in the finished building. The activities, in turn, derive from the mission of the organization that occupies the building. While it is true that some avant-garde architects have emphasized form at the expense of functionality, it is still the point that a house is a residence, a church is for worship, and an office building is for conducting business. In a sense, architecture is like a folk art in which the art objects, though decorated and beautified, are nonetheless initiated for utilitarian purposes.

The function of libraries is to make knowledge and information accessible, and so those who design their form must take this into account. And since the formats of knowledge and information have changed and increased in number so much in just the last two decades, this book will see if the architectural form of new libraries is somehow fundamentally altered by these changes in information. The book ventures one step farther, however, and assumes also that whatever their form, the new library buildings reflect the nature of our profession as it will be in the next century. For it is one thing to generate article after article in library journals that proclaim the direction our buildings and profession should take. It is quite another thing to amass the public confidence and treasury to cast those philosophical positions into permanent, multimillion-dollar edifices. And public sentiment for funding support may not change quite as rapidly as technology.

In addition, the social stature of certain types of buildings always seems to demand more concern with form and significance, and less with formula. For instance, state capitols, churches, university buildings, especially those donated by a generous benefactor, and other noble subjects provoke the architect more toward artistic inspiration. Library building projects seem especially to invite architects to grand design, even at this time when electronic information can be widely spread without the intervention of librarians and independent of customary library functions and facilities. According to some, pleasing form may be as unnecessary for future libraries as it is now for service stations, and future library design may be reduced to mere architectural formula, or even to a virtual existence in hyperspace.

Library Significance

The architects of the buildings in this book are not out of touch with reality or with the changing nature of information delivery. Their continuing predisposition to grandness in library design is deliberate, and exists precisely because of the library's long and noble history. Reverence for libraries has to do with what I have elsewhere called "symbolic librarianship" (Webb, *Public*, 222–23). By that I mean that the library has assumed the stature of a social institution, a cultural shrine, and a symbolic form because of society's respect for knowledge and the services to knowledge seekers that libraries render. So prevalent are the respectful attitudes toward libraries that they are present among library users and non-users alike (see *Buildings* in Works Cited). Those prevailing attitudes are actually society's expectations for libraries, and have become a set of myths about librarianship and knowledge. In these mythic expectations, the library stands for the preeminence of order and rationality in society; for the knowableness of the universe; and for the ability of society, as represented by libraries, to accommodate all knowledge, even knowledge as yet undiscovered.

Library users often assume the library to be a repository of all information. Whether or not they eventually find what they need, users come to the library with the attitude that it holds, or at least can hold, all answers to all questions. In this respect, a large part of the practice of librarianship is not determined by any professional or scholarly discipline, but by those myths about what knowledge is, what it can do, and how it is best stored and acquired. The chapters in this book are replete with the mythic significance of libraries; the myths are built into the new library facilities right along with the conduits, the mortar, and the foundation.

Symbolic librarianship takes the position that librarians must be aware of and manage the symbolism of libraries. In this era of doubt about the longevity of libraries, our future depends on rendering services and utilizing the new technologies in innovative ways so that society's mythic respect for libraries will not be discarded or replaced the way so many other symbol systems have been abandoned even before they outlived their usefulness.

The End of Libraries?

There are voices, even some within the profession, proclaiming the end of libraries. The library community in general, however, not to mention architects and planners, is evidently unconvinced by the "library without walls" concept, because we are still building libraries, some of them massive. Nevertheless, the pervasive calls for paperless, electronic, and virtual libraries would seem to herald a new design phase for libraries. The case studies in this book will show whether information technology is really transforming the design of libraries, or whether the technology is being subsumed in more traditional library services.

An especially large number of new, grand libraries have been built in the 1990s around the world. And because this comes on the very threshold of the virtual library, the proliferation of great library building projects provides a rich opportunity to study the contradiction. An examination of notable new library buildings and the thought that went into them should help us see the future of libraries and perhaps, by extension, the societies that will use them.

The Present Book

The idea for this book arose during the four years I spent planning and constructing a library facility that integrates several information and media technologies into a single system. The planning team had to contend with perplexing issues that emerged in the process of designing and building a new library and what those issues portend for librarianship. Grappling with the problems and professional implications of building a library for the 21st century developed into the notion that the practice and even the philosophy of librarianship are either being reinforced or transformed as librarians adapt to new technologies, societal change, increased user expectations, and numerous other social, economic, and professional conditions, and then encase them in new, rational spaces. It followed that the design of new library facilities may provide the clearest indicators of any substantive changes in the practical and philosophical currents of professional librarianship.

This book explores the reasons for the paradox of building new libraries in the dawn of the virtual library era by examining several new library facilities to see how modern expectations for libraries are being translated into concrete, steel, and space. Each chapter covers a different library, and was written by a librarian who actually worked on the project. Chapters were also obtained from professionals in other fields who had critical roles and special insight into library design and construction. Contributors were asked to write on design and building concerns that were particularly relevant to their libraries: philosophy, technology, construction, architecture, budget, administrative issues, or any other concern they faced in the process of planning, building, and providing services in their new facilities. Each chapter, therefore, presents a unique and candid selection of issues, constraints and opportunities encountered, so that readers can gain a good understanding of the intentions, decisions, outcomes and compromises involved in building libraries for the next century.

The views expressed in these chapters about library purpose, user needs, library cooperation, information vs. knowledge, access vs. ownership, funding, technology, etc., and the incorporation of these views in a new library, have enormous implications for facility planning because they affect space allocation, equipment placement, staffing patterns, mission, and even traffic within the building. Such views also may clear the way for our collective future.

The contributors were invited to use this writing project about the process of planning and providing services in their new facilities as an opportunity to share their experiences and philosophies with the library community. They were asked not to exclude discussion of pertinent circumstances that might have been unique to their respective building projects; for example, abundant funding, spectacular location, special mission, or pre-determined shape of the building. I hope that those who read this book will clearly see from this that their own library planning must be accomplished within the broader context of their specific management circumstances.

From the practical-professional dialectic of the compromises inherent in building a new library in this high-tech age, a set of common values and projections about the future of librarianship will emerge. Since libraries are the artifacts of the library profession, the shapes of our time, an examination of the libraries constructed to take the profession into the future should provide good insight into what is and is not occurring in librarianship.

The libraries selected include public and academic libraries of varying sizes from around the world. Because large libraries are often the first to acquire and develop new methods, practices and technologies that later reach the profession at large, they are more numerous here. On the other hand, because large libraries, like other large organizations, are hard to re-direct, smaller libraries often can adapt to new methods more effectively, more cheaply, and more quickly. So smaller libraries are included as well.

The book documents the convergence of modern, computer-age librarianship and architecture by providing in-depth treatments of actual efforts to bring the library of the 21st century into being from the ground up. The book includes a variety of viewpoints, and I have tried to provide a unifying commentary to dig at the professional issues behind various designs. Through detailed treatments of professional considerations that affected outcomes of the construction, each in-depth case study is a separate voice on the library planning/building process. These voices together say what well may happen to libraries in the near future. Perhaps "libraries for the 21st century" is after all a near-contradiction in terms, like "form follows function." The chapters in this book should make clear whether this is true or not.

The chapters are grouped into four units. The first unit is called Function, and includes chapters that emphasize the mission or purpose of certain library building projects, and chapters that concern the people of librarianship — library users and staff, governing bodies, and the general public. The second unit is called Form, and includes chapters that deal more with the construction itself, especially the physical layout and arrangement of library services within a spatial enclosure. The third unit is Style, and examines library projects from the perspective of librarians who work on the projects and the architects who designed the buildings. The last unit is Significance. It focuses on the meanings conveyed by the libraries beyond the knowledge and information contained in the materials gathered and organized within their walls.

Although I have grouped the chapters into these units, all the contributors speak to one extent or another about function, form, style, and symbolism. That they all do so, without instruction from me, shows that their new libraries are intended to be more than examples of an architectural formula. They are intended not only to be rational embodiments of a functioning profession, but also artistic and symbolic expressions in their form and presentation.

Unit 1
FUNCTION
Mission, People, and Places

Unit Background

In December 1996, within the space of a few days, the official openings of the new, sparkling white Shanghai Library and the magnificent new Mitterrand Library of the Bibliothèque Nationale de France in Paris took place, and administrators began to move into their offices in the bold new British Library in London after thirty years of stop-and-go planning. The completion of these monumental edifices capped a building spree that within a few short years saw four massive public libraries completed and at least a dozen large ARL library building projects underway in the United States alone, not to mention the numerous library construction projects abroad, some of which are described in this book (see Michalak, 95).

Library literature is packed with reasons why this construction should not be happening: technology is making the need for library buildings questionable at best; print is obsolete; from their homes and offices, our users will go online to personal information providers for direct information access; the role of librarians has become unclear, and we had better carve ourselves a new niche, or we will become simply curators of old books.

Yet the construction continues. And as the arguments against it become common and shopworn, other voices are rising to reassert the library's primacy as a preserver of accumulated knowledge, as an information provider, and as a social institution. This reasoning generally contains certain themes: the continued relevance of library mission; providing service to the information have-nots; access vs. ownership of information resources; the need for facility and organizational flexibility to meet an uncertain and changing future; the opportunities to be gained by partnering with other agencies; and the sense of place that a library gives its users. The builders of new libraries are of course of this persuasion; they are literally attempting to shore-up the library profession with their edifices. In so doing, they are trying to temper the technology-rampant arguments by subsuming them under the library's larger purposes.

This book examines the position of the builder-librarians to see if their new

13

facilities do in fact tame raging technology and embody an efficient, justifiable, and workable vision for librarianship that can carry us forward and into the next century. The four chapters in this unit illustrate how some new libraries have attempted to address these concerns in their facilities.

The Persistence of Mission

In Phoenix, there is a little park on Washington Street where the city's Carnegie library was built in 1908. That library was vacated when a new, much larger library was built in 1952, featuring air conditioning, elevators, and other new building technologies. Now the 1952 library has been demolished because the new Central Library was completed in 1995 at a location only a few blocks away, but still within view, and incorporating a variety of new information as well as construction technologies (see Unit 3).

The last time I drove down Washington Street and saw the Phoenix Carnegie was in the early 1980s. Round, with an Ionic portico, it was no longer used as a library. It served some function or another for the city's parks department. In fact, the park was more heavily used than the building, mostly by homeless persons seeking shelter from the heat by camping under the trees. The "Carnegie Public Library" carved in the frieze above the front steps was still visible, but some city parks worker with a compulsion for correctness had painted out the "Library" with black paint, and daubed "Park" instead.

That image alone convinces me that libraries have in fact changed considerably during this century in their scope, sophistication, and size. These quantitative changes are of such dimension as to become qualitative. The changes have been in reaction to concomitant change in the needs of the public, change in the sheer abundance of information, change in scientific inquiry and in technology, and change in the publishing industry, too. In other words, the library as a social institution has a proven history of successful adaptation; and so far, it has incorporated change without relinquishing its mission.

Sarah Michalak states, "In the current climate of almost ceaseless change, it is important to note how little has changed in the academic library's fundamental role and mission" (96). And although she speaks from academe, the services she cites as elemental in the continuing purposes of academic libraries fit other library types also:

- Provide access to materials from their own collections and from other libraries as well;
- Organize collections for easy access to information;
- Preserve knowledge in collections for future generations;
- Provide reference and information services to users;
- Maintain a safe and comfortable space for users and staff;
- Operate a highly functional organization dedicated to meeting user needs [96–97].

The building projects of the libraries in this unit certainly attest to the continued relevance of conventional library mission statements. For the British Library, in fact (see chapter 1 of this Unit), the building was that institution's first "scientific purpose-built home," according to the Minister for the Arts, Richard Luce (quoted in Nelson, M., 11). But as Jane Carr states in chapter 1, the new location and new facility did *not* come with a new purpose attached. Similarly, Wu Jianzhong's chapter on the Shanghai Library specifically addresses his library's continuing mission to provide reference services and to be a sort of people's university, one of the most resilient planks in the social platform of the public library (see chapter 2 of this Unit).

Yet the chapters of Unit 1 demonstrate also that the methods for achieving a library's mission are more complex now, and more numerous than we once thought, and that flexibility is now a very necessary and an advantageous part of mission implementation. The managers of these new facilities articulate their conventional missions more expansively than before, and have assembled more diverse means to implement them. Wu, for one, exuberantly describes a variety of such innovations built into the new Shanghai Library, including televised information delivery, a reading café, ATMs, and other novel user services. There is also an ambitious plan to digitize portions of the library's collections. And the new library will feature open stacks for much of the collection to make the materials more available to the public. As other chapters in this book describe, some of these same features appear in other libraries around the world, and this attests to the effect of modern communication and even travel technologies on international librarianship and library planning.

Organizational Resilience

A flexible mission requires a resilient organization to absorb the expansion. The chapters in Unit 1 and throughout the book indicate that redepartmentation or even major reorganization may be necessary components of new library construction, one that should be part of the planning but is often overlooked. Planning new spaces requires the re-evaluation of departmental boundaries, staffing patterns, professional skills, security, and a host of other concerns, some of which are hard to predict. In a survey of recently opened libraries, Peter Wiley found that "Invariably, the new buildings require more staff, larger training budgets, and greater investment in the purchase and maintenance of electronic equipment" (113).

For instance, in preparation for the opening of its new facility, the staff of the San Antonio Public Library built a "wow factor" into their planning, and increased the number of public services staff, expecting huge crowds to see the building designed by Ricardo Legorreta, a renowned Mexican architect (Wiley, 110). This was a shrewd move, but even so, as Craig Zapatos describes in chapter 3, they could not have anticipated the patron response. The daily usage rose 275 percent, from 800 to 3,000, after the opening. Increases of this magnitude impact every library function, from circulation and reshelving to reference and automation, to air conditioning and security.

Zhu Qiang of the library at the prestigious Beijing University would probably concur (see chapter 4 of this Unit). His chapter describes the library's plans to handle a number of management problems, including those that arise in the linking of two facilities, and the management adaptations that must be made when adding something new to something old. The Beijing University Library expects to reorganize its staff and services to adjust to the new technologies and to an anticipated increase in the demand for their services from all over China as well as the world.

The British Library, because it consolidates in one place over a dozen operations previously conducted in various locations around London, likewise is establishing synthesis. But in so doing, as Carr's chapter explains, the new building is essential to the fulfillment of the British Library's role as the national library. It provides not only a suitable place to store and access the collections, but "a visual manifestation of the knowledge and history" the building contains.

Partnering

As libraries march toward the next century, we are finding that the establishment of partnerships with outside agencies is a natural correlative to the traditional mission of a library, and may bring considerable benefits. The Beijing University Library's undertaking of an information clearinghouse role in the humanities, social sciences, science and technology for all university libraries in China will propel the Beijing University Library into a new position of leadership and unprecedented interlibrary cooperation there.

One of the most intriguing aspects of the Shanghai Library chapter is the consolidation of the Library with the Institute of Scientific and Technical Information of Shanghai (ISTIS). The merging of these two entities that were in many ways quite similar, but in many ways also quite different, constitutes a unique venture into partnering on a scale formerly unknown in China, and perhaps in the world. It sets an ambitious example, however, and Wu provides some enlightening details of the advantages and difficulties that can come of such a merger.

Partnership is one of 12 "revolutions" that James Neal says will shape the future of library organization and service delivery (76). Of course, partnering includes even greater cooperation between libraries, as in the case of the Beijing University Library, but more importantly, it means partnerships with agencies outside the library that have something to offer and something to gain from cooperating with a library, such as occurred in Shanghai.

Although it is not a new library (and so is not included in this study), the Carnegie Library of Pittsburgh (CPL) has embarked on a type of interlibrary partnership that seems a natural outgrowth of 1) the increasing involvement of libraries in information technology, and 2) the lack of certain important types of information on the Internet, despite the glut of other types of data there. CPL addressed the glaring lack of local and community information on the Net by forming the Electronic Information Network (EIN) with the other public libraries of Pennsylvania's Allegheny County. Eschewing any appearance of becoming a digital or electronic library, however, CPL instead expects the project to bolster its more traditional services while providing its users with a much needed collection of materials online. Because of the dearth of online local information that could help build a county-wide sense of community, CPL staff "learned that libraries must become the publishers, editors, and distributors of local culture and local information to the world" (Hubbard *et al.*, 45).

The need for local information is becoming so apparent that some online information providers are already working with libraries to publish local community information on the Internet (St. Lifer and Rogers, "Online," 12–13). Similarly, discussions of the possibility even of establishing partnerships between libraries and publishers is increasing. Panel members at the 1996 Finding Common Ground conference, for instance, floated suggestions of joint ventures, possibly involving electronic publishing, between libraries and publishers (see McKinzie, 366). James Neal predicts that libraries will produce "vast amounts of digital information" (76), and the Benton report on libraries in the digital age found that some library leaders also expect libraries to "create, publish, and manipulate information" in digital formats (*Buildings*, 9, 14), largely resulting from cooperation with other agencies.

Some libraries, on the other hand, are bypassing conventional publishers altogether and partnering with faculty, researchers, professionals, business firms and government agencies directly to collect and electronically publish information that either is not available or not widely accessible through conventional publication channels. For instance, the Cornell University law library is electronically publishing the actions of the World Court; the University of Ulster library is digitizing previously unpublished documents about the conflict in Northern Ireland on its Website to support conflict resolution studies internationally; and the Kapiolani College library is publishing curricular materials, such as course syllabi and bibliographies, in a variety of Asian and Pacific subjects to support the College's mission (Webb, "After").

These developments are highly relevant to the current study, partly because of their implications for future services and products that will be expected of all libraries, but also because funding for such innovative initiatives seems to be readily available. For instance, CPL received several million dollars for its project, and the Kapiolani Library received nearly $20,000 from its various projects, enough to finance the equipment and software to launch its www digitization and publishing ventures.

Of course partnering with outside groups or agencies entails a host of compromises, entanglements, and controversies, as the San Francisco Public Library (not included in this book) learned, and as some of the chapters in this study illustrate. But it seems that partnering is inevitable and may be very advantageous if handled adroitly. We must learn from the successes and misfortunes of others.

A Sense of Place and Community

According to Neal, "The use of dedicated or shared collection storage facilities and the expansion of digital network delivery … minimizes the need for new building construction" (76). But according to Frank Allen, "libraries exist and continue to prosper because people value place and proximity, and because there is an economy and efficiency in agglomerating related functions and services in close physical proximity to one another" (373). But then Sarah Watstein counters this with, "Today, place is about connection. It is about access to all types of information," and "Today, proximity is about online collaboration. It is about networked communication." She adds that information technology has "reframed" our conceptions of place and proximity, and that desktops and workstations should be recognized as "places in their own right" (373).

Speaking for academic libraries, however, Michalak states that

> there will be a continuing need for the library as a social and intellectual commons, an integrative location, which, in its accessible and accommodating environment, provides for the university a symbol of continuity between the past and the future [105].

Yet according to a 1996 study conducted by the Benton Foundation, while 65 percent of a general public sample believed that maintaining and building public library facilities was *very* important, only 34 percent felt that providing a place for community groups and public activities was more than *moderately* important (*Buildings*, 27).

The opening of new libraries may shed a great deal of illumination on this otherwise endless dispute. For Wiley found that attendance and requests for reference services usually soar far beyond expectations during the first year after a new library comes online. And though the activity then declines to more manageable levels, those levels are still higher than they were in the old libraries (110, 112).

As was the case at the San Antonio opening, Wiley's interviews with librarians at other new facilities found "an instantaneous, huge increase in patronage as the most dramatic change to which those who open a new building must adjust" (110). The extreme rise in usage in new libraries shows that users *do* come to libraries presumably seeking a public space, or to strengthen their sense of community per se, but certainly also, and primarily, as a personal information agora. According to Will Bruder, architect of the new Phoenix Main Library (see Unit 3), people are "starved" for good access to libraries. He adds, "Our community is starved for a public place, for a place to be seen and a place to interact" (quoted in Wiley, 112). Judging from chapter 3, Zapatos would no doubt concur.

Nor should we forget that the library provides a sense of place for its staff, too, and a focus for their efforts. Some persons and some workplace activities do not adapt well to telecommuting, despite Neal's easy argument that an "array of library operations and services will be performed from home, enabling improved competitiveness for the recruitment and retention of talented staff" (76). The library as a place important for the practice of librarianship may persist in society even if its importance as a community institution and icon should disappear from society's list of valuables. The staff of the new British Library rejoice in the "purpose-built" sense of place that adheres to the new facility. This enthusiastic reaction to the completion of a library building project is common to many of the chapters in this book, and amounts to no less than a staff renewal.

The Shrouds of Controversy

Perhaps the most important lesson emerging from the project to build and run the new San Francisco Public Library is that controversy hovers around a library building project. The SFPL's unhappy climax should send shudders through library directors faced with a building project. The users, the budget makers and the staff are always watching. Some of the libraries in this unit had their own dissenters.

For instance, expansion of the Beijing University Library was desperately needed, and received full support from the students. But as I learned during a visit there even before construction began, the students strongly disapproved of attaching the new addition to the front of the old library, where it would obliterate a grassy, tree-lined open space that was a favorite place for students to congregate and relax. Zhu's chapter explains how the builder-librarians in Beijing resolved their controversy to the mutual benefit of both sides. This kind of direction during a strenuous, 'round-the-clock construction project maintained the Beijing University Library's high reputation. As a result, the opening of the new building, accompanied by an international conference on 21st-century missions of academic libraries, became one of the featured events of Beijing University's 1998 centennial celebration.

In London, public criticism of delays, scale-backs, and rising costs became oppressive at times, and even Prince Charles, who dislikes modern architecture, inveighed against the proposed design, comparing the look of the new library to that of an academy for secret police (see Adler, 72, and Nelson, N., 4). But the British Library's public relations strategy to "unwrap" the Library a piece at a time, discussed in Carr's chapter, is an ingenious approach that can serve other library administrators well. Numerous controversies also plagued the Mitterrand of the Bibliothèque Nationale de France, but that library, too, appears to have subdued the storm and won its acceptance, as discussed in Unit 4.

Carnegie Park

Amid the public and professional controversies, the image of the Carnegie library in Phoenix becomes a symbol to me, reminding me how closely dissolution shadows adaptation. The old Carnegie outlived its usefulness, and as the ragged black paint on the frieze announced, the library became a fixture for the park that once was its adornment. After a two-year renovation project that began in 1984, the Phoenix Carnegie reopened as the Arizona Hall of Fame Museum, which celebrates "the people of Arizona: her pioneers and astronauts, soldiers and poets, yesterday's scalawags and tomorrow's leaders." And according to the museum's brochure, "Who knows how many of them discovered and nourished their dreams in Andrew Carnegie's Library" (Museum).

Fortunately, the Phoenix Public Library system, like the other libraries in this study, is thriving, its mission intact, because it possesses resilience, and so has adapted well to change. The allegorical lesson of the Phoenix Carnegie and the fine library system that grew from it is that libraries must change in order to preserve and achieve their mission. Otherwise, they will eventually surrender to someone else's purposes.

1. The British Library

Jane Carr
Director, Public Affairs, The British Library

When His Royal Highness the Prince of Wales formally laid the foundation stone for the new British Library building (not, incidentally, at the site of the building itself next door to St. Pancras station in London, but in the then headquarters of the Library in a building built by and for the Novello Company in Soho), he brought to a close some 15 years of planning for the future of the Library and, as it has subsequently emerged, inaugurated a further 15 years or more of building work.

The origins of the British national library and of its collections and services are rich and varied and can be traced back through many centuries. A brief historical introduction is, therefore, necessary to pull together the various threads and to explain, at least in part, why the new building is so important to the successful fulfillment of the national library's role now and in the future.

In 1753 the British Museum was formed by Act of Parliament and, appropriate for this present day, endowed by a public lottery which, even after charges of corruption, raised the princely sum of £75,194. 8s. 2d. The government of the day had finally agreed to finding a permanent home for three great collections of books and curiosities which had been left to the nation and should now "remain and be preserved therein for publick use, to all posterity" with free access to "all studious and curious persons"—those of Sir Hans Sloane, Sir Robert Cotton and successive generations of the Harley family. More collections were to follow, most notably with the donation in 1823 by George IV of George III's library under terms which mean that it will still be on public display in the new building at St. Pancras in the 21st century (in a smoked glass tower which has become the center piece of the ground floor public spaces—a living sculpture in itself).

The 18th-century scheme for the national library was replaced in the 19th century by Antonio Panizzi's vision of the universal library in which all human knowledge might be found. It was Antonio Panizzi who, as Keeper of Printed Books and thus Principal Keeper of the British Museum (a status which reflects the relative importance of the Library collections at that time), conceived of a circular domed building with the catalogue at its center and the books stored in

ironwork tangents around it. His energy resulted in the construction of the Round Reading Room, which remains, even now after its final closure, as perhaps the most powerful ever architectural symbol of the universal significance of libraries and librarianship.

A century later, as publishing output in the United Kingdom and elsewhere exploded, it was all too evident that the ironwork stacks of the Round Reading Room could no longer contain the British Museum Library's collection. Leslie Martin and Colin St. John Wilson were commissioned in 1972 to develop their ideas for an extension to the south of the British Museum which would house the Library and the Department of Prints and Drawings, with their exhibition galleries. The design took the form of a 400 × 400-foot atrium for the library, an open court for the exhibition galleries and conference center, and a large courtyard extending from the British Museum forecourt to incorporate Hawksmoor's St. George's Church.

Even as these ideas were being considered, however, views on the role of a national library in the 20th century were being reconsidered by government and by the academic community. The transfer of the Patent Office Library collection to the British Museum Library in 1966 and the establishment of the National Library for Science and Invention within the Department of Printed Books was an additional design task for the architects, but was also a reflection of the demands and expectations of the scientific community for a national library service which recognized their particular needs for access to current scientific and technical information.

In 1976 the designs for development south of the British Museum were finally rejected due to strong opposition from those who wished the character of the area and its architecture to be preserved. Ironically, this decision in the interests of conservation may well have acted as the spur to those whose objective was to bring change to the traditional, historical and literary-based atmosphere of the British Museum Library, and thus brought about the final separation of the library collections from the rest of the Museum departments and the end of a 200-year era.

In 1971, in response to the recommendations of the Report of the National Libraries Committee chaired by the then Sir Frederick, now Lord, Dainton (1969), and an earlier Report on the Committee on Libraries by the University Grants Committee (1967), a government White Paper had been published which proposed the setting up of an entirely separate British Library. The Committee had found that:

> Except in sharing a common aim to collect and make available information for which an existing or potential demand has been demonstrated, the many different library and information services do not at present form a well-ordered pattern of complementary and cooperating

Opposite: Entrance to the new British Library from Euston Road showing the gates designed by David Kindersley and Eduardo Paolozzi's statue of Newton, inspired by William Blake. (Copyright British Library Board.)

> parts ... even among the national institutions themselves, the variety
> of their administrative arrangements is not conducive to cooperation.
> Each institution enjoys either complete or a very considerable degree of
> independence from the others and from the other types of information
> service which it complements.

The White Paper proposed that the British Museum Library should be amal-
gamated with the National Central Library (for the humanities and social sciences), the National Lending Library for Science and Technology (which had
been set up in 1962 in Yorkshire and was already one of the world's largest suppliers of documents), the British National Bibliography (formed in 1950 as a non-
profit organization) and the Office for Scientific and Technical Information
(previously part of the Department of Education). Together they would provide
"the best possible central library services for the United Kingdom," to include:

> preserving and making available for reference at least one copy of every
> book and periodical of domestic origin and of as many overseas publica-
> tions as possible...

> providing an efficient central lending and photocopying service in sup-
> port of the other libraries and information systems of the country....

> providing central cataloguing and other bibliographic services related
> not only to the needs of the central libraries but to those of libraries and
> information centers throughout the country.

This was distilled in the 1972 British Library Act to "the national centre for
reference, study and bibliographical and other information services, in relation
both to scientific and technological matters and to the humanities," and brought
the British Library into being in 1973.

Although it had been recognized that the British Museum Library was burst-
ing at the seams, it was only with the final rejection of the proposals to extend
the British Museum site that an alternative and wholly separate site for the London operations was sought. It had always been the intention to develop the Yorkshire site at Boston Spa into a single center for the efficient and speedy delivery
of documents, although the degree to which the site has now expanded — to
accommodate not only a much-expanded lending and document delivery service with an annual turnover of £22 million, but also bibliographic, cataloging,
administrative and computing support services — was certainly not envisaged
then.

A goods yard beside St. Pancras station, in use as a coach depot at the time,
was purchased by the government for £6 million and Colin St. John Wilson, who
had already been working on plans for the Library for 12 years, was asked to present plans for the new site. His new scheme, designed to be constructed in three
phases, occupied 200,000 square meters with space for 3,500 readers and 25 million books. It was a monumental conception which would have ensured that all
the Library's vast collections, out-housed at some 18 locations around London,
could be brought together under one roof, with space for future acquisition into

the 21st century and the opportunity to provide much greater access for readers and for the general public. To secure government commitment to any part of this, the first phase was itself divided into three parts, the first of which Mrs. Shirley Williams, then Secretary of State for Education and Science, agreed to fund in March 1978. The Department of Education and Science press release at that time reads:

> The Government intends to start the construction of a substantial first stage of the new British Library building in the Euston Road in 1979–80.... The building has been designed to the requirements of the Library for the Department of the Environment by the nominated architects, Colin St. John Wilson and Partners. The first stage is expected to be occupied towards the end of the 1980s, enabling a substantial part of the Library's unique collections to be housed in satisfactory conditions and providing a greatly improved service to readers. The estimated cost of the first stage, which will be spread over ten years, is £74 m (at June 1977 prices)....

The "Notes for Editors" attached to that press release give lack of accommodation and poor storage conditions as explanation for the need for the building, and anticipate that the new building will provide space for readers and storage well into the 21st century at an estimated total cost of £164 million at June 1977 prices. It was agreed by the Royal Fine Art Commission to be "a brilliant solution to an extremely complex problem" in which space would be found for about 3,500 readers, 2,500 staff, collections which were expected to grow to about 25 million volumes, and "a large number of public visitors."

Although the project has undergone many vicissitudes since those decisions were made, including widespread press criticism, major reductions in scale alongside equally major increases in construction costs, and public criticism of the architect and of the management of the project, the essential purpose has remained unchanged. The building was and is needed to provide safe, environmentally controlled storage of, and access to, the Library's unsurpassed collections and, in doing so, to provide a visual manifestation of the knowledge and history across the arts and the sciences contained within it. Colin St. John (Sandy) Wilson's approach was always an essentially modernist one; he has designed the building from the inside out in order that it can work successfully for the purpose for which it is intended. Although the Library staff were not formally included in the project management until very late in the program, the brief for the building was developed with them and contained, when the detailed design stage began, over 800 separate specifications. At least some of the success of the building and of the British Library within it, should be attributed to this approach, which produces spaces which are not only esthetically pleasing but which have the added esthetic and practical satisfaction of being appropriate for purpose.

Thus, the reading rooms are soaring and light-filled and carry echoes of the Round Reading Room within them, but they also have chairs specially designed

for maximum comfort for the reader and are supported by systems which will ensure quicker and more efficient delivery of the books or information the readers need. Since all the currently dispersed reading rooms of the Library in London, with the exception of the Newspaper Library in Colindale, will be brought within the single St. Pancras building, it will also be possible for readers to have access to different kinds of books and information across a range of subject areas in whichever reading room they are working. And the reading rooms themselves have been designed in different ways to accommodate the working needs of the readers.

In the humanities reading rooms, where books and special collection materials are brought to readers who may spend several days or weeks working on a small group of books or manuscripts, the rooms are full of desks or catalog access and inquiry points. In the science and business reading rooms, where speed and currency of information are the key requirements, the center of each reading room contains shelving for current periodicals and monographs.

The great front hall immediately draws the eye up to the light-filled ceilings and clerestory windows, but is also designed to provide clear direction to all those who pass through it — whether members of the general public or readers.

For the first time the Library has a truly modern auditorium and conference center, and purpose-built exhibition galleries, which allow it to respond effectively to the increasingly important objective of providing wider public access to, and interpretation of, its collections. New or enhanced services have come into being as a result of the opportunities for wider public access created by the purpose-built surroundings. An Education Service has been established to provide services for school and life-long learning both on-site and remotely. An Events Office will arrange and coordinate events for the public and for professional groups, and a Visitor Services section will insure that visitors of all kinds are welcomed warmly and reach the destination they require or receive the information they want. Alongside these, in an increasingly difficult financial environment, has also come the need for fund-raising on an ever-increasing scale — but even in this area, the building has offered new opportunities, such as the hiring of the conference center space for commercial use, as well as more traditional forms of fund-raising.

The book storage areas illustrate clearly the benefits of the architectural approach. Four basement storage areas, which are the equivalent of a ten-story building aboveground, provide a stable environment for the collections to the precise specification of the Library's preservation staff. Temperature control is made more simple by the underground location but is reinforced by a computer-controlled air conditioning system. The storage spaces in the British Museum

Opposite: The main humanities reading room with its soaring ceilings echoing the dome above the great Round Reading Room in the British Museum. Above the main reading room are two further tiers of reading rooms — one for general humanities and one for the map collection. (Copyright British Library Board.)

The main entrance hall of the Library showing the information desk, the Readers Admissions Office, the gates that allow reader access and the smoked glass tower in which the King's Library — King George III's collection — is housed in environmentally controlled conditions. The tapestry on the wall was made by the Edinburgh Tapestry Company and is the largest hand-woven tapestry to have been made in this century in the United Kingdom and is based on Ron Kitaj's painting, *If Not, Not.* (Copyright British Library Board.)

building were romantic memorials to the age of gaslight and the days before we understood the effect of light, heat and moisture on paper, but they shortened the life of some parts of the collections almost daily. In the new surroundings in St. Pancras their life expectancy is expected to increase four-fold.

Inevitably, in a 15-year building program, there have been changes to the brief to respond to changes within the Library, within the library profession or in society itself. Changes to a brief are easy targets to support criticism of delay but, in the case of this building and the phased and drawn-out approach to its construction and funding, were unavoidable and, if they had not been responded to, would have considerably diminished the long-term value of the building.

Chief among these must be the changes that have resulted from the rapid introduction of new technology into our lives, and specifically in the provision of information. When the brief for the building was prepared at the end of the 1970s, there were a small number of computer-based cataloging projects but no CD-ROMS either for bibliographic or for full-text products. During the life of the project, therefore, we may find that CD-ROM as a medium for communication may have both come and gone! Even now we are unable to specify the appropriate environment or systems for the long-term storage of computer-based information, but at least the new building will be able to respond to some of the requirements for delivery of electronic information.

Each reader desk contains power and an ADP point so that personal computers can be used by readers anywhere in the reading rooms, and locations have been provided for networked access to CD-ROM or online publications and information. Satellite and video-conferencing can be accommodated, although issues such as the provision of Internet access for all readers are still the subject of careful consideration in terms of operational viability. The ability to access other national and international collections in digital form can be achieved technically if funding allows.

One of the great difficulties for the British Library has been the close public association of the Library itself, and its management, with the difficulties and escalating costs of the building project. The irony of this has been that, while the building provided the national library with the first real, tangible opportunity to establish its identity and role as a separate institution, that identity has until now been colored almost exclusively by the problems of the building or criticisms of its architecture — all of which were, until the closing stages of the project, largely outside the Library's control.

The British people and the British press enjoy, as a national pastime and almost to excess, public exposure of national institutions, and the Library and the architect have, perhaps unjustly, been victims without the right of reply until comparatively recently. The effect of a constant barrage of criticism on staff and reader morale was considerable and will take time torestore.

But a psychological barrier was broken through with the beginning of the book moves at the end of 1996, and internal and external reactions have improved since then as staff and visitors have seen the building as it unfolds. Few, even of the press, have been able to resist some of the building's very fine points, and the public relations strategy has so far been to unwrap the building slowly for carefully targeted audiences and stakeholders, piece by piece, and to build a tide of goodwill and support for its essential messages in the process. This approach began with the involvement of authors and readers in the first book moves — household names such as P. D. James and Lady Antonia Fraser — and continued with the unveiling of the first two works of art which are to be permanently displayed in the building, the largest hand-made tapestry woven in this century after Kitaj's *If Not, Not*, which hangs in the front hall, and Paolozzi's statue of Newton, which was unveiled by the Prime Minister's wife, Cherie Blair, and which dominates the piazza at the front of the building. Staff parties, and parties for readers and staff to mourn the closing of the Round Reading Room and to celebrate the opening of the first humanities reading rooms are all part of the continuing process of building confidence and support.

If all can agree, as *Newsweek* expressed it in July 1997, that the British Library is "the perfect place to curl up with a volume of Ruskin or Wordsworth," or as Lisa Jardine suggested in the daily *Telegraph* in October 1977,

> Forget the delays and the politics. Sandy Wilson's new library is designed with the needs of the reader resolutely in mind.... The confrontational architecture of the British Museum belonged to an Age of Imperialism — its monumental style celebrated British power. Today's library is not empire-orientated but access-orientated; the old scale threatened, the new invites. Confrontation is, after all, the last thing readers need as they coax their precious thoughts into coherent arguments over a pile of inspiring, carefully chosen books.

then we shall all be content.

Some facts and figures about the new British Library:

1. The British Library is funded by government (c. £85 million in 1996/7) and earned revenue (c. £35 million).

2. There are more than half a million reader visits per year.

3. Over four million documents are supplied to remote users per year.

4. Some three million titles are added to the collection each year.

5. The collections moving into St. Pancras include twelve million monographs and serials, eight million stamps, two million maps and more than one million sound recordings. They also include major national and international treasures such as Magna Carta, the Lindisfarne Gospels and no less than four copies of the Gutenberg Bible.

6. The shelving stretches for 270 kilometers.

7. There are 11 reading areas in the new building, with 1,206 reader seats, and 23 linear kilometers of open access shelving.

8. The four basement levels descend to a depth of 23 meters.

9. The Online Public Access Catalogue (OPAC) will contain over 12 million records. Ordering will be via an Automated Book Requesting System (ABRS) and a Mechanical Book Handling System (MBHS), both of which are linked by

computer to the OPAC and to the Reader Admission System (RAS) which will issue readers with a pass which secures access beyond the public areas of the building.

10. There are three exhibition galleries, a bookshop, and a 255-seat auditorium.

2. Constructing the New Shanghai Library

Wu Jianzhong
Deputy Director, Shanghai Library*

Situated in the heart of the city, along the busiest shopping street, the old Shanghai Library is perhaps one of the most attractive cultural institutions in the city. The Library, with its holdings of about 10 million volumes, ranks second in the library world in China. But although the European-style building looks elegant and beautiful and is listed among the city's protected cultural buildings, it was too old and too small to house this fast-growing institution. Furthermore, the plans to build a new facility led to the consolidation of the Library and the Institute of Science and Technology of Shanghai (ISTIS). It was the most important event in the history of the Library, and could not have occurred without the prospect of constructing a new library building.

The New Building Project

The new building project commenced in the early 1980s. In March 1983 the National Planning Commission of China authorized the project. In 1985 the Shanghai Planning Commission decided that the floor space of the new building would be 83,000 square meters. To draw upon all useful ideas for constructing a modern library, the municipal government invited many architects for an architectural competition. The judging panel finally selected the Shanghai Institute of Architectural Design and Research to draw the architectural plan. Between 1986 and 1989 the Institute and the Library organized a number of study tours at home and abroad to see other new libraries and their modern facilities, and to get ideas of modern library development and management elsewhere in the world. Also, well-known architects and librarians were invited to modify and optimize the

*This is an expanded and revised version of a paper delivered at the 62d International Federation of Library Associations and Institutions General Conference, Beijing, 25–31 August 1996.— T.D.W.

The main entrance of the new Shanghai Library and the Institute of Scientific and Technical Information of Shanghai. (Courtesy of the Shanghai Library, photographer Yu Li.)

plan. Among the invited figures were Mr. Dai Nianci, the former vice minister of the Ministry of Construction; Mr. Ni Tianzeng, the former vice mayor of Shanghai; and Mr. P. J. Schoots, the former director of the Rotterdam City Library.

In March 1989, the Municipal Construction Commission finally authorized the plan. Later, the Institute of Architectural Design and Research further modified the plan according to the opinions made by the former mayor, Mr. Zhu Rongji (now the vice premier of the State Council of the People's Republic of China), who visited the Library in 1990. The secondary technical design and the working drawing started in 1991 and 1992, respectively. The foundation stone-laying ceremony was held on March 25, 1993, and the new building of the Shanghai Library, one of the city's ten great cultural projects in the last decade of the 20th century, officially opened in December 1996. The city of Shanghai now has a beautiful modern library that people have for years been yearning for.

The new institution is located in the city's educational and academic center, surrounded by a group of the best-known universities and research institutions of China. With a total floor space of 83,000 square meters, the new Library is composed of two tower buildings of 11 and 24 stories respectively, modeling itself somewhat after the old Library's European-style building. The new building is about 20 to 50 meters away from the noisy streets. Around the building is a green area of over 11,000 square meters, a long band of sloping grassland along the streets, two big squares called The Wisdom and The Knowledge, and a group of eye-catching sculptures. The broad and wide stone steps lead visitors directly to the entrance hall on the first floor. The idea of this design is to bring out a striking contrast to the crowded streets of the city. Paintings, calligraphic works, and bonsai will be on display throughout the building to make the Library elegant and magnificent. The Library will surely be one of the city's most striking symbolic architectural structures and the most attractive meeting place.

Open Access

Many libraries in China still keep their books on closed shelves. But we can see a trend of opening stacks to the public in some university libraries and new libraries recently. The new Shanghai Library is built on the concept of open access, and as many as 1,000,000 books will be displayed in its 23 large-scale reading rooms. All the new materials published within 10 years will be openly shelved and easily accessed. Books and periodicals in the reading rooms are for reference only, but multiple copies of the local materials are kept in the closed stacks to support circulation. A rapid, automated book-carrier system connecting all the stacks in the building makes the access easier. This system is exactly the same as the one used in the new National Library of France. There is also an open-stack lending department for Chinese books. As many as 300,000 of these books will be put on the open shelves for readers to take home.

Flexible Service Departments

Most libraries in China are room-based, and books are kept in many small rooms. But the new Shanghai Library introduced a new modular system so that the reading rooms can be freely reconfigured. In a large-scale room of, say, 2000 square meters, there may be a number of reading rooms or special subject corners separated by shelves or by low furniture, not by walls. When a reading room or a subject corner needs a bigger space, we can move the shelves or furniture to change it freely.

There are 23 reading rooms and 3,000 individual study places distributed over all floors. For those who want to study quietly, the new Library also provides 32 closed study carrels where readers can keep a group of the Library's materials for a certain period, but the carrels have to be booked in advance. Reference desks are scattered all over the reading floors. Exhibitions to display the Library's special holdings will decorate the reading rooms. For instance, a book history exhibition with a different theme each time will be regularly held in the Chinese Rare Books Reading Room.

One of the 25 reading rooms in the Library. (Courtesy of the Shanghai Library, photographer Yu Li.)

The Electronic Library Project

The Library will introduce the latest technology to form a first-class information management system. The Library is cooperating with the Ameritech Company (USA) to have its Horizon library system customized for Chinese users. The new system will have five modules: acquisitions, cataloging, circulation, serials and OPACs. A CD-net will be installed to have the Library's special collections scanned and stored into the optical database systems. A bibliographic system will be developed, and the original bibliographic systems of the Library and ISTIS, such as the Index to the Periodicals and Newspapers Published in China and the patent information system, will be upgraded. Administration work will also be automated and networked. All the systems will be integrated within the Library's local area network and connected to the world's major networks, such as the Chinanet, Cernet and Internet. The Shanghai Library will be an important node in the library world.

Audio and Visual Services

There is a large area for multimedia and A/V services. The Shanghai Library maintains the country's largest phonograph records collection of 140,000 pieces, including most of the Chinese local operas, dramas, and musicals, and all these materials are going to be recorded into an optical database. A music appreciation room, a sound laboratory, and many individual and group rooms are prepared to meet the users' various needs. There is also a large studio for producing sound recordings, videos, and dramas. Here ISTIS can continue producing its long TV series entitled "New Sci-Tech," which covers interesting scientific stories for broadcast on Shanghai TV. The new A/V Department will take advantage of newly installed A/V facilities, satellite receivers, and library networking system to make multimedia programs for television broadcasting stations and other social and educational activities.

For instance, the Library has already made two educational TV series for a TV station in Shanghai, and they have been very successful. The Library has a rich information resource and a skilled team of cameramen for making the programs. By opening its resources to the public, the Library can publicize itself to the public and make some profits as well. The programs are contracted by the TV stations.

Cultural Activities

To make the new Shanghai Library the city's symbolic cultural center, the building provides various cultural and recreational facilities. An 872-seat lecture hall, a 300-seat multi-functional hall and four seminar rooms are well furnished and equipped with simultaneous interpretation facilities. Two exhibition halls of up to 1,800 square meters are prepared to display the Library's favorite holdings, hold cultural exhibitions, or host various social meetings. The Library will open a Reading Café, a bookstore, and a library shop as well as automatic teller machines, telephones, and other facilities for public use. Many social activities can be held in the new building, such as press conferences, new release meetings, new product demonstrations, and art auctions. A friends of the library group will also be organized to attract more people to support the Library.

Merging the Shanghai Library and ISTIS

October 4, 1995, was the most important day in the Library's history. On that day, the Institute of Scientific and Technical Information of Shanghai (ISTIS), one of the city's leading information centers, was joined with the Library, resulting in the first combination of a library and an institutional information service in the country. This was an epoch-making event in Chinese librarianship. The new Library will administratively and physically combine the two organizations, which will complement strengths of each to provide first-class information services for the research community as well as for the general public. The merger has provided a significant chance for the new institution to restructure itself towards a new direction: the Library as a center of information resources, an information clearinghouse, a "think tank," a school of social education for personal self-improvement, and a meeting place for recreation. The new Shanghai Library will also serve as a coordinator among all kinds of libraries and information services in the city because it acts as a back-up library for all the other libraries in Shanghai in terms of resources, cataloging, training, etc.

Rational Allocation

The new building now accommodates the two institutions, including the 10 million volumes of the Shanghai Library and 30 million items in the ISTIS collections. To put such a huge resource in order, the architects and the librarians had tried many proposals before a comparatively rational plan was adopted. Now the new plan has the following features: first, the Shanghai Library and the ISTIS holdings have been combined; second, departments are arranged according to the frequency of library use, which means heavily used materials are on the lower floors and not so frequently used materials are on the higher floors; and third, reading rooms are laid out compactly and so that readers will not feel that their required materials are far apart. A signage system was designed to lead readers to the very places they want. Lifts are available to all the reading floors, and escalators carry people to the second and third floors.

Reference and "Think Tank" Services

Both the Shanghai Library and ISTIS have reputations for providing reference services for the city's social and industrial development. The Shanghai Library has participated in many of the city's major industrial projects by providing information services. For instance, the Library assisted with the construction of the tunnels across the Huangpu River by providing information from the archives of subsurface structure. And ISTIS often organizes information research, or "think tank" projects for the academic community and the municipal government. The first draft of "The Information Port Project" (the information superhighway project) of Shanghai was done by the ISTIS staff. The new organization will effectively exploit the considerable strengths of each institution to the fullest, and set up a new reference department combining the resources and expertise of both. The department will continue to organize research projects and also answer readers' daily inquiries.

More Benefits

The merging of the Shanghai Library and ISTIS has already brought many additional benefits. For instance, many years ago the municipal government asked the Shanghai Library and ISTIS to be the coordinators for the acquisition of foreign periodicals among libraries in Shanghai, with the Library taking responsibility for the materials on social sciences and humanities and ISTIS for science and technology. Every year in the season of subscribing to the foreign periodicals, the two institutions separately organized meetings to reduce duplicates among the participating libraries. Each May the acquisitions librarians from all the libraries gathered to work out plans for the following year's acquisitions. The aim of such cooperation was clear: avoiding duplication of expensive foreign materials. During that earlier period, duplicates were normally controlled to fewer than approximately five duplicate subscriptions for any one title among all the libraries. But as the two organizations worked separately, some comprehensive libraries had to attend two different meetings, and the Shanghai Library and ISTIS had to perform their coordination efforts as separate institutions.

Then the Shanghai Libraries' Consortium of 30 academic and research libraries was set up in 1994, aiming at sharing information resources and reinforcing interlibrary cooperation. The Shanghai Library and ISTIS, the city's two major information organizations, took the leading role in the Consortium, and developed even more effective methods of cooperation than before. One of their major activities continued to be a cooperative acquisitions program. Before the subscription season, the two organizations worked together to coordinate purchasing of expensive foreign materials as in the past, but they still had their separate meetings, agendas, and organizations to work across.

When the Shanghai Library and ISTIS merged, however, the coordination became that much easier and efficient. In 1996, for instance, coordination of subscriptions for both social sciences and science and technology became one meeting. As a direct result of the merger and the more efficient cooperation and planning, duplicate subscriptions to 200 foreign periodicals were eliminated so that more new titles could be added during the 1997 subscription period.

Thus, as a result of the merger, the two organizers of acquisitions became one, the two acquisitions meetings were combined, and the two leading institutions in the Shanghai Libraries Consortium merged. Now a comprehensive university library no longer needs to send librarians to meetings held separately. Attendees at the Consortium meetings are from libraries all over the city, including libraries that are not official members of the Consortium, but the non-members are small libraries.

The new staffing pattern also benefits both institutions. Before the merger, the Library was considering a public recruitment plan for another 500 new staff. How could the Library find so many qualified staff? Where would they come from? ISTIS has a staff of 400, and most of them have experience providing services in the science and technology fields. On the other hand, the staff of the Library, totaling 500, graduated mostly from social sciences and humanities areas. Therefore, the Library needed a staff with science backgrounds, and the merger provided a very good solution. The new institution now has a good balance of subject specialists.

Now, the Library gives its attention to social sciences and humanities while

ISTIS lays particular stress on scientific and technical work, and its services are more practical. Although the Shanghai Library is a comprehensive institution and has a good portion of scientific and technical information resources in its holdings, the Library's activities are heavy in social sciences and humanities. It has closer links with historians, writers, novelists and artists. ISTIS mainly serves the industrial and technical community, and has a solid foundation for scientific and technical development. The institution provides a variety of science and technology information services ranging from searching to translation, from industrial surveys to research projects.

ISTIS also has a group of specialists covering various scientific and technical subjects. Every employee has his or her own specialty of one or two subjects, and is trained to be a subject information specialist. They are required to undertake follow-up researches in their own areas. But libraries, on the whole, provide more general services for their customers and have less experience in answering specific research needs from readers. But developing consultation services such as these in libraries seems likely to be a general trend of librarianship in the 21st century, and the new Shanghai Library is now in an excellent position to undertake this new type of service.

The Library has clearly benefited by expanding its services and coverage into new subject areas and user groups. By the same token, ISTIS can enjoy the increased information resources and the addition of social science workers from the Library. Also, because the Library has more funding resources from the municipal government, ISTIS will benefit from this as well.

Problems

Despite the benefits of the merger, problems have appeared. The space allocation problem was solved by rational use of the available space in the new building. But some problems are more persistent. The libraries and information agencies in China are under different administrations. The public libraries are administered under the cultural departments (or bureaus), while the information research institutions are under the science commissions. They follow different instructions and have different funding sources. When the Shanghai Library and ISTIS were merged into one, they were divorced from their own higher-level authorities and placed directly under the municipal administration. Although the merger is expected to be beneficial to both institutions, putting the new organizations in order surely will take time. The merger is the first such case in the country. Unless the new organization balances itself nicely with other government agencies, there will be a lot of administrative problems to deal with.

Another problem that must be dealt with involves fee-based services. The Shanghai Library is a public institution and provides basically free services to the public, so all of its services for salaries and library materials are regulated by the Shanghai Price Control Bureau. Although ISTIS is also a non-profit institution, many of its services are provided on a fee basis. Some jobs require overtime, and salaries are floated according to individuals' actual achievements. Furthermore, ISTIS is divided into many small groups, and quality services are encouraged on a basis of competition. As a result of these conditions, the average income of ISTIS staff is naturally higher than that of the Library staff. Merging the two organizations means that many fee services of ISTIS have to be changed, following public library practice. The new institution is more a public library than an information agency, and many of its practices will be less profit oriented. As one organization, it will be difficult for the leadership to produce a fair and balanced policy for staff compensation.

And although the new building was spacious enough to accommodate both institutions, as described above, another problem presented by the consolidation is that the building now provides less space for future growth. But from the Library's point of view, the increase in materials and collections from ISTIS compensates for this problem. Among the most valuable additions are the ISTIS collections of patents, industrial standards and technical reports. So now there is a special industrial reading room in the new building for these materials. Other ISTIS materials are being merged into the Library's.

The main problem faced in the consolidation is to re-allocate and reorganize the resources of the two institutions. And so far the merge goes on successfully.

Conclusion

The new Shanghai Library is continuing the traditions of the old library, but has also added many new features, including new technologies, services, and staff. But most importantly, the new Library now has a new identity and a strengthened capacity to provide services as a result of the merger with ISTIS.

3. *The San Antonio Public Library*

Craig Zapatos
Central Library Administrator

May 20, 1995, was a typical late May day in San Antonio. The weather was sweltering in the nineties, and hundreds of people were sitting on folding metal chairs as hot as the color of the new Central Library building they had all come to see. Another three thousand people lined the street leading to the building and watched the requisite parade of school children, dignitaries, and media. In spite of the heat, the energy level and anticipation of the crowd was apparent. They had come to see what the brightest building on the San Antonio skyline was really like. Even those who were not regular library users had to come see the building reported in *Newsweek* magazine three months earlier under the headline, "You Say Tomato, I Say I Hate It," and what the local paper had dubbed in a contest, "The Big Enchilada."

Most in attendance had probably seen the building under construction in the last twenty-two months, or at least had heard of the bright colors from numerous newspaper articles and presentations from Library staff and Library Foundation staff. Indeed, it was the most striking building on the skyline. Bright red, with accents in yellow and purple, it definitely made a statement among the mostly bland limestone buildings and modern glass high-rise office buildings prevalent in the downtown area.

In 1989 the voters of San Antonio passed a library construction bond issue for approximately $40 million. Of that amount $28 million was earmarked for construction of a new Central Library, with the balance used to enlarge existing branch libraries and construct two new branch libraries in parts of the city that were under-served. The $28 million was not enough money to construct a building of the size recommended in a Main Library Space Needs Assessment report presented to the San Antonio Library Task Force in 1990. That report, commonly referred to in San Antonio as the "Beach Report," suggested in its executive summary that a Main Library of approximately 340,000 square feet would be the ideal size. Recognizing that $28 million was not enough money to fund a building

41

View of the Central Library's eastern elevation showing geometrical forms and Bradford Pear trees. (Courtesy of the San Antonio Public Library, photographer Celine Casillas Thomasson.)

of that size, the report recommended that the new Main Library be built in a phased approach, with initial space allocations totaling 254,000 square feet. At that time it reiterated the need for future expansion to an eventual 500,000 square feet. The "Big Enchilada" Central Library that stood before the citizens on May 20, 1995, actually totaled 238,000 square feet. Throughout the project, the name Central Library was used to distinguish the new building from the "old Main Library" located less than two miles away.

The new Central Library was a significant departure from the square, three-story Main Library building which was located in the heart of the downtown area on the Riverwalk. Most obvious, of course, were the color and unusual architecture that immediately identified it as a building designed by the famed Mexican architect Ricardo Legorreta. Its bright colors, simple geometric forms used on a grand scale, and preponderance of glass and outdoor terraces reflect many of the design features used in Legorreta commercial and private residence projects throughout the world. It was unique, too, in that the Legorreta design was chosen as a result of a limited design competition. This approach to architect selection had not been used for a city building project in anyone's recent memory, and a project management firm would be retained to oversee the design competition as well as program planning, design development, contract compliance, and project completion.

The Central Library was also the end product of a public/private funding initiative in conjunction with the San Antonio Library Foundation. This nonprofit support group for the San Antonio Library System eventually raised private funds and pledges totaling $5 million, which were matched by an equal amount of additional funds added to the project by the City of San Antonio. Of course, these facts were far from the minds of most in the opening-day crowd. They wanted to see the interior, the new materials, and the new computers.

As with all significant buildings, there are many interesting stories about how the final product came to be. I would like to focus the remainder of this chapter on some of those stories, and some of the issues that came to play in the project's completion. They are stories of the efforts of many people to create a building that reflected the constituents' sometimes conflicting desires. It is not my intent to focus on the events that led to passage of the 1989 bond issue, site selection, or process for selection of the project management firm. Those events preceded my tenure with San Antonio Public Library and are well documented in the public records and memories of those who were employed with the system at the time those events occurred. The interpretation of events is my own and does not necessarily reflect the feelings and beliefs of others involved with the project.

In November of 1990 the final draft of the Main Library Program, focusing on schematic design, was delivered to then Director of the library system David Leamon by 3DI, the firm hired as the project managers. In that document were many of the germinal ideas leading to the finished building that would open in May of 1995. Incorporated in the report were ideas gleaned from community focus groups organized in preparation of the Beach Report, Beach Report authors' recommendations, members of the library's administrative staff, input from the Library Board's Library Advisory Committee and from library staff. The primary focus of the report was to begin defining square footage for public and non-public areas, critical adjacency requirements both within and between library subject departments, and projected seating estimates.

Among the design concepts that prevailed throughout project design were that the spaces should "create a dramatic, yet inviting, sense of arrival and a sense of entry," that the floorplans were to be open and flexible, that there would be comfortable reading and lounge areas, and that there would be a feature throughout the various floors to provide a sense of orientation. Consideration was to be given to providing escalators to invite patrons to the upper floors.

Library administrative staff were most concerned that the building have flexibility, so that it could be reconfigured in the future, and incorporate technological changes within its anticipated thirty-year life span. As the project progressed into design development, the "thirty-year life span" mindset would exert itself in many ways.

In the spring of 1991, 3DI, with Milton Babbitt as the library's project manager, initiated a limited design competition for selection of the design architect.

Each of the architectural firms submitting designs had San Antonio architects as a portion of its team. A jury composed of the Library Director, Library Board members, an urban planner, a library building consultant, and others reviewed four design concepts for the site. It was their feeling that the design submitted by Ricardo Legorreta best addressed the objectives stated in the program, and made best utilization of the near-trapezoidal shape of the building site. The selected site at that time was occupied by a vacant Sears retail building with an adjacent three-story garage. The jury felt the Legorreta scheme took best advantage of the site by proposing demolition of the existing Sears structure, and renovating the adjacent garage to provide convenient and easy access to the building. The Legorreta scheme was believed also to best address the varying scale of the surrounding buildings, a historical park across the street, and the nearby skyline of the central city. It proved critical in the course of the project that the local columnists who frequently wrote about city architecture and urban design issues were invited to view and discuss the attributes of each scheme. The newspaper articles discussing the proposals were very important in generating the enthusiasm for the Legorreta scheme. The submitted models and presentation boards were left on display in the old Main Library for public viewing and attracted many users and non-users alike.

As the selected design put forth by Legorreta Architecturas, Johnson Dempsey Architects (JDA) Inc., and Sprinkle-Robey Architects made its way through confirmation by the Library Board and City Council, proposals for award of the construction contract were solicited and evaluated. Upon recommendation from the project management team and approval by the Library Director, Library Board, and City Council, the firm of H. A. Lott (Houston) was selected to construct the building. Later, the local architectural firm of Ford, Powell, Carson would be selected, using the same process, to design the interiors.

Milton Babbitt, project manager, believed that a "partnering" session would assist all the firms involved to better understand each other's project priorities and concerns as well as those of the Library represented by the Director, the Central Library Administrator, and the Library Facilities Manager. A two-day session was scheduled at the conference facilities of a local hotel and each party had a chance to present its concerns about schedules and coordination among the subcontractors, and anticipated areas of concern in the design. Of course, the priority of the Library's team was that the building be a functional, durable, technologically forward-looking structure that would be an important tool in delivering exceptional library service.

An equally important goal, from the Library's perspective, was that the building be finished on time and in budget. The mayor at the time, Mr. Nelson Wolfe, was serving his last term of office as a result of San Antonio's term-limit restrictions. Mayor Wolfe had been a strong supporter of the library's efforts, both publicly and privately within the community. The Library staff and the Library Board very much wanted to deliver a product the City and he could be proud of, and one that would honor the Mayor's and the City's commitment to the project. The term-limit restriction placed a non-negotiable constraint on the project timeline if it were to be completed within Mayor Wolfe's term of office. In meeting that timeline, design completion, construction, and move-in would have to occur within twenty-two months.

San Antonio is fortunate in having two very active support groups. The Friends of the San Antonio Public Library has a large membership throughout the city and serves as the "umbrella" organization for the various individual branch library Friends groups. The San Antonio Public Library Foundation is a separate, non-profit fund-raising and support organization whose membership includes corporate supporters' representatives and other influential members of the community. Together these two groups were instrumental in the passage of the 1989 bond issue, during Henry Cisneros's mayoral term, that would fund the construction of the Central Library and branch library system improvements.

As design development progressed, and revised cost estimates became more accurate, it became clear that bond funds were adequate to construct the building, but not to provide the level of finish to ensure long-term durability, new furnishings, and interiors that were on a par with Legorreta's world-class design. In November 1992, the Library Foundation enlisted the help of a major corporate sponsor to design a fund-raising campaign which was titled the "Central Library Enrichment Campaign." The objective was a campaign structured as a public/private initiative. The Library Foundation pledged to raise up to $5 million in the private sector if the City would provide additional funds to the project in a dollar-for-dollar matching agreement.

Working with the library staff and the project management team, the Library Foundation identified "naming opportunities" that contributors could take advantage of. It was the desire of the library team that the naming opportunities correspond to areas or architectural features of the building that would be permanent in nature. Naming of individual pieces of furniture was eschewed because of the problems of replacing damaged or lost items in the future after donated funds had already been expended. Because of Legorreta's minimalist interior design it was decided that the only art objects in the building would be those integrated into the architecture, and funds for individual art pieces or donations of artwork would not be accepted. The Library Foundation commissioned two artists for the project. A large interior entry featured the neon work of Stephen Antonakos from New York, and a large mural near the auditorium was created by the nationally known local artist, Jesse Trevino.

Prior to presenting the "Enrichment Campaign" to the City Council for approval, the Library Foundation called on their corporate sponsors and individuals in the community to enlist their commitment and contributions to the effort. By the time the Library Foundation approached City Council they had already secured over a million dollars of private sector support.

The City Council approved the City's willingness to participate in the Enrichment Campaign and engineered additional financial support in the form of increased budget commitments in future materials budgets, additional staffing for the Central Library, and in-kind support of the project from other City Departments. The end result was that the City mandated materials budget increases for the Central Library of $200,000 for five years, paid for renovation of the parking garage, and provided landscaping on the site. The funds previously budgeted for those items were re-directed towards enhancing the interiors, providing durable finishes, and upgrading the automation system. Had additional funding not been secured, the Central Library would have been a much different place. Furniture from the old Main Library would have to have been used, as well as the old shelving. Staff and the public would have to use many of the same furniture pieces that the old Main Library opened with thirty years ago.

With the City Council's commitment to the Enrichment Campaign, the Library Foundation set out to secure the rest of its $5 million pledge. Under the tireless and enthusiastic leadership of Maria Cossio, Executive Director, a number of meetings were held with corporate sponsors and wealthy individuals. In an effort to encourage participation from all sectors of the community, the Foundation's Annual Telethon was devoted to the campaign. Literally dozens of presentations were made by Foundation and library staff to Lion's groups, Chamber of Commerce meetings, and nursing homes. Each presentation involved an overview by the Central Library Administrator of the project and the benefits that could be expected from the new Central Library, followed by a short presentation from an estate planner or attorney who could discuss various mechanisms that could be employed to donate. At the same time tours of the building under construction were conducted for potential donors who were interested in one of the naming opportunities located throughout the building.

As the fundraising continued, the Central Library Administrator and Dennis Rice, the library's Facilities Manager, met regularly with the project management team, architects of record Johnson Dempsey and Associates, and the general contractor to review the plans and the progress. There were regular weekly meetings, in addition to daily site inspections by the library staff.

The local architecture firm of Ford, Powell, and Carson was retained for the project, beginning in October 1993, to design the interiors. Architects John Gutzler and Mary Bartlett would lead the FPC design team. The interiors were of particular interest to the library staff. Besides the esthetics, the "thirty-year mindset" was an important perspective used in the selection of furniture and finishes. Of equal importance was selecting furniture for staff areas that would be comfortable, ergonomic, and durable. It was made clear early in the project that money set aside for staff furniture would not be sacrificed at the expense of high-priced public furnishings. The rationale for this approach was that it would be much harder to get funds in the future from either the City or the Foundation to replace or upgrade staff furnishings. It was felt that this was the opportunity to secure the type of office furniture that would both benefit the staff in the long run and help to make their transition to the new building that much more enjoyable.

By the time FPC was onboard, the architectural plans had progressed and a number of questions were raised about maintenance of certain features of the building. It was decided that a visit would be arranged to the Marco Museum of Art in Monterey, Mexico, which was also designed by Legorreta and featured many design elements similar to those of the library design. The trip helped the

Aerial view showing the third- and fourth-floor outdoor terraces, and palm tree planters. (Courtesy of the San Antonio Public Library, photographer Celine Casillas Thomasson.)

interior team to get a better sense of the interior spaces and scale of a Legorreta building. A trip to Legorreta's "Solana" complex, outside of Dallas, was made for the same purpose.

Library staff, in particular, were interested in the ongoing maintenance and repair of certain building features. It is not uncommon in Legorreta's designs to have large windows with an exterior casement with vertical bars, and the San Antonio design had them, too. A similar feature was proposed in the San Antonio design for the glassed portion of the atrium from the fourth to the sixth floors. Staff concerns had to do with cleaning the glass on the inside surfaces of the atrium located behind tall vertical bars. The eventual, and labor-intensive, method involved installing a track around the top of the atrium from which a window washer could hang in a sling to clean the glass. The vertical bars necessitated the workers' turning their squeegees ninety degrees to pass between the bars, and then make a single cleaning stroke downward. Then, they would move over to repeat the process around the entire atrium interior. Likewise, to clean the windows on the exterior of the building one would hang from roof divots to repeat the procedure.

Four outside terraces were incorporated into the library design, one of which has a fountain with two reflecting pools. The terrace fountain is located on the third floor, creating a very dramatic view from the Children's Department inside

View of the fourth-floor terace with architectural cylinders and contrasting wall. (Courtesy of the San Antonio Public Library, photographer Celine Casillas Thomasson.)

the library. The fountain also happens to be located directly above the area of the second floor where the library's Reference Department is located. The selection of the terrace surfaces was important because of concern that the fountain might leak, or the terraces might flood during San Antonio's periodic downpours. The eventual surface chosen was actually a roofing scheme using stamped pavers that can be lifted to keep the drains below on a regular maintenance schedule. The challenge of the design was to space the pavers close enough that high heels would not get caught in the gaps, and yet allow for adequate drainage. There is an additional fountain located in the center of the motorcourt entry to the building. With water being a valuable commodity in the San Antonio region, it was decided to design the air conditioning systems to recycle condensation back into the fountains.

San Antonio, like most urban areas, has suffered a rash of graffiti in the last few years. A feature designed into the building to combat the problem was a stone wainscot approximately nine feet high around the entire base of the building. Legorreta chose a stone which was quarried in Mexico and shipped to San Antonio. Extensive testing of "sacrificial" coatings was performed on the samples until one was found that would allow easy removal of graffiti.

As the selection and testing of durable exterior finishes continued, selection of the interior finishes and fabrics began. Each fabric used for public seating was subjected to staff testing involving ease of cleaning, and puncture and tear resistance. Most of the public seating incorporated easy to clean nylon fabrics, and the larger pieces, like couches and arrangements of ottomans, were done in a ballistic fabric similar to that found in soft-sided travel luggage. With the additional funds available from the Library Foundation's Enrichment Campaign, all of the end panels for the shelving were custom-made of solid Corian (the kitchen countertop material). This was chosen for its ease of cleaning and molded-through color to resist damage from bookcarts.

Most of the small tables used throughout the building feature rubber inlays around the edges, again to guard against delamination due to booktruck damage. Whenever possible, manufactured seating with welded frames was chosen for the public so that it wouldn't become loose over time. A carpeting scheme was chosen that would use different color and texture in the main walkway areas from that under the stacks. In this way, as those areas wore quicker they could be replaced without unloading the books and dismantling the bookstacks. In the restrooms, graffiti-resistant tile and surface finishes were used, and wall structures to support the stall doors were built rather than installing panel systems attached to the floor and ceiling. The concern was that the panels would only loosen over time. Full-length hinges were used in hanging the stall doors to ensure the integrity of the structure over time.

Design of signs for the interior was developed concurrent with the interior planning and selection of furniture. The Legorreta building design lacked a common footprint among most floors. Combining design features which encouraged "discovery" of the building spaces rather than a common logic among the floors presented challenges in anticipating how the public would move through the building. In designing the signage, the overriding qualities sought by the project managers and architects were that it provide useful direction and not detract from the architecture. From the staff point of view, additional concerns addressed in the final designs were that the signs be damage-resistant and easy and inexpensive to replace or change. Although collections and service areas were specified in the building program developed by staff and architects, staff were not certain that the scheme would prove to be the best to encourage patron access and efficiency of delivering services.

The resulting signs were of four basic designs: wall-mounted identification for service areas and recognition of donors; free-standing, "ladder-framed" signs to be used in open areas; similarly designed signs that were wall-mounted near elevators; and large orienting signs showing the layout for each level of the building to be located on every public floor. The wall-mounted signs were of a clean and uncluttered design of polymer with silkscreened letters, whose edge thickness was painted purple to relate to one of the common accent colors used throughout the design. The ladder-framed signs were constructed of steel painted white, with magnetic strips within the individual frames to hold white metal plates with applied silkscreening. The design would allow replacement of individual panels to reflect changes in the arrangement of collections or additional services without reconstructing the entire sign. The panels could also be replaced at reasonable cost if they were damaged or subjected to vandalism or graffiti.

The large orienting signs on the public floors are of a horizontal design and incorporate a sectional structure for each floor supporting a glass panel, with the floorplan represented by an appliqué affixed to the back side of the glass. The development of this design came about through discussions of how to cheaply reconfigure possible changes to the collection arrangement, easy repair of the appliqués that patrons might damage by reaching around behind the glass, and the ability to add additional sections to the unit if the building were ever to be expanded.

Installation of the automation system began in earnest in January of 1995. Battery backups as well as a separate air conditioning system for the room housing the processors had been prepared. The backup power for the processors was additionally supported by the ability to switch over to the diesel generator which supplied emergency lighting throughout the building. The automation system for San Antonio Public Library System is located at the Central Library and drives the terminals at the eighteen branches throughout the city. The data handling infrastructure of the building incorporates fiber-optic cable coming to the building and a fiber-optic spine running vertically through the floors. Fiber-optic cable was chosen in anticipation of providing web-based Internet access with its increased bandwidth requirements. Level 3 twisted pair wire was chosen to run laterally on each floor from the fiber to the individual terminals. Aside from the service desks and staff work areas, wire was pulled to identified catalog areas with large groups of terminals and to large reading tables that are designed to be converted to catalog areas if needed in the future. Wiring for data was also pulled to selected meeting rooms, the Auditorium, and the Art Gallery. Two and a half years after opening, the library supports 92 terminals, mostly PCs, in the public service areas. An additional 23 PCs are awaiting installation.

Installation of the shelving was started in early April of 1995 and completed in early May. As the bookstacks were completed on one floor, staff immediately started working with the contract movers to relocate the materials from the old Central Library. Staff had worked for almost two years previous to this, inventorying the collection to update the database of holdings and to weed the collection of outdated materials and those not in a condition to be placed out for the public. The old Main Library had approximately 20 percent of its collection in closed stacks that necessitated retrieval of materials by library staff. In the new Central Library there would be no closed stacks except the climate-controlled "vault" for rare and valuable materials. All other materials, including government documents and back issues of periodicals, would be available for unencumbered access by the patrons.

The process of planning for the move was complicated by the reorganization of the collection. The old Main Library collection and staffing were arranged by the traditional subject departments of Literature, History, Arts and Music, Business, and Children's. Books and magazines and selected newspapers were also divided among those departments. In the new scheme for the Central Library there would be departments of Telephone Reference (a non-public area), Media, Circulation, Reference (whose selectors would also oversee development of the non-fiction circulating collection), Fiction, Government Documents, Special Services (to serve primarily the vision-impaired), Periodicals, Children's, and Texana/Genealogy.

The scheme for the Central library required planning for combining all the circulating non-fiction from the old departments into an arrangement starting with the Dewey Decimal Classification of "000" on the first floor and the books shelved in classification number all the way up through the sixth floor. Each department counted the number of shelves for each non-fiction classification in the Main Library and merged them into a master map of the shelving in the Central Library, overseen by the Central Library Administrator. Planning for arrangement of the collection in the Central Library had to have logical breaks such that "Dewey hundreds" were not broken between floors. Once moving the collection was begun, staff were assigned in groups to monitor the orderly removal of the books by the mover from the Main Library and to monitor their correct placement on the designated shelves in the Central Library. Because broad Dewey classifications (like the 300s and 000s) existed in several departments in the Main Library, they had to be mapped to their new location in the continuous Dewey arrangement at Central Library on a shelf-to-shelf basis.

Once the move began, and with the Main Library closed for the move, staff were assigned from morning until midnight to oversee the movers, the transport of approximately four hundred thousand items, and to shift the collection as needed upon arrival. Neither top nor bottom shelves were used in order to allow for up to 20 percent growth of the collection without serious rearrangement. Special care was given to rare and fragile materials that were moved to the museum-quality climate-controlled vault constructed in the Central Library's Texana/Genealogy area.

Finally, all the pieces were coming together in time for the grand opening on Saturday, May 20, 1995. Staff worked tirelessly up until opening time to make sure all was in order. The audience which had waited so patiently in the heat that morning in anticipation of the opening were overwhelmed by the size and interiors of the Central Library compared to the old Main Library. During that first weekend ten thousand people visited the building and six hundred new library cards were issued. Numerous programs and presentations were planned in the building for the remainder of the month in celebration.

The first year of opening was one of discovery for both patrons and staff. Patrons became acquainted with the new arrangement of the collection and the building layout, while staff fine-tuned the processes of delivering exceptional service in light of overwhelming response. At the old Main Library, due to a lack of parking and its location in the heart of the downtown area, a busy day was one in which eight hundred people visited the library. During the first year, the daily average door count showed three thousand people visiting the new Central Library. In addition, the opening of Central Library coincided with the switch from a microfiche catalog to an online catalog, which required extensive patron education about its use. Hundreds of tours for the public were given by staff and a specially trained volunteer corps of docents.

Two and a half years after opening the building has held up surprisingly well. The upgraded finishes and furniture fabrics have withstood the traffic and day-to-day abuse, and we hope the planning efforts in those areas continue to result in an attractive and inviting facility for many years to come.

In hindsight, there are a number of modifications we wish we had incorporated in the design. We totally underestimated the popularity of the building as a meeting place for the public. Soon after opening, it became apparent that a staff position of Events Coordinator was needed to schedule room use and tours, work with caterers and audio-visual providers, and continue coordination of the docent tour guides. The library would have been better able to accommodate the huge number of receptions and events if it had a staging area for use by the caterers, and for use in the assembly and take-down of exhibits in the Art Gallery. A staging area would have proved helpful, too, for the unanticipated use of the building as a backdrop for filming of several Tejano and Christian music videos and filming of segments of the movie *Selena*. Had we anticipated the popularity of the Auditorium use, an area able to accommodate twice our capacity of two hundred would not have been wasted space.

An on-going problem is that the walkways between the library and the covered parking garage are a source of complaint on rainy days, and result in patrons constantly trying to exit through the entrance, by-passing the materials security system. Although a computer training room was designed to accommodate sixteen terminals for ongoing training of staff in electronic resources, a separate similar room would be helpful now that the Central Library has begun Internet training classes for the public so that they can better utilize the library's increasing resources.

These, though, are small things that can be remedied in the future with available funds, and most likely don't detract from the public's very positive response to "The Big Enchilada."

4. The Construction of the New Peking University Library*

Zhu Qiang

Professor and Deputy Director, Administrative Center
China Academic Library & Information System (CALIS)
Peking University Library

Translated by Yao Kuangtien

An updated version of a paper presented at the May 4, 1994, Seminar at Peking University Library.

Facts about Peking University's New Library

Architect:	Professor Guan Zhaoye
Director:	Professor Dai Longji
Total Area:	25,500 square meters
Capacity:	3,000,000 volumes
Reader Stations:	2,400
Total Budget:	$17,600,000

Necessity for Constructing a New Library

Peking University Library was founded in 1902 and is one of the oldest modern libraries in China. It was first named Capital University Book Collection Building and then renamed Peking University Library.* In the course of the past century, many people have left their marks on it, including revolutionary heroes such as Mao Zedong and Li Dazhao, as well as many renowned scholars.

Peking University Library has long been the largest university library in China in terms of its collection, staff, budget, and space. The old library alone houses 3,500,000 items including a large number of rare books, and a wealth

In pinyin transliteration, "Peking" is now rendered as "Beijing"; however, Professor Zhu prefers "Peking University," which is still the University's official English name, as approved by its administration.— T.D.W.

South side of the new PKU Library. (Courtesy of PKU Library.)

of contemporary Chinese and foreign books and journals. Another one million items are allocated to more than 30 departmental libraries and other storage places at the university. The operation, technology and service of the library are among the best in China. The library has established agreements for material exchanges and library cooperation with more than 50 countries and over a hundred libraries all over the world. It has won great prestige domestically as well as internationally.

The existing library was constructed in 1975 with a total building area of 24,500 square meters and floor area of 11,289 square meters. Its maximum capacity is 3,000,000 items, and maximum seating is 2,000. The usable floor area for reading and staff offices is 13,000 square meters. The library is old-fashioned in its structure and design. It impedes the work of the staff, and has simple and rather crude facilities for users and staff. After 18 years of operation, due to steady increases with the collection and users, and the expansion and changes of library operation, it is no longer able to meet the demands of staff and users with respect to space and technology. The capacity of the stacks has reached its limit, and seating for readers has decreased to a ratio of ten students to a seat. Under such difficult circumstances, it is extremely hard for the library to operate and function effectively. Since we are the largest academic library with the most important collection in China, we are providing service not only to more than 20,000 of our own students, staff and faculty members, but also to large numbers of foreign users every year. In addition, the library has also undertaken the responsibilities of Peking University Center of Humanities and Social Sciences and the Station for Checking and Searching New Achievements of Science and Technology. These bodies are under the direction of the State Education Commission and serve all the concerned institutes throughout the country. To make Peking University Library a first-class library in the 21st century and to further provide contributions to the development of education, science, technology, and culture in China, it was urgent to build a new library that would be among the best in the world.

In 1992, Mr. Ka Shing Li, a well-known Hong Kong entrepreneur and an Honorary Doctor of Peking University, visited Peking University and the library. The contrast between the abundant treasures and out-dated facilities in the library made an indelible impression on him. After his visit, Mr. Li expressed his willingness to donate 10 million U.S. dollars to help Peking University build a new library with first-rate facilities and equipment. The Peking University new library project has also received great support from the State Education Commission of China and the Peking Municipal Government. The construction for the new library has been included as one of the major initiatives that make up "Project 211" for Peking University.

Project 211 is a nationwide project initiated by the State Education Commission of China and approved by the State Council. The purpose of the project is to enhance higher education in China by allocating extra funds to about 100 key universities, so that they will achieve an international level of quality by the year 2010. "211" implies "21st Century" and "100 key universities." Peking University is one of the two universities first approved to enter the project.

After a lengthy competition, the design task was assigned to the Architectural Design and Research Institute of Tsinghua University. The architect responsible for the overall design was Professor Guan Zhaoye, an academician of the China Academy of Engineering, from the Architecture Department of Tsinghua University. The preparation work for construction officially began during the latter part of 1993. After more than two years of preparation, the construction commenced in June 1996, and was scheduled to be completed by May 1998, just before the celebration of Peking University's centenary.

Guiding Principles for Constructing the New Library

1. The new library should become an important document and information center for student and faculty study and research. It should guarantee to provide effective and timely document and information service as well as graceful, comfortable, and peaceful internal and external environments.

2. The new library will operate mainly with open stacks. It should provide easy access for users, and facilitate management by staff members. It should carry

out a scientific and logical management system and service style. The arrangements for shelving and storing, lending and borrowing, reading and browsing of the library materials should be in accordance with their contents and types.

3. Whenever possible, the new library should have modern facilities and equipment to provide first-class library collection, management, preservation and user services.

4. The new library should be practical and flexible. It should also be adaptable to future operational development and functional changes in the future.

The Scope and Basis of Construction

CONSTRUCTION AREA: 25,500 M²

According to the development plan of Peking University, it has targeted to have 10,000 undergraduates, 5,000 graduates, 1,000 foreign students, and 10,000 continuing education students by the end of this century. The ratio of faculty to students will be 1:10. We will need approximately 5,000 seats in the library to provide an average of four students per seat, and 10 faculty and staff members per seat. Among them, 2,400 seats will be provided for the old library, and 2,600 seats will be needed for the new library.

Currently, the library houses 3,500,000 items. Approximately 60,000 new items, annually, have been added to the present collection during the past few years. And because we have undertaken the responsibilities of Peking University Information Center of Humanities and Social Sciences of the State Education Commission of China, approximately 100,000 new items will be added to our collection every year in the future. Furthermore, we will be acquiring more audio-visual materials and electronic publications. Even with calculating items withdrawn, mutilated and discarded, we will still add 90,000 new items to our existing collection every year in the future. Within 30 years, without considering any further expansion, we will expect to have approximately 7,000,000 items in our collection. After the renovation of the old library, it will be able to house 4,000,000 items, and the new library will be able to accommodate 3,000,000 items.

The new library will be acquiring large amounts of modern equipment and providing new service facilities for users; therefore, it is essential for the library to have spacious rooms to accommodate the demands. Moreover, we will have approximately 100 staff members working in the new library, and it is equally important to provide them with spacious offices.

Selecting the Library Site

The new library site is located on the south bank of the Unnamed Lake of Yan Yuan, and it is linked to the east side of the old library. It is centrally and conveniently located in quiet and graceful surroundings without much air pollution.

A reading room in the new PKU Library. (Courtesy of PKU Library.)

It will be easier to manage and utilize because of its location next to the old library. The new library is 100 meters in length from east to west, and 130 meters in width from north to south. It occupies a total area of 13,000 square meters. Previously, this was a green area, and the new building now occupies parts of it. According to the master construction plan for Peking University, two classroom buildings nearby were demolished and replaced by a green area to form a new open area on campus. Land has also been reserved for future library expansion.

The Design Requirements for New Library

The construction of the new library should give an impetus to the development and reform of Peking University Library; therefore, it was essential that the architectural design of the new be consistent with the renovation of the old.

STRUCTURE, SCALE AND SHAPE

The building has a 7.5 × 7.5 meter modular structure. Lightweight partitions were used. The uniformly distributed load is 500 kilograms per square meter for each floor and 1,000 kilograms for the foundation.

Facing east, the new library comprises three parts, including a central building, and south and north wings in a symmetrical layout. A frontage road of 51 meters leaves the library with a wide-open and quiet green area at the front. Two out of the eight stories of the central building are underground. The fourth story from the ground is at the same height as the fourth floor of the old library. The height from the ground does not exceed 30 meters. The west side of the new building is 7.5 meters away from the old one, and is connected to it by corridors. The area between the corridors is reserved for a glass-roofed garden. There are two sunny gardens at south and north corners that provide natural light and ventilation for the two underground stories. The two wing buildings are also integrated with the central building by corridors.

After its completion, the structure of the new library not only harmonizes with its surroundings, but also reflects the simplicity and the dignity of the campus' artistic style. It plays a dominant role at the center of nearby buildings. And most importantly, it is a fitting symbol for Peking University.

The total building area combined, for the new and the old library, is 50,000 square meters.

General Requirements

The new library is a first-rate building with an eight-degree anti-seismic, top-quality fire-resistant structure, and a Class-A quality construction.

Colored terrazzo flooring is used in most areas, but carpet will be installed in some rooms. Floor color varies for each floor. Granite materials were used for major stairways. Ceilings and inner walls have sound absorbent insulation. Heat insulation, anti-seepage treatment, and lightning-resistant equipment are installed on the roof.

A central air-conditioning system with individual controls is installed in the library. Airtight windows are installed to prevent dust. However, they also open for natural ventilation in case of malfunctioning of the air conditioning system. Thermal insulation and heat-resistant materials have been installed in the external walls and roof.

The Class-A civil defense planning design and structure were applied to the basement construction. It has top-quality waterproofing.

Natural lighting as well as artificial lighting are used. Illumination levels are 220 lux at the work surface during the night, and 200 lux on the bottom shelf of the book stacks.

Connecting plugs, at least four sets between each modular structure, were installed for the multi-purpose cabling system, built-in power, lighting fixtures, broadcasting equipment, and telecommunication system.

Stairways, two passenger (1,000 kg) elevators, and two passenger-cargo (600 kg) elevators were installed. Handicapped access is also available in the new library.

Fire-resistant materials were used. An automatic security monitoring and alarm system, and automatic as well as manual fire extinguishers are installed.

Fireproof partitions were installed for each floor. Fire exits and emergency lighting equipment were also installed.

Lockable garbage disposal shoots are provided for each floor. A garbage removal passageway was installed in the basement, and it will also be used as a fire fighting passageway.

THE RELATIONSHIP BETWEEN THE NEW AND THE OLD LIBRARY

We made an effort to unify the architectural structures of the new and the old library; however, because of differences in their space and arrangement, responsibilities were assigned individually to each library with respect to their official functions and operational activities. Corridors connect both libraries on each floor. This not only provides users easy access to both libraries, but also provides a convenient means for staff members to move books, journals and other materials. The subject coverage and materials arrangement is divided between the new and the old library. The new library emphasizes attracting teaching and research faculty and staff members, while the old library attracts mostly students. The new library will be responsible, mostly, for the public services, and the old library is responsible for the internal operation of the library. The collection of the new library will emphasize ancient Chinese books and documentation, recent publications published after 1975, new audio-visual materials, and electronic publications, while the old library is mainly responsible for periodicals, special subjects documentation, and books published prior to 1975.

TRAFFIC BETWEEN THE NEW AND THE OLD LIBRARY

Two entrances are available separately to facilitate a smooth operation of the library. One is for staff members and library materials. The other is for users. The library workflow will avoid interfering with student activities in the library. Floors are flat and smooth, without stairways; passenger elevators are close to the users' main entrance as well as the main connecting corridors for the new and old libraries. Passenger-cargo elevators were installed in the internal work area where they are invisible to users. Traffic guides and signs are used according to international standards.

INTERNAL ENVIRONMENT OF THE NEW LIBRARY

Room temperature and humidity
Winter: Temperature: 18-20°C. Relative Humidity: 50%–55%.
Summer: Temperature: 28-30°C. Relative Humidity: 55%–60%.

Air exchange

Air exchange: 25m³/hour per person.
Dust filters installed for ventilation.

Internal lighting

Energy-efficient lighting fixtures were installed in the ceiling and can be individually controlled. Desk lamp may be used if necessary. Decorative lighting fixtures were installed in some special function rooms. All lighting fixtures are easy to maintain, clean, repair and replace.

Interior decoration

Flooring coloring is different for each floor, and it is pleasant, elegant and quiet. Light shades of colors have been used for furniture, and to coordinate and harmonize with the surroundings. Glossy paint and shiny metal were not used for interior windows and doors to prevent glare and dazzle.

External environment

Approximately 1,000 square meters of open space was reserved for parking bicycles and motorcycles. There will be an underground parking area for them. A wide-open space has been reserved for a green area in front of the library. Traffic lights will be installed outside of the library. Special lighting will be installed at the front of library to illuminate its facade. The inner courtyard connecting the new and the old library will be an artistically designed garden.

Public Facilities

Electricity

A multi-purpose cabling system is installed. Important areas of the library are equipped with emergency power.

Heating

A hot water heating system was installed. Some areas of the library are air conditioned.

Water supply

A fire-fighting water tank with automatic fire pump was installed on the top of the new building.

Drainage

Drainage pipelines in the new building were connected to a nearby sewage system. The basement also has drainage.

Communication

The new library will install hundreds of telephones. Communication cables are connected to the main switchboard.

The Management and Service of Both New and Old Libraries

ORGANIZATIONAL STRUCTURES, FUNCTIONS AND DISTRIBUTIONS

———————— NEW LIBRARY ————————

Administration Office
> Responsible for managing and coordinating administrative work and business, receiving domestic and foreign guests, and providing secretarial services and maintenance of files, etc.

Ancient Book Collection
> Responsible for acquiring, cataloging, preserving, maintaining and servicing all ancient Chinese books, manuscripts, rare books and other special materials.

Audio-Visual Department
> Responsible for maintaining, preserving, photocopying, storing, inventorying, and discarding all Chinese and foreign audio-visual materials.

Automation Department (Center for applying and developing new modern technology)
> Responsible for managing various types of new information, recommending and introducing processing technology, and installing, maintaining and utilizing equipment.

Circulation and Reading Department — Two
> Responsible for circulation, reading room, reference information, maintenance, shelving, inventorying and discarding Chinese and western-language books and other materials.

Information and Consultation Department (Document Information Center)
> Responsible for providing general help and consultation, special subject consultation, and service of domestic and international electronic publishing. Also responsible for construction, maintenance, inquiry service, user accounts, management of various document information databases and other electronic databases.

———————— OLD LIBRARY ————————

Acquisition Department
> Responsible for acquiring, recording, receiving, exchanging all types of Chinese and foreign materials.

Automation Department (Center for applying and developing new modern technology)

Responsible for managing various types of new information, recommending and introducing the processing technology, and installing, maintaining and utilizing the equipment.

Cataloging Department

Responsible for cataloging and maintaining all types of Chinese and foreign materials.

Circulation and Reading Department — One

Responsible for the circulation, reading room, reference and information, maintenance, shelving, inventorying and discarding of all Chinese and western-language books, and other materials.

Document Printing and Photocopying Service Department

Responsible for typesetting, printing, photocopying, binding and mending book and journal materials for users and library use.

Office of General Affairs

Responsible for providing logistic support to the administration, and security of the library, allocating benefits for the employees, and maintaining and repairing furniture, etc.

Serials Department

Responsible for acquiring, recording, receiving, binding, cataloging, maintaining, and preserving all types of materials. The department is also responsible for maintaining, allocating, storing, inventorying and discarding serial materials as well as maintaining its reading room.

Layout and Management of Library Materials

——— NEW LIBRARY ———

Ancient Thread-Bound Books (including rare books, manuscripts, rubbings, calligraphies and paintings, etc.):
Volume: Approximately 1,200,000 volumes
Type of Stack Area: Closed

Chinese and Western Language Books Published after 1975:
Volume: 1,200,000 volumes
Type of Stack Area: Open

Audio-Visual Materials:
Type of Stack Area: Closed

Electronic Materials:
Type of Stack Area: Closed

———————— OLD LIBRARY ————————

Beida Wen Ku (Peking University Documentation Center):
Type of Stack Area: Closed

Chinese and Foreign Periodicals:
Current Subscription: 7,000 titles
Type of Stack Area: Open
Back Issues: 700,000 volumes
Type of Stack Area: Open — current issues and recent back issues
                    Closed in the storage — back issues of old newspapers
                    (Faculty members with rank of assistant professor
                        or higher may have access to items of newspapers
                        in closed stacks)
                    Closed — periodicals published prior to 1949

Chinese and Western Language Books Published Prior to 1975:
Volume: 1,200,000 volumes
Type of Stack Area: Closed
(Faculty members with rank of assistant professor or higher may have
access to items in closed stacks)

Chinese Reserved Books:
Volume: 100,000 volumes
Type of Stack Area: Closed

Dissertations:
Type of Stack Area: Closed

Microforms:
Type of Stack Area: Closed

Russian and Japanese Books:
Volume: 100,000 volumes
Type of Stack Area: Open

NEW LIBRARY FACILITIES—AREA, LAYOUT AND FUNCTION

Ancient Books Storage and Utilization Area
  Ancient Books Stacks:
    Area: 5,000 m²
    Volume: 1,200,000 volumes
    Location: 2nd floor Basement
    Lighting: Artificial lighting with ultraviolet filter
    Temperature: Air Conditioner
    Winter: 15°C. Summer: 22°C. Relative Humidity: 50%–55%
    Facilities: Electronic compact shelving, moisture absorption equipment,
                drainage, emergency power, automatic security monitoring
                and alarm detection, automatic fire extinguishers, passenger-
                cargo elevator, escalator

Ancient Books Reading and Display Room:
    Area: 250 m^2
    Employees: 2
    Displaying Case: 10
    Seating: 40
    Location: 1st floor in the basement near the courtyard
    Facilities: Automatic security monitoring and alarm detection, automatic
        fire extinguisher

Ancient Books Administration Office: (containing a workroom for repairing and binding):
    Area: 150 m^2
    Employees: 8
    Location: 1st floor in the basement next to its reading and display room
    Facilities: Automatic security monitoring and alarm detection, automatic
        fire extinguisher, water supply lines and drainage

Chinese and Foreign Language Books Open-Stack Circulation and Reading Area

Western Language Books Circulation and Reading Room:
    Area: 3,000 m^2
    Volume: 300,000 volumes
    Employees: 10
    Seating: 300
    Workstation: One Circulation and Information Desk
    Location: 1st floor in the basement
    Facilities: Automatic security monitoring and alarm detection, automatic
        sprinkler

Chinese and Western-Language Reference and Index Room:
    Area: 900 m^2
    Volume: 100,000 volumes
    Employees: 6
    Seating: 150
    Workstation: One Reference Desk
    Location: 1st floor
    Facilities: Automatic security monitoring and alarm detection, automatic
        sprinkler

Chinese Literatures Books Circulation and Reading Room — First:
    Classification: A–F
    Area: 2,800 m^2
    Volume: 300,000 volumes
    Employees: 10
    Seating: 300
    Workstation: One Circulation and Information Desk
    Location: 2nd floor

Facilities: Automatic security monitoring and alarm detection, automatic sprinkler

Chinese Literatures Books Circulation and Reading Room — Second:
Classification: G–K
Area: 2,800 m²
Volume: 300,000 volumes
Employees: 10
Seating: 300
Workstation: One Circulation and Information Desk
Location: 3rd floor
Facilities: Automatic security monitoring and alarm detection, automatic sprinkler

Chinese Humanities and Social Sciences Books Circulation and Reading Room:
Area: 2,800 m²
Volume: 300,000 volumes
Employees: 10
Seating: 300
Workstation: One Circulation and Information Desk
Location: 4th floor
Facilities: Automatic security monitoring and alarm detection, automatic sprinkler

Chinese Current Accessions Reading Room:
Area: 600 m²
Volume: 30,000 volumes
Employees: 3
Seating: 150
Workstation: One Information Desk
Location: 5th floor
Facilities: Automatic security monitoring and alarm detection, automatic sprinkler

Public Searching Area — Located on 1st Floor
General Information Desk:
Area: 50 m²
Employees: 3

Online Searching Area:
Area: 240 m²
Employees: 2
Terminal: 50

CD-ROM Searching Room (Room will be locked after closing):
Area: 160 m²
Employees: 4
CD-ROM Workstation: 20

Facilities: Automatic security monitoring and alarm detection, fire extinguisher

Audio-Visual Circulation, Listening and Viewing Area —
Located in the South Wing

Facilities: Acoustic insulation, automatic security monitoring and alarm detection, fire extinguisher

Multimedia Room:
Area: 300 m²
Multimedia Microcomputers: 60

Audio Room:
Area: 150 m²
Employees: 2
Seating: 60

Film Projecting Room:
Area: 100 m²
Employees: 2
Seating: 40

Video Viewing Room:
Area: 200 m²
Employees: 2
Seating: 60

Audio-Visual Materials and Equipment Room:
Area: 240 m²

Broadcasting Control Room
Area: 50 m²
Employees: 2

Research and Study Area

Document Class Room:
Area: 100 m²
Location: 1st floor

Research Room:
Located on each floor with different designs, equipment and sizes

Equipment Room

Facilities: Fireproof partition, acoustic insulation, automatic security monitoring and alarm detection, fire extinguisher

Power Distribution and Safety Control Room:
Area: 50 m²
Location: 1st floor in the basement (in a concealed area with lightning-resistant equipment)

Air Conditioning Equipment Room:
　　Area: 150 m^2
　　Location: 1st floor in the basement

Computer Equipment Room:
　　Area: 340 m^2
　　Location: 6th floor
　　Facilities: Lightning-resistant equipment, radiation protection, electro-
　　　　magnetism protection

Includes:
　　Mainframe Room:
　　　　Area: 60 m^2
　　　　Facilities: Static guard floor, optical cables connected to computer
　　　　　　room in the old library

　　Terminal Room:
　　　　Area: 80 m^2
　　　　Facilities: Static guard floor

　　Magnetic Tape and Disk Room:
　　　　Area: 30 m^2
　　　　Facilities: Static guard floor

　　Data Processing Room:
　　　　Area: 50 m^2

　　Software Room:
　　　　Area: 50 m^2

　　Utility Room (computer spare parts and tools):
　　　　Area: 30 m^2

　　Duty and Reception Room:
　　　　Area: 40 m^2 (a suite)

Offices — All Located on 1st Floor, Except Conference/Seminar Room
　　Facilities: Automatic security monitoring and alarm detection, automatic
　　　　sprinkler

Director's Office:
　　Area: 40 m^2 (a suite)

Office:
　　Area: 50 m^2 (doorway to the Director's Office)

Guard Room — close to Main Entrance
　　Area: 20 m^2

Guest Receiving Room — close to the Director's Office
　　Area: 110 m^2
　　Seating: 20
　　Includes a Conference Room (wall-to-wall carpet) with seating for 30.

Conference/Seminar Room:
> Area: 150 m²
> Seating: 50
> Location: 6th floor
> Facilities: Wall-to-wall carpet, long-distance television conference equipment and other audio-visual equipment, acoustic insulation

Public Activity Area — Located on the 1st Floor and the North Wing
> Facilities: Automatic security monitoring and alarm detection, automatic sprinkler

Entrance Hall:
> Area: 200 m²

Lecture Room: (in the north wing)
> Area: 400 m²
> Facilities: Lecture theater with step seating, opaque curtains, automatic screen on the platform, white writing board, simultaneous interpretation workroom, acoustic insulation

Multi-function Room: (in the north wing)
> Area: 300 m²

Lounge (for library users):
> Area: 200 m²
> Facilities: Washrooms (located on each floor, except 2nd floor in the basement)
> Drinking fountain outside of the washrooms
> Handicapped access
> Low-noise ventilation
> Passageways, elevators, stairways

Construction Dates and Implementation Schedules

The library's grand opening was held in conjunction with an International Library Conference and was a major event of the university's centennial celebration.

Schedules planned as follow:

March 1994–April 1994:
Drafting design proposal. Discussing design requirements.

May 1994–August 1994:
Researching, adjusting the proposal and ratifying the construction proposal.

September 1994:
The plan is ratified and confirmed. Public bidding for construction design.

June 1995–May 1996:
Examining and approving construction design. Public bidding for construction.

June 1996–April 1998:
Constructing the library.

August 1997–December 1997:
Investigating, selecting, ordering and purchasing furniture and equipment.

March 1998–June 1998:
Decorating interior, arranging furniture and installing equipment. Landscaping of external area. Construction checked and accepted.

July 1998–September 1998:
Shifting and moving library materials.

October 1998:
Grand opening.

Construction Budget

The project required approximately $17,600,000, including the $10 million for architectural design and construction donated by Kai Shing Li. The remaining amount was funded by the Chinese government.

The Benefits of the New Library

INCREASED SIZE

Upon completion, the library doubled its size in terms of area, seating capacity and collection volume, making it the largest university library in Asia. None of the ten top libraries in Asia exceeds 40,000 square meters. The combined area, for the new and the old library, is 50,000 square meters. The library has a total of 5,000 seats, and is able to collect over 7,000,000 books.

IMPORTANT TRANSFORMATIONS WITH RESPECT TO ITS MANAGEMENT AND SERVICE

The old library has always relied on traditional lending and borrowing methods with closed stacks because of its old, structural limitations. The new library utilizes advanced library management processes. The new library adopted a multipurpose cabling system, offers electronic information networking, CD-ROM databases and indexes, digital information and audio-visual service, and has automatic security and alarm detection and calamity-resistant systems, and other modern equipment.

The new library provides open-stack services, computer online terminals, electronic information services, and other media materials and services. Faculty members and graduate students will have the privilege not only to use carrels specially designed for them in the library, they will also be able to access the Internet

President Clinton addresses PKU students in front of the new PKU Library during the ceremony for his donation of 500 books to the Library. (Courtesy PKU Library.)

for inquiring and obtaining the latest information, domestic and foreign, in their offices as well as dormitories.

AN ARTS AND SCIENCES DOCUMENT AND INFORMATION CENTER FOR ALL LIBRARIES IN CHINA

After its completion, Peking University Library will become the arts and sciences document and information center for all university libraries in China. This will allow it to offer modernized information services to all universities in various subject areas, such as providing the newest, domestic and international, document and information services in the social sciences and natural sciences, and checking and searching new achievements and projects of science and technology. In the future, the users, on-campus as well as off-campus, will be able to use telephone, fax machine, e-mail, and other communication means to inquire and obtain the latest worldwide information through our library network and services. Through these enhancements, the wealth of documents that pass through Peking University Library will be commonly shared by the other university libraries in China.

An Important Research Center for Chinese and Asian Studies

After its completion, Peking University will strengthen its classical and ancient Chinese collection. This will not only allow us to make Chinese culture more widely known, but will also allow us to provide information service to the world. Peking University has an abundant collection of traditional Chinese thread-bound rare books. Many of them, either matchless in the world or treasures of great value, are rarely seen anywhere else in the world. The new library will maintain its tradition of enlarging this special collection. And if we can convert these Chinese classics and rare documentation to CD-ROM, we will be able to preserve them further and disseminate them widely to all users. This will not only make us an important research center that exerts a tremendous influence on the organization, preservation, research, and use of Chinese classics and culture, but will also allow us to promote international cultural exchanges.

A Base and Source for Practicing Library Sciences and Information Studies

By combining the advanced facilities and practice of the new library with the teaching and research activities of the Information Management Department of the university, Peking University Library will become an essential base for teaching and researching Library Sciences and Information Studies in China. Furthermore, the library will become a domestic and international study and research exchange center for all librarians, and a major bibliographical center for all users. Thus, Peking University Library will become the leader among all libraries in China.

Foreseeable Difficulties and Insufficiencies

Although we are striving to establish Peking University Library as a world first-class university library, we see difficulties and insufficiencies due to various limitations and restrictions.

1. Distinct contrast between the old and the new building structures.
   Because of the fixed shape and structure of the old library, even after its renovation and improvement are completed, the distinct structural contrast between the new and the old will still exist.
2. The application of new technology to the library may be restricted by the infrastructure development in China.
   Although China is thriving economically, we are still behind other, more developed countries. Funding shortages will surely have an impact on our application of new technology and equipment in the library. For instance, "The National Information Infrastructure Project" in the United

States has already been implemented. We may not be able to fully enjoy the benefits of this advanced hi-tech application due to certain communication and technological limitations and policy restrictions in China. Therefore, we may still have to use the traditional methods side-by-side with the advanced modern technology and equipment for some time in order to adjust to our own infrastructure.

3. Financial difficulties.

Building a first-class university library requires a substantial amount of funding. Budget for construction was a fixed amount which was calculated rather conservatively. Moreover, to maintain a first-rate library operation, we also need to have a substantial budget for daily library operation and maintenance. The funding, $2,000,000, originally budgeted for the daily library operation and maintenance, has been cut to fund the current building construction. Without any budget for its daily operation and maintenance after its completion, it will be difficult to add new equipment to keep abreast with the advanced modern technology of the future.

4. Availability of qualified personnel.

To operate and maintain a first-rate university library, we need librarians with the highest qualifications. They should have backgrounds in various specializations and administrative skills, be able to exchange, directly and equally, with library professionals abroad, and have received some international recognition. To provide qualified personnel, the library should concentrate on an in-depth training program. Also, the library should try to attract qualified personnel from among Chinese students studying abroad, in countries such as the United States, Canada, Great Britain, and Australia. We may also be able to attract foreign library professionals and experts to work for the library. However, it is rather hard for us to keep the present qualified personnel working for the library because our wages, benefits and hiring policies still do not match those of other countries.

Although difficulties and insufficiencies do exist, we can still overcome them if we strive harder. Peking University has made great improvements in all areas. Faculty and staff members and students are working hard together to maintain the university's reputation as a world class institution. The construction project for the new library will help sustain Peking University as a first-rate university. The development of teaching and scientific research at Peking University has also made urgent, new demands on the library. That is also the driving force for the development of the library. The construction project was an inseparable link to the construction and development of the university as a whole. We are greatly encouraged by support from faculty members and students of Peking University, as well as from our friends, domestic and abroad. We will definitely make the best use of our funding to get the most desirable results.

Additional Readings

Peking Daxue Tushuguan Guancang Wenxian Diaocha Pinggu Baogaoji (The Investigation and Evaluation Report of Peking University Library). Peking daxue tushuguan bianyin, October 1992.

Beijing Diqu Xinjian Gaoxiao Tushuguan Xuanli (Shiyi yu cankao ziliao) (Selected Examples of New University Libraries at Beijing Areas [Sketches and References]). Beijingshi gaoxiao tushu qingbao gongzuo weiyuanhui jianshe yu shebei zixunzu xuanji, 1993.

Shan, Xing. *Tushuguan Jianzhu Yu Sheji* (Architecture and Design of Library). Dalian: Liaoning shifan daxue chubanshe, 1992.

Edward, Heather M. *University Library Building Planning*. Metuchen, N.J.: The Scarecrow Press, Inc., 1990.

Guoli Taiwan Daxue Tushuguan Jingtu Zuoping Zilaioji (The Collection of Plans and Works of the Library of Taiwan National University). Guoli Taiwan daxue xiaoyuan guihua xiaozu zongtushuguan gongwu xiaozu huibian, 1991.

Yang, Zhi-min. *Beijing Nongye Daxue Tushuguan Jianzhu Gongneng Tanxi* (Survey and Analysis of the Constructional Function of the Library of Beijing Agriculture University), December 1993.

Unit 2
FORM
Arranging Services in Space

Unit Background

John Perry Barlow, cyberspace "guerrilla" and Grateful Dead lyricist, has said,

> Librarians should understand that what they do is create space, cognitive space in the environment. It can look like a public library, a web site ... or whatever. Librarians need to make sure that they provide a rich space, where human beings can gather, interact, and become more than themselves. If librarians can do that, and do it well, they will be a part of the future. I know a lot of them are doing that right now [quoted in Chepesiuk, "Librarians," 51, ellipsis in the original].

Barlow leaves librarians a lot of room for space-building, so to speak. He encourages us to enlarge our thinking, if we can, even beyond walls and web sites, beyond the "architecture" of mere buildings and computerized systems. Sarah Michalak might concur. She states, "In the current environment, no particular arrangement of functions within library spaces can be considered mandatory or permanent" (100), and adds that library buildings "must be organized in a logical fashion according to the typical patterns users must follow to locate the information and materials they need" (101).

In the modern parlance, then, the rules of library design have changed. Builder-librarians must incorporate an intuitively friendly order in their design of library spaces, whether those be areas inside physical structures in real space, or the menus, search engines, and hyper-connections within a library's online resources residing in virtual space. Some of the libraries in this book are clearly rule-breakers; instead of designing their new buildings to accommodate standard library departmentation and conventional library staff work flow, they designed the facilities according to their perceptions of how their users approach library materials and services. The libraries in this unit are no exception, and because they happen to be academic libraries, this translates into how college students study and learn. But the same consideration for the users and their needs is also appearing in public library building projects as well. The Shanghai Library and San Antonio Public Library in Unit 1 provide examples; the Phoenix Public Library in Unit 3 is another.

Changing the Rules

The libraries at Kapiolani Community College (KCC) and George Mason University (GMU) both looked to student patterns of study and learning to guide the design of their new facilities, and arranged their internal spaces accordingly. GMU wanted to reflect these patterns, and KCC wanted to influence them. There are other similarities as well: both libraries wanted to help students see the relevance of their classroom learning to the larger community and to the world; both saw the need for a variety of seating to suit different learning styles; key design elements came from the top administrators of the respective institutions; both libraries intended to blend several electronic information formats with a basic or core print collection; and both libraries have noisy and quiet zones.

Also, both KCC and GMU saw the task of building a library for the 21st century as more than simply a matter of accommodating new technology. As Charlene Hurt states in her chapter, defining the library of the future at GMU meant physically "taking the library" to the place where its users congregate, in order to open "a new entrance to the library system." For KCC, designing a 21st-century library meant organizing the space around a variety of information formats, which would be arranged and integrated in a meaningful succession to take the most advantage of their best features.

Yet despite the remarkable similarities, the resulting buildings are very different because user needs are so varied that the KCC and GMU libraries arrived at very different floor plans and arrangements of services to meet them. The KCC library worked from the traditional model of the academic library, and so is the more conventional of the two: to assure security, there is only one public entrance/exit; no food is allowed in the library; and aside from computer labs operated by the College's computing center, the library is the only "tenant" of the building.

The GMU library, on the other hand, is part of a new student center that resembles popular public meeting places like shopping malls and trendy café-bookstore combinations: the GMU library has multiple entrances and exits; food is allowed in library areas; and the facility is shared with other student services, study centers, retail shops, a theater, and even a food court. In a bold statement that appears to be much less than coincidence, Will Bruder, the architect of the new Phoenix Central Library (see Unit 3), also is reported to have designed the new Phoenix facility according to "a popular bookstore culture of easy access" (quoted in Wiley, 112).

Obviously, designing libraries around the habits and tastes of the users opens the door to many possible variations. For instance, KCC designed its library as an information "buffet" leading students from televised coverage of the most current events to print sources for researching the distant past. GMU, on the other hand, emphasized collaborative, even convivial, learning. And if the Benton Foundation's findings are accurate in reporting that the people who frequent commercial bookstores are among the library's loyal supporters, the GMU design may in fact be a model library for the future (*Buildings*, 6, 17–18).

Interlibrary Borrowing

Just as the Shanghai Library officials studied other libraries around the world as part of the planning for their new library, the GMU planners were familiar with several other newly constructed libraries, including the new library at Indiana University–Purdue University Indianapolis (IUPUI; see chapter 8) and the Leavey Library at the University of Southern California (USC).

The similarities between USC's Leavey Library (not included in this collection) and the GMU library appear most strongly in their combination of moderate print collections with extensive electronic information access; in their designs that promote collaborative learning among students and collaborative instruction involving librarians and faculty; and in their emphasis on a teaching mission. The interior of the Leavey was "specifically designed to facilitate finding and managing information and to encourage students to explore the networked systems that will be critically important in the next century" (Commings, 19). According to Charlene Hurt, the design of the GMU library began as "a desire to create a new kind of learning environment for undergraduates ... and an interest in supporting new ways of teaching undergraduates that depended on collaborative learning [and] extensive use of media and technology" (quoted in Davis, 277). Yet for all the similarities, the GMU library, again, is very much its own library, an original and provocative creation, like the other libraries in this book.

Flexible Positioning

This phrase from the GMU chapter refers to one of the most often repeated advisories in all the chapters: build flexibility into your library's space, from the shape of the place, to the allocations of its internal spaces, to the allowance for new technologies. For example, movable partitions and modular interiors are appearing in libraries from Beijing to Paris. And ample cable raceways in the floors or in the ceilings, to facilitate the installation of additional or new technology, or to permit the reconfiguration of furnishings and service areas, is as common now as plumbing.

As an example, the new IUPUI library is a $30 million facility built for a smooth transition into multi-format electronic information delivery, with over 120 miles of optical fiber packed into the structure to network more than 1,700 work sites. Access to the library's online resources and the Internet is available through the many public work stations and also through in-house connections for persons who wish to bring their own computers or borrow a laptop from the library (Koopman and Hay, 12). Directives from the university administration regarding the building included

> commitments to deliver information regardless of format, and to deliver that information to virtually every seat in the building. This meant that the library building had to be constructed to provide delivery of text, video, audio, and graphics to individual sites throughout the facility [Koopman and Hay, 12].

Yet one of the important lessons the IUPUI staff learned quickly was that even with all the provision for electronic information access, "demand for computing always swells to meet and exceed supply" (Koopman and Hay, 14). It is a lesson that all future builder-librarians should keep in mind.

A distinct lack of flexibility surrounded the construction of some of the libraries in this unit, however. For instance, the basic shape and size of the new KCC library were predetermined by the college's master plan, which was completed years before planning for the building began. But at least the internal spaces could be allocated and outfitted to our specifications. Conditions for the new library at California State University, Monterey Bay (CSUMB) were even more restrictive than those at KCC. Because of a ten-year moratorium on new construction at CSUMB, the library was constrained to use existing buildings on the old Fort Ord site, which became the CSUMB campus after the Army closed the base as part of its downsizing effort.

The CSUMB library made national news when the Chancellor for the California State University system was quoted in *Newsweek* as saying, "You simply don't have to build a traditional library these days" (Hafner, 62). Librarian Jeannette Woodward portrayed the statement as a potential "death knell" for academic libraries, because it was uttered by a very potent decision maker and carried in a very widely read national news magazine where its message could infect the minds of other decision makers (Woodward, 1017). But Woodward was no doubt exaggerating for effect, because new libraries everywhere, and certainly every library in every chapter in this book, are examples of an attempt to get beyond the "traditional."

The CSUMB library is no exception; it is another rule breaker. John Ober relates in his chapter that instead of using electronic resources to supplement the print collection, CSUMB uses a small core collection to supplement its full-text electronic subscriptions. This places the CSUMB library, he says, in a transformational middle ground between a traditional library and a wholly virtual one. Ober's fascinating chapter also demonstrates how quickly a library can be assembled in the digital age when its mission statement prefers access to electronic information sources over ownership of print materials. Like a pontoon bridge floating on an impassable river, the CSUMB library was staffed, wired, connected, automated, and equipped with books and e-subscriptions in a little more than six months.

Ober also makes us question another "rule," namely, that only purpose-designed library spaces are suitable environments for providing effective library services. While a purpose-built facility was necessary to consolidate the vast resources of the British Library, the same may not hold true for libraries with capped collections designed to support a largely electronic mission. Ober outlines a number of benefits that the CSUMB library has derived from occupying a space that was designed with practically no librarian input whatsoever. Functional layout, not to mention form, style, and significance, were hardly elements in the genesis of the CSUMB library. Yet the CSUMB staff counts the advantages of their physical circumstances in terms of the institution's politics, their efficient staffing patterns, and the economies of managing a small book inventory.

Perhaps more than any other, then, the CSUMB chapter questions not so much the future of libraries with walls, but the need for complex form in libraries of the future. The CSUMB chapter suggests that even if a library's form is little more than happenstance, library function will remain the same. For despite the technological preferences of the CSUMB library mission statement, its mission and functions are unchanged. Likewise, the persistence of customary user expectations indicates that the library's social significance is also intact.

Size and Adaptability

This unit includes chapters from some smaller libraries of under 150,000 volumes, and smaller libraries have certain adaptive advantages that become apparent in the process of conceiving and designing new library facilities. For the simple reason that smaller libraries need less space and have smaller collections, their new buildings can incorporate innovations more quickly and economically; because they have fewer staff members, training in new technologies and methods can proceed more quickly, include more of the staff, and move more rapidly into sophisticated operations; and because staff members in smaller libraries generally perform a broader range of tasks, departmentation tends to be less rigid, which facilitates boundary-spanning, project team formulation, and organizational communication.

Technology can give smaller libraries access to, if not ownership of, resources equal to those of much larger libraries. For example, using technology, the library at the Hong Kong University of Science and Technology (HKUST; not included in this study) supplemented a collection too small to support the university's global ambitions, and helped make HKUST a world academic power almost overnight. When it opened in 1991, HKUST intended to streak to research prominence through: 1) its massive funding, 2) recruitment of an internationally renowned faculty, and 3) development of a library that would prefer electronic access to research sources instead of ownership (see "Global"; Hertling; "Fact Sheet").

Hovering above Clear Water Bay, the HKUST library's dimensions were too small for the size of collection necessary for the faculty to compete with other institutions with research collections amassed over generations. But electronic access was the equalizer. As Chang and Wassink state, "We were fortunate to be building a library at the right time, when technological advances made implementation of the electronic library concept practical and desirable" (2). Now "owning" just over 6,000 journal titles in print or electronic format, the library's holdings are small by their own admission for an aggressive institution like HKUST. But the library's CD-ROM indexes and abstracts provide faculty with access to over 50,000 journals.

In addition to solving its space limitations, the HKUST library has experienced cost savings in subscriptions, staff time, and binding, and offers faster, more powerful and more accurate access to research journals than is possible with print. Access vs. ownership has drawbacks, however. For instance, electronic versions of journals often lag weeks behind the print issues. Also, canceling an e-subscription could jeopardize access to the back issues as well. But Chang and Wassink sum up their experience this way: "We emphasize ownership of monographs, but access to journals. With this philosophy ... we have been able to optimize our materials budget to build a collection rapidly while providing the necessary journals for our researchers" (5).

The HKUST library was, of course, generously funded. But the building funds available for most smaller libraries tend to be less than those for larger libraries, and monies raised through external funding campaigns are generally more meager, too. The IUPUI chapter, on the other hand, demonstrates the kind of funding a large institution can attract, and provides a good lesson for all libraries to follow in raising external funds. The IUPUI library's fund-raising campaign was highly successful, in large part because the campaign developers were able to assemble a steering committee made up of stellar civic and business leaders with significant influence and numerous contacts in the community.

Space and Cyberspace

Barbara Fischler's chapter on the new IUPUI library clearly articulates a concept that is implied in the other chapters in this book, but is never made quite as explicit. It is this: in order to do the things that libraries are expected to do in the digital age, a library building is required. IUPUI was clearly committed to evolving into a digital library. In fact, development of a new work station and information system was as much a part of the building project as the construction of the 270,000-sq. ft. facility. In a way, the new work station and information system were intended to virtually enclose virtual space by providing abundant access to the digital realms. But cornering virtual space did not negate the need for a real location in space from which to do it.

In John Perry Barlow's words, the IUPUI library building is creating rich "cognitive space" in both the real and digital environments. The result is a model facility for the future that is not so much a library *without* walls as a library that reaches *beyond* its walls. Other libraries in this study are effectively pursuing the same goal.

The Macroergonomics of Libraries

Walt Crawford and Michael Gorman make the terse and trenchant observation that "libraries are not factories" (149). This fact struck me suddenly at a conference on macroergonomics in Stockholm several years ago. Ergonomics is a field of design that applies a knowledge of human characteristics and needs to the creation of objects, spaces, facilities, and processes so that people and things can operate safely and efficiently together. The field is sometimes called "human engineering" or simply "human factors," and its techniques are applied in activities ranging from appliance and furniture design to management techniques and organizational development. *Macroergonomics* is the field of designing efficient and satisfying sociotechnical systems — people and things interacting well together throughout extended processes and within expansive spaces.

All the other presenters at the conference were macroergonomists. They talked about flow-through, output, increasing production, maximizing efficiency, and manufacturing technology in the factories and assembly plants they had been retained to design or re-engineer. My talk about designing an academic library by matching the processes of reading and learning to the characteristics of diverse information delivery formats left everyone a little baffled, because the direct outcome of the library experience for library users is not tangible. Our product — learning — cannot be measured except indirectly or anecdotally, and the return on our investment does not accrue to us, but to our users. And the benefit we seek for them is not just that they become better library users; our mission is not to make librarians out of our users. Instead, our mission and hope is that by utilizing the library effectively, our users will do better in the very diverse aspects of their lives conducted outside the library.

Yet the conference taught me that macroergonomics has something of value for builder-librarians, because industrial design has customarily focused on the well-being and also the efficiency of the industrial employees, the factory workers, the manufacturers. Likewise, the larger part of library design in the past has been concerned too much with the comfort of the staff and the accommodation of customary library processes and materials. But those processes are now changing; new job titles are appearing; job descriptions are being re-written; and library materials are becoming more diverse and complicated. And all of this is in response to the intensified needs users have for information. They must figure more largely in library design.

Mapping user intuitions into facility design may not lead to great efficiency. But we are really seeking effectiveness more than efficiency. Effective learning takes time, and effectiveness is not the same as efficiency or convenience. The human factors that architects and builder-librarians must build into any library design have to include the user dimension with an emphasis on effective learning. As Crawford and Gorman said, libraries certainly are *not* factories. Librarians and those others who design and build libraries must be aware of that. What works in industry may be a bad fit for a learning facility. Our output is not reducible to direct measurement and calculation because our intended product is the human betterment of our users, and this cannot be directly measured inside the library itself. More than ever before, librarian-builders must look beyond library walls to the users when designing a library.

5. The Johnson Center Library at George Mason University

Charlene Hurt
University Librarian, Georgia State University

In October of 1995 George Mason University opened a new building which featured, among other things, a four-story atrium, food court, movie theater, bookstore, computer labs, and a library. The library is fully integrated into the building and accessible to students looking for a place to eat their just-purchased food. Its seating is designed to encourage collaboration, and its dominant feature is its use of technology. Although it has been described as a library that "breaks all the rules," it is in fact the result of careful thought about how people learn and what role libraries should play in learning communities. To truly understand the building, one must understand its history.

George Mason University

George Mason University is a rapidly growing, publicly supported comprehensive university in the northern Virginia suburbs of Washington, D.C. Founded in 1957 as a branch of the University of Virginia, it began offering graduate programs in 1970, and achieved university status in 1972. In many ways it has grown *despite* the wishes of the Commonwealth establishment, by staking out a claim to innovation and interdisciplinarity that could not be interpreted as competing with Virginia's more well-established universities. One of the consequences of that growth is that funding was never available for basic infrastructure, and the university is chronically short of space. Recent funding initiatives have enabled the development of a high-capacity network and substantial growth at two additional campuses, but space on the Fairfax campus remains tight. During the 1995–1996 term, George Mason University had a total enrollment of 24,172 and

North side of the George W. Johnson Center, a fully integrated building on the Fairfax Campus of George Mason University. (Courtesy George Mason University Publications. Photographer Judith Desplechin.)

offered 54 undergraduate, 41 master, 13 doctoral programs and 1 professional (law) degree program. The average student age is 29, and approximately 90 percent of the students commute; 75.9 percent work, 42.7 percent work full time. For 24 percent of the students English is a second language.

The University Library

In 1986 George Mason University was denied funding for an addition to Fenwick Library, the only library on a campus then serving 17,652 students. The general consensus was that it would be difficult to secure funding for an addition without support of the Council of Higher Education (SCHEV), the state agency charged with making budget recommendations for capital projects. SCHEV had been looking at its formula for deriving space needs and realized that the current rate of collection development would require that the state build twenty-seven acres of shelving in the next ten years.[1] They concluded that the Commonwealth of Virginia could no longer afford to house these ever-increasing collections and should look to shared warehouses and the use of electronic collections for a solution. George Mason was already pursuing these solutions through its membership in the Washington Research Library Consortium, which was funded to build a book storage facility for the academic libraries in the D.C. area, and through development of an "electronic library," but neither solution addressed the greatest needs, which were for patron seating, space to expand the periodicals and media collections, adequately wired space for consultation, and staff space. Fenwick had become the "home away from home" for many of its commuter students, and the building and staff were straining to serve the contradictory roles of research library and student hangout in the same space.

Preliminary Planning

The University administration had charged us with developing an "electronic library," and we were committed to doing so, but we were still uncertain about how that fit with the traditional library mission we expected to serve for many years to come.

In 1986 we went on a retreat with the goal of defining the electronic library, and began instead imagining the library of the future, as we recognized that our focus needed to be on service implications for a library combining print, media, and electronic collections. One of the most memorable events of that day was when we talked about our own memories of those moments in learning when the light suddenly goes on and we begin a love affair with learning. For most of us, those moments did not happen in the environment libraries traditionally provided: the single scholar alone with a book. Instead, they often happened in conversation, and frequently with some sort of beverage close at hand. How, we wondered, could the library of the future accommodate this need for human contact?

Within this context, in 1988 George W. Johnson, the president of the university, appointed a GMU Library Taskforce to investigate and write a report on the Library of the 21st Century. That faculty committee was chaired by one of GMU's distinguished professors, John Paden, who had played a pivotal role in the development of Northwestern University's African collection and was familiar with Northwestern's undergraduate library. As Director of Libraries I served on the committee and was able to suggest needs and possible solutions, but the report which was produced was very much the product of the faculty who wrote it. This was pivotal in the report securing the support of the university's president, which was essential to any future requests for expanded facilities.

The report recommended a strategy of "flexible positioning," with a "triple track" approach consisting of building strength in three broad areas:

- increasing holdings in print media, which would include broad coverage of undergraduate and graduate needs including a "core" library;
- increasing electronic facilities to provide for the bibliographic referencing of resources within an entire network of linked library systems, and the

electronic transference of an increasing number of journals and specialized publications through subscription arrangements; and
- facilitating dispersed access to the "main library" and work stations throughout the university, and in multi-site locations.

In addition they made two general recommendations:

- the library should be regarded as a central facility in any future development of the university (and hence as a high priority in planning funding requests and capital campaigns)
- the university needs to acknowledge a "triple track" approach: in the "books vs. electronic media" debate the Task Force suggests the necessity of *both*, and in the centralization/decentralization debate it suggests a "main library" at the Fairfax campus, but with the possibility of branch libraries in future dispersed-site developments.

Two recommendations were particularly important to the planning of the University Center:

> Undergraduate Student Needs — Design and implementation of an undergraduate "core library," with approximately 50,000 volumes comprising a "multi-cultural" library with emphasis on global linkages. An extension of library hours and library space, with seating capacity ratio of about 1:5 student enrollment and seminar and other collaborative learning/teaching spaces. Provision of media facility which will include audio-visual services, microcomputer and language labs, which eventually will be merged as the technology becomes standardized.

> Graduate and Professional Research Needs — As the number of graduate programs expands each year and existing programs are strengthened, a major effort will be needed for the development and accessing of professional collections, including the recruiting of specialized librarians....[2]

A Library in a Student Union

In 1989 George W. Johnson, president of the university, called me into his office and told me he wanted me to think about a library in a student union — maybe one with a bowling alley, even. Despite the quixotic phrasing of the request, it was in fact a very practical solution to two problems George Mason faced:

- It was very hard to develop a sense of community at GMU when many of our commuter students couldn't find anywhere to sit before or after classes except in their parked cars, and
- The Commonwealth of Virginia was disinclined to build any traditional space on our campus except in small increments (generally 100,000 square feet at a time).

It was also a serious attempt to address a long-standing concern of the president's, which he described as the "egg carton" problem, whereby the various parts of academic life were isolated from each other, making it impossible for students to make connections between classroom learning and the rest of their lives. He wanted a building that would help integrate all aspects of student life, demonstrating that learning takes place in many ways.

Even without the bowling alley, thinking about a library in a student union was not an easy task. Fortunately, many of the librarians had participated in the earlier retreat and were enthusiastic about the challenge of designing the library of the future. They had also participated in a series of faculty planning teams working on a new general education curriculum, and had begun thinking about the library's role in a new curriculum committed to diversity and relying heavily on the use of media and technology. The great respect staff had for the president and members of the GMU Library Task Force also contributed to their willingness to "think outside the box." Nevertheless, as library staff began discussing what kind of library might be located in a student union, some staff kept hoping the idea would go away.

The first working hypothesis was that we would build an undergraduate library designed to support the emerging general education curriculum, with special emphasis on media and technology. Although we were sympathetic to many of the goals of undergraduate libraries, as exemplified by the one at Northwestern, many of us had also had experience with the problems such libraries faced, including the tendency to be viewed as second-class citizens in the library system. Nor did we like the linguistic distinction between "undergraduate" and "research" libraries, since we knew that many of our undergraduate students engaged in complex research. We were also convinced that technology would allow us to deliver information to multiple locations without duplication, thereby blurring the distinction between materials available in research libraries and those available elsewhere. What we really needed was a new entrance to the library system, one that could accommodate the technology we found hard to shoehorn into our present facility. We also needed student seating that was designed for different learning styles than those provided for by our current library. And we needed space for collections, but not space dominated by its collections. So we conceived of the University Center Library as an electronic library with an undergraduate paper collection—a library for which we didn't have a name ("beginning library," "starter library," "media center," and "instructional resources center" were all speedily rejected), but for which we were beginning to have a mission.

Several assumptions about the future of libraries were important to our thinking, and each ultimately impacted on the design of the building. These were:

- Paper collections will decrease in importance as electronic collections grow, but there will continue to be a demand for books, especially non-research level monographs.
- The computer will be ubiquitous, serving as the vehicle to deliver information and as the tool most library users will use to utilize that information.

- Media and data will blend, and work stations will be expected to deliver all forms of information.
- Learning is collaborative, and will become more so in the future.
- Learning is interdisciplinary, and information resources must reach beyond traditional disciplinary limits.
- Universities will "distribute" themselves to other campuses, corporate training centers, and students' homes, and the library must be part of that presence.

Expanding Campus Involvement

Another Faculty Taskforce, this one on University Life, appointed a subcommittee to further develop the concept of what we were now calling the University Center. This subcommittee consisted of several faculty members, including John Paden, who had led the earlier Library Task Force, and Arthur Chickering, a distinguished professor with an international reputation for his work on collaborative and experiential learning. Other members represented Student Affairs, University Unions, Facilities Planning, and the Library. I represented the Library, and brought to the meetings the results of wide-ranging discussions among librarians as they began development of a preliminary building program. On May 7, 1990, the University Life Taskforce adopted a proposal for University Center which included the following statements:

> The University Center concept embodies the philosophy of George Mason University, which is to be learner-centered, interactive and engaged with its community. By placing the library in the University Center, thereby taking the library to the students and faculty, we are disavowing the cloistered notion of a library separate from the rest of the university. In the University Center students and faculty will be able to read, do research, collaborate, and socialize in one unified space.
> The University Center is designed to encourage active engagement in the academic enterprise by all elements of the university. The architectural design will encourage interaction with the resources provided throughout the building, and with others engaged in the learning process. The small book and materials collection of the library will be pertinent to the general education core. These resources will support a common core of knowledge around which students and faculty can interact throughout their academic careers.
> The design of the University Center is informed by the work of the General Education Committee of the University, which has developed a core curriculum to help students develop verbal, reading and mathematical abilities, critical thinking abilities, multi-cultural understanding, content related understandings, and resource utilization abilities. Since learning is continuous, and significant portions take place outside the classroom, the University Center integrates library resources and student activities designed to encourage those outcomes.
> The library in the University Center will be a model Library of the Future, serving as the central node of an information system that reaches

outward to the wider world of information. The latest in technological systems will maximize access to information for students and faculty. The University Center will incorporate the latest in information technology, recognizing that technology is a *supportive mechanism* for *human* learning. Computer work stations will be networked to increasingly more complex and distant systems: students begin work with a limited sphere of information and spiral outward to larger, more sophisticated systems as they develop the ability and need. Expert systems technology applied to automated systems in existence will support this process. The system design also will enable researchers to contact other students and faculty interested in the same research areas, thereby encouraging the human collaboration so important to effective learning.[3]

Already the planning for the library was reinforcing the truth of our belief in the power of collaboration, as our ideas were increasingly enriched by the perspectives of others. In recognition of the importance of this cross-fertilization, Sarah Looney, the Vice President for Student Affairs, and I organized a series of meetings that included staff from all groups that were expected to have a presence in the building: auxiliary enterprises, food service, libraries, police, print services, student services, university computing, and university relations. We identified areas of the building that seemed to us to require interdepartmental thinking, and asked for volunteers from each area to work on defining the issues. Eventually we had groups on the Information Desk, Loading Dock, Meeting Rooms and Lounges, Security, and Technology. These were in addition to planning groups for each of the functional areas.

The selection of architects for the building represented another important step in the development of our thinking, because the university chose the Boston firm of Shepley Bulfinch Richardson and Abbot (SBRA), partnering with Marcellus Wright Cox and Smith of Richmond. SBRA had wide experience with academic libraries and student unions, and was the architect of record for the planned new library at the University of Southern California, with which we had much in common. Over the next several years we became members of another, highly informal collaborative group — people who were building "different" libraries. A major source of contact was Geoff Freeman of SBRA, who told us about each other, thereby leading to further contacts. GMU borrowed freely from the pioneering work of USC in the development of the concept of a "teaching library," and from the Maricopa Community College District in Arizona in its use of "computer commons," as well as from the planning for an intensively networked library at Indiana University–Purdue University at Indianapolis. Although each of us developed surprisingly different libraries, each incorporates many of the same basic assumptions.

The University Center

In order to provide a context for the discussion of the University Center Library, some general information about the building itself will be helpful. The

University Center (UC) is a four-story building containing 320,000 gross square feet (296,000 net assignable square feet). It occupies the highest point of land on the campus, and is surrounded on the north by a large general classroom building, on the east by three classroom buildings (two Science and Technology), on the west by an Arts complex and administrative offices, and on the south by a newly constructed classroom building for Business and Public Administration. Further expansion in academic buildings will be to the south, beyond a wooded area behind the UC, which will be retained because a creek runs through it. The lower floor is built into the hill and is underground for over half of its length. There are five entrances to the building: one on the ground floor, south, and one each on the first floor east and west, and at the northeast and northwest corners. The location of the building and its doors make it convenient to walk through as one travels between classes.

The building has two large open staircases which benefit from the natural lighting of the clear story at the top, and which are designed to encourage foot traffic between floors. There is a fountain at the bottom of the north stair, which marks the perimeter of the food court. A large Information Desk occupies the center of the second floor, between the east/west doors and the two staircases. The most important breakthroughs in the design of the building were the agreement by the bookstore to occupy two levels on the northern end, with their textbook sales primarily on the first, windowless floor, and the agreement by the library to locate its "open" library along the eastern sides of the atrium on floors three and four and its "controlled" library at the southern end of the second and third floors. This opened up the second (main) floor for development of a variety of retail spaces, including an art gallery, bank, computer store, copy center, credit union, and travel agency. The movie theater and a 1,000-seat Multipurpose Room share the lower level with a "Bistro," a student hangout serving beer and wine and providing large-screen TV and a dance floor. A "white-tablecloth" dining room is on the top floor, as are a series of meeting rooms, library stacks and seating, and extensive computer labs.

The building cost $30 million and took two years and five months to build. Once funding for the building was secured, the University's Associate Vice President for Operational Services, Stanley Taylor, established a series of advisory committees to develop policies, procedures, and budgets for the various areas. The committees included faculty and student representatives and reported to a large central committee called the University Center Task Force. The other committees were:

Programs and Activities Planning Groups:

Multi-Cultural and International Programming and Activities

Major and Special Events Planning Group

Opposite: Large open staircase in the Johnson Center which benefits from the natural lighting of the clear story at the top. The fountain marks the perimeter of the food court area. (Courtesy George Mason University Publications.)

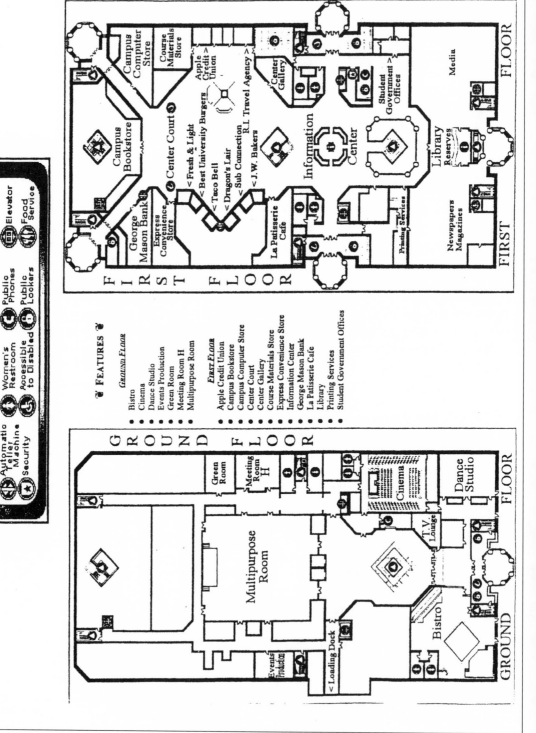

KEY

Information
Automatic Teller Machine
Security
Men's Restroom
Women's Restroom
Accessible to Disabled
Library Book Kiosk
Public Phones
Public Lockers
Stairway
Elevator
Food Service

🏛 **FEATURES** 🏛

Ground Floor
- Bistro
- Cinema
- Dance Studio
- Events Production
- Green Room
- Meeting Room H
- Multipurpose Room

First Floor
- Apple Credit Union
- Campus Bookstore
- Campus Computer Store
- Center Court
- Center Gallery
- Course Materials Store
- Express Convenience Store
- Information Center
- George Mason Bank
- La Patisserie Cafe
- Library
- Printing Services
- Student Government Offices

FIRST FLOOR

FIRST FLOOR

Campus Computer Store
Course Materials Store
Apple Credit Union
R.I Travel Agency
Center Gallery
Student Government Offices
Media
Campus Bookstore
Center Court
< Fresh & Light
< Best University Burgers
< Taco Bell
< Dragon's Lair
< Sub Connection
< J.W. Bakers
Information Center
Library Reserves
George Mason Bank
Express Convenience Store
La Patisserie Cafe
Printing Services
Newspapers Magazines

GROUND FLOOR

GROUND FLOOR

Multipurpose Room
Green Room
Meeting Room H
Events Production
< Loading Dock
Cinema
T.V. Lounge
Dance Studio
Bistro

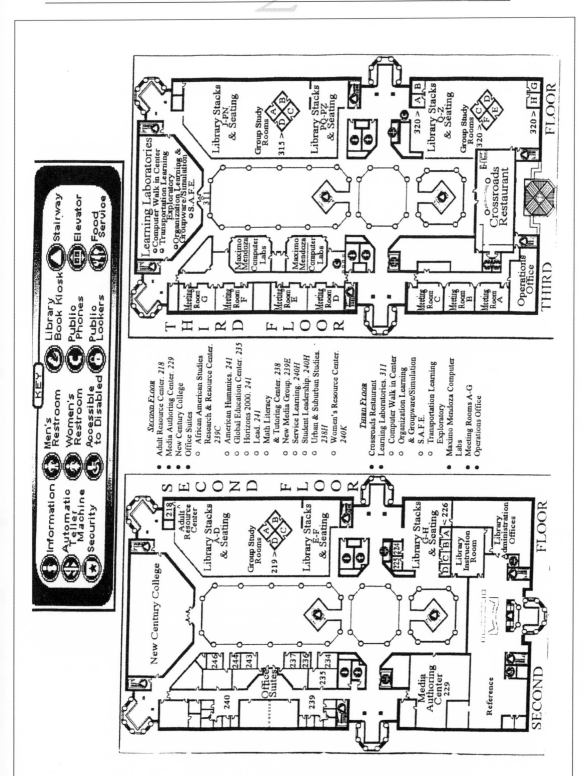

Social Events Planning and Activities

Artistic and Cultural Programming and Activities

Film Programming and Activities

Athletic & Recreational Programming and Activities

Information Technologies

Information Center

Access and Security

Maintenance and operations

Auxiliary Enterprises

Even as the building was being constructed, ideas about how it should work and who should occupy it were evolving. President Johnson, whose original idea had inspired the building, had insisted from day one that it be a building for students and not a building for offices, and that it be designed for flexibility, with minimal interior walls. As the reality of the building took shape, the President announced that no one would be given space in the building unless they demonstrated that their occupancy would somehow contribute to the creation of a learning community. This announcement was translated into a proposal process, led by Professor Arthur Chickering, with proposals judged by the University Center Mission and Programming Criteria Task Force, which included seven faculty members, the head of University Unions, the Director of the Center for the Arts, a representative of Auxiliary Enterprises, and the Johnson Center Librarian. The committee decided that no one would have a permanent right to space in the building, and that as "leases" came up for renewal, the units would be evaluated for their contributions to learning and the appropriateness of their use of space in the University Center. Although this development was consistent with the original idea for the building, student groups were upset that space they believed had been "promised" to them was now part of the proposal process. Ultimately, some groups that had assumed they would be in the UC were not offered space, in some cases because they failed to take the approval process seriously. This continues to be a source of student unrest on campus, and of continuing pressure to change space allocations.

The President's announcement was, however, a critically important decision for the library, because one of the groups to move in was New Century College, an innovative new undergraduate program that relies heavily on collaborative and experiential learning, learning communities, and team teaching. The building is also home to the Women's Resource Center, the Center for New Students, African American Studies Research and Resource Center, Global Education Center, Horizons 2000, Center for Service Learning, Student Leadership, and Math Literacy and Tutoring Center, all of which provide wonderful opportunities for collaboration with library programs. Although the library had planned an outreach effort to any programs moving into the UC, the emphasis on learning made that connection easier to make.

The University Center Library

The UC Library that we ultimately planned and built consists of three units: 1) an open library containing stacks and study space, 2) a "controlled library" containing reserves, multimedia, a small periodical collection, casual reading, the reference collection, and service desks for circulation/media and reserves, and 3) staff workspace. In addition, we share responsibility for the management of the Information Desk, which functions as the first line of referral and provides circulation assistance, including at five self-checkout stations located at the doors. The assumptions that influenced our decisions evolved over time, but were very consistent with our initial vision. Those assumptions were:

- teaching and learning are becoming more collaborative, and will continue to be;
- learning should be free of artificial space constraints;
- the new information environment will require constant training and updating;
- everyone will want to be connected;
- text and media will merge;
- electronic resources will change the role of paper.

The design implications of these assumptions resulted in very specific decisions for the University Center Library. Many of them are described in the sections that follow.

Teaching/Learning Needs to Be More Collaborative

The UC Library has 32 group study rooms, each fully networked and wired and provided with white boards. Most of the group study rooms are in the open library, and are provided with locks but currently not locked, since the "first-come, first-serve" method is less staff-intensive to manage. A sign containing Library policy for use of group study rooms is posted in each room; it includes a statement that groups have priority over individual users and can ask that an individual (or materials left to "hold" the space) be removed. Several of the rooms are equipped with viewing and sound equipment; these are in the controlled library. From the first day we opened these rooms have been full. The rooms serve an unintended function: as one walks around and looks at what is written on the white boards, the very diverse nature of our student body becomes evident in the many languages represented.

There are 14 "super-carrels" in the closed building, each with four work areas. The four work areas can accommodate two to three people each (basically designed for two seated and one standing). We purchased regular library chairs for them, but as we add other seating we're converting to office chairs with wheels. These are the areas where we provide reference consultation, help in using various library systems, and small group teaching. They are also the site of much of the peer teaching/instruction and group work.

Although we originally designed media carrels to be single work stations, we revised the design of several of them to become two- or three-person media carrels by taking out the intervening panels, recognizing that many students like to view videos together. Each carrel is equipped with multiple earphones.

We have a mix of 40 percent seating in carrels, 50 percent seating at tables, and 10 percent seating in lounge furniture. In addition, the tables along the atrium wall, which are not part of the library's "official" seat count, are heavily used by library users. We worked with acoustical engineers to design elements to manage the spread of noise from the atrium, so the space gets noticeably quieter as one moves away from the atrium and towards the outer walls. Shelving is interspersed with seating throughout the open library. Placement of library furniture generally follows the assumption that people near the atrium will want to work in groups, and people closer to the windows will want quiet. It is important to repeat here that we have a research library a block away where quiet is enforced. Many library carrels have rather playful roofs that serve to absorb sound and create a sense of privacy; they also serve to identify carrels that are wired for network and electricity and prevent glare of computer screens.

Learning Should Be Free of Artificial Space Constraints

We started out with a library adjacent to a student union, but separated by the traditional single entrance to all library space. It soon became apparent that this wasn't responsive to the charge to break out of our individual boxes, and we started wondering how we could fully integrate ourselves into the building. To do that, two rules of library space planning had to be re-examined:

- in order to provide security to collections the library can only have one door (except for fire doors with alarms).
- patrons should not have food and drink in the library.

These two ideas were deeply embedded in library culture, and most library staff and users were inclined to consider any threat to them as equivalent to heresy. A number of factors, some of which are unique to GMU's Library System, allowed us to reconsider the security issue:

- The collection at the UC Library was not intended to be an archival collection (see further discussion under *"Electronic resources will change the role of paper"*).
- GMU has an Honor Code for students that can be invoked in the event of book theft.
- GMU is located in a wealthy suburban area and has a fairly affluent student body.

- GMU's administration was willing to accept the proposition that an open collection might lead to greater need for replacement dollars.
- There was a budget line for security for the building.
- The Information Desk in the building could handle circulation tasks and would be open every hour the building was open.
- The Bookstore is in the same building.
- Local retail malls had exit control systems that were not close to service desks and that appeared to discourage theft.
- The availability of self-checkout systems enabled multiple circulation points (one near each door) so that checkout became, we hoped, more convenient than theft.

The food and drink issue caused the most consternation, but few could deny a number of relevant facts:

- Library staff almost never stopped students from bringing food or drink into Fenwick Library, or consuming it. I tested this out for myself by following (unobtrusively, I hoped) various staff as they walked past students with food, and I never saw a library staff member say anything about the rule breaking. In a staff meeting we talked about this issue, and agreed that none of us wanted to be in the role of rules enforcer. So we decided to take down our signs forbidding food and drink and see what happened. The answer, as measured by custodial trash collection, was nothing much different than had been happening all along.
- Various libraries had begun experimenting with allowing covered beverage containers in libraries, and reported satisfaction with their efforts.
- Someone pointed out that patrons took books home with them, where we had no control over their proximity to food and drink.
- There was a commitment to purchase furniture and schedule custodial staff for the whole building with the assumption of food and drink consumption.
- Bookstores were beginning to follow the example of a long-time D.C. bookstore, Kramerbooks & Afterwords, and serve food and drink on premises.
- Again, the UC Library collection was not designed to be an archival collection.

With these major hurdles overcome, the majority of UC Library space was located on the eastern side of floors three and floor, fully occupying the space between the atrium and the exterior walls and completely open to all areas of the building. A student can (and does) get food at the food court and carry it up to the library to consume, or get a book in the library and carry it down to the food court to read. A book from the open shelves can be checked out in the controlled library, at the Information Desk, or at any of five self-checkout kiosks. Students working on a project in one of our group study rooms or one of the reservable meeting rooms or at a table in the food court can easily move to information resources if needed, and those browsing in the library can easily get a cup of coffee while deciding whether they want a book. And, as our Provost requested, a student engaged in a social activity can look up and see a student engaged in research, and vice-versa.

As part of the freedom from space constraints a decision was made to network the entire building at a level of intensity not generally expected in student unions. There are network connections in the coffee shop and along the atrium walls, as well as in all meeting rooms and lounges. There are, in fact, very few spaces where a power and network connection is not close at hand.

The New Information Environment Will Require Constant Training and Updating

The JC Library contains a classroom designed for interactive instruction using laptop computers. The classroom opens onto the second floor of the controlled library, where there are six super carrels at which small-group instruction can take place, as well as 20 additional computer work stations and a reference desk. All work stations in the library and at the information desk are similar, and use the World Wide Web as their organizing principle. A library patron can get help using any of the library system's networked resources, including its CD-ROM LAN, plus any resources on the Web, including the university's campus-wide information system, at any work station, and can readily find help if first attempts at self-directed learning fail.

In the building itself are a number of services which are not the responsibility of the library but which are closely linked to the library and share a common reporting relationship to the Vice President for Information Technology. There are four computer labs on the top floor (deliberately placed there to keep traffic moving to that floor all hours), a Computer Store, a Multimedia Authoring Center, and a Computer Walk-In Center/Learning Lab. There is also a computer lab for New Century College students and a math tutoring lab, to which access is restricted. This year the Information Technology Group collaborated on a budget proposal for an Information Literacy project that would be presented to all new students as an introduction to the Information Technology environment of the university. The availability of a multitude of teaching environments in the University Center enabled us to propose a combination of large-group instruction followed by small-group tutoring, using the large multipurpose room and all the electronic classrooms and computer labs in the building, in a massive effort during new student orientation. If funded, that project will begin next year.

The Information Desk in the center of the building is surrounded by a ring of work stations that are connected to the Web, with their default Home Page a specially designed University Center Home Page. Visitors to the building can click to calendars, maps, campus and building events, the library information system, or out to the Web. The work stations are set to preclude using telnet or FTP functions, in order to avoid their use as e-mail stations, and do not have printers.

Some of our cleverer students manage to override any limits we place on them, however, and this continues to be a problem. Staff at the Information Desk are trained by University Relations to answer general university information questions, and by the library to assist users of library systems and provide circulation assistance. The staff are trained to give basic assistance (looking up a title, for example) and to know where to refer patrons with more complex research needs. Early on we discovered that people who asked, "Where's the library?" were automatically being directed to the UC Library, leading some visiting parents to assume we had only the one small library; now the staff asks what they're looking for. The cross-training and shared management of the Information Desk has been more difficult than we anticipated and still needs improvement, but the library is committed to making the desk its first line of inquiry, and trying to establish the concept that every question is potentially an opportunity to teach. We've also discussed having a technology expert stationed at the desk to field questions about the building's technology, help students with computer problems, and hand out connectors to the building network, but demand has not been great enough yet to justify such a position.

Everyone Will Want to Be Connected

The building was designed for ubiquitous technology use, and is intensively wired for electrical and network connections. Technically, it has fiber to the floor and unshielded Category 5 twisted pair to the outlet. It was designed with the intent of converting to ATM when that became available. All of the seats in the controlled library are wired for power and network; some carrels and study rooms also have analog connections. Tables and carrels were custom designed to provide connectivity, and to protect the connections from possible spills of liquid. Except for carrels built around columns or very large groups of carrels, the furniture is plugged into floor or wall outlets so it can be moved if desired. In the open library 60 percent of the seats are wired, and all group study rooms are wired. The Computer Lab checks out network adapters to students who need them for their laptops and provides instruction in how to set up their computers to use the network.

Text and Media Will Merge

The rapid advances in digitizing images led us to conclude that the network connections and the work stations we installed must be capable of receiving multimedia, so we designated the work stations we would order "super computers" and waited till the last possible minute to order the most advanced work stations we could find, with 17" screens and sound cards. We had already decided to house our entire Media Collection in the UC Library because of expected heavy use of media in the new general education core, and we supported building a movie theater which could be programmed for group viewing of required videos and films.

In addition we planned a Multimedia Authoring Center adjacent to the library, which contained a Media Distribution System for the entire building (with potential to expand to the entire campus), a small TV studio, and a series of work stations for producing multimedia products. This MAC was intended for students preparing classwork and presentations, since other facilities existed on campus for faculty. It also houses part of the AV Distribution service for the campus.

Electronic Resources Will Change the Role of Paper

Since the UC Library collection was intended to serve an evolving general education core and was not intended to be archival, the least important function of the UC Library is to hold and secure collections. We decided to locate only current newspapers and periodicals in the library, with any archiving do be done in the research library. In order to make this work, we committed to purchasing as many electronic collections as we could afford, and to making them available in all university libraries (we have campuses in Arlington and Prince William counties as well as Fairfax). Fortunately for us, the Commonwealth of Virginia had asked the libraries of its academic institutions to develop a proposal for cooperative collection development, and that proposal for "The Virtual Library of Virginia (VIVA)" was funded at $5.2 million for the 1994–96 biennium, and $4.9 million for the 1996–98 biennium. GMU therefore has access to an exceedingly wide range of electronic resources, mostly via the Web, at little or no cost to our base library budget.

The collection development process for the book collection has been described in an article titled "Collection Development Strategies for a University Center Library."[4] The library is designed to hold 100,000 volumes, and opened with about 25,000 on the shelves. In order to provide maximum flexibility of space usage we decided to avoid seven-foot shelves. We installed five-foot shelving, which keeps the appearance of the space much more open and casual, and can be moved if we ever decide we need to reconfigure the space. It also provides much better accessibility to the collection for students with disabilities.

One Year Later

On April 12, 1996, the University Center was renamed the George W. Johnson Center, in honor of the President, who had announced his retirement effective at the end of the academic year. As part of the celebration of this event, the newly renamed Johnson Center Library (JCL) set up a guestbook on the World Wide Web, and invited friends near and far to share their reactions to the Johnson Center. We also recorded the event with a digital camera and loaded new images regularly throughout the day.

At the time this is written we've been in the building 1½ years, and had time to learn what's working well and what's not working as well. The good news is that the building is busy all the time. From January to May 1997, 561,003 people entered the Johnson Center and 52,791 people entered its library. The library is heavily used. After years of library staff complaining about students eating at library tables, we saw the tables turned when Food Services put up signs on the tables in the food court asking students not to study at the tables during the lunch rush. Reports from Parking Services suggest that more cars are parked on campus longer at night, because students are arriving at campus earlier and staying longer. This has created pressure on parking lots near the Johnson Center. Perhaps most gratifying, the campus underground newspaper, which seldom finds anything to praise, reported the Spring after we opened that students seem happier, and are staying on campus longer.

From the perspective of Fenwick Library, the best news is that the number of people entering the library is down 40 percent, but the number of people using their services is down only 10 percent. Although Fenwick's traffic decreased precipitously at first, it has begun building again, and more growth is expected when installation of work stations comparable to those in Johnson Center is completed. The building has become manageable, and much of the stress produced by overcrowded facilities has been reduced. The custodians report that they're carrying out less trash. On an average Sunday before the Johnson Center opened, 35–40 bags of trash were taken from Fenwick Library. Now, the weekend trash coming out of Fenwick Library is down to 10–15 bags. Even the elevators are working more reliably. Although Fenwick staff had thought they would go back to some restrictions on food and drink once JCL opened, they have not done so yet, though they are considering a "hot food" ban.

System-wide circulation of books and media, consultation with reference staff, and attendance at library instruction sessions has increased. In 1994–95, 258 instruction sessions and tours were offered; in 1995–96 there was an increase in instruction by 25 percent, with 322 instruction sessions and tours given. Use of library systems, especially through the Web, skyrocketed. We've conducted tours of the building for people from universities all over the world, and various elements of our building are being incorporated into libraries of many types. Students and faculty are proud of the building, and bring visitors to see it and especially to demonstrate its technology. The University was the site of the 1998 World Congress on Information Technology, in large part because of the availability of the Johnson Center's facilities.

The most significant success story is one we hadn't really planned, although it is the logical consequence of decisions made. New Century College (NCC), an innovative undergraduate program which was not even envisioned when we began planning, moved into the building the same time as the library (other programs were phased in over the Fall and Spring). Since the initial goal of the library was to be more closely integrated into the programs of residents of the building, we immediately assigned a librarian to be the liaison to NCC. The first-year curriculum for NCC uses six-week blocks and team teaching, and an important element in the first year is teaching students to use information resources. Subsequent years focus on the development of "learning communities." Librarians are now full participants in the teaching teams, participating in the development of curriculum, teaching, and evaluation of student work. We also assigned librarians to work with various learning communities for developing the appropriate collections to support them, including moving materials from Fenwick to JCL as appropriate. Although we always seek to be closely linked to the teaching programs of the university, we've never been as successful at gaining full partnership, and we believe that our co-location in a building is a significant factor. Despite all we say about "virtuality," proximity still matters, and it's hard to ignore people you run into all the time.

Some things don't work as well as we'd hoped. Five items stand out:

- We built a large reference desk, one that was the envy of the Fenwick reference staff. In the JCL, however, it's too monolithic, too imposing, and too formal. Its location on the second floor of the controlled library is a mixed blessing; it allows us to use the entire floor as a "teaching floor" and deflects directional questions from the reference staff, but it's not as visible as we'd like and raises concerns about how to avoid bouncing a patron from desk to desk to desk. We experimented with a small desk on the first floor during the first academic year of occupancy, but finally decided to move reference services up to the second floor. Part of the desk was converted to a work station for patrons using databases that require password sign-on. We consider the location of the reference desk to be an open issue, though we agreed not to change it for at least one full academic year.
- We had minimal experience in joint management of a service desk, and have not yet worked out all the issues related to the Information Desk's dual role as a source of university information (essentially a public relations function) and of library information. The library would like the Information Desk staff to be able to refer patrons to whichever desk at whatever library would meet their needs, and to help with simple holdings information. This creates a significant training issue, especially for students who work 10–15 hours/week.
- The philosophy "all work stations are equal" has definite advantages, but sometimes interferes with our need to keep the work stations available for use of information systems instead of being tied up by e-mail, applications like word processing, downloading of large files, or frivolous use for games or miscellaneous mischief. Although clever students seem to be able to figure out ways to defeat our controls, we've made progress in solving most of the problems, especially e-mail access and downloading of massive files, but we don't intend to try to function as censors of what sites students can access on the Web. Although we have not been asked to restrict web access, library staff worry about the possible consequences of someone deciding to make an issue of this.
- We tried to design a flexible library instruction room by purchasing laptops instead of fixed work stations, but the inconvenience of handing out laptops and worrying about their security has probably discouraged their use by some librarian instructors. We're currently rethinking the entire

design of the room, perhaps combining fixed terminals along the walls while retaining movable furniture and laptops in the center of the room.

• Printing has turned out to be a massive headache in all libraries, and we chose not to install individual printers with work stations, relying instead on networked printers. The maintenance of these heavily used printers is a source of constant frustration, and the cost of paper and toner is escalating rapidly. This year we convened a Campus-Wide Printing Solution Committee to propose a solution for all public printing; our budget request is now pending. Our hope is to implement a charge-back solution that will encourage users to take responsibility for the number of prints they generate, since the libraries and labs all observe substantial waste.

The biggest problem has been security. The exit control gates go off so frequently that no one pays any attention to them, and the Security guards the campus contracted with have failed to effectively patrol the gates. Students and faculty are convinced that the library collection is being stolen, although our first inventory, nine months after opening, revealed about a 3 percent loss, not inconsistent with what we experience at Fenwick, where control is much tighter. We assigned library staff to stop people at the doors and ask for help in a survey, and found that most of the alarms were caused by bookstore books; we're now working with the bookstore to get them to desensitize books as they sell them, and have provided them with the necessary equipment. They don't currently use a security system, but are considering either adding a security system themselves or at least routinely desensitizing the books. The number of alarms has already decreased. We also discovered that the self-checkout units we were using were not adequately desensitizing paperback books. This problem will be resolved by replacing the current equipment with different equipment that appears to be more effective. The design of the self-checkout units is also a problem — they look quite impressive but don't provide a place for the user to put other books, bags, etc., and are therefore awkward to use.

Not all universities could or should build a library like that in the Johnson Center. Local conditions and needs vary tremendously, and what works at George Mason University might not work for others. Our major contribution may be that we broke some rules that should no longer be automatically accepted, and that we discovered one way for libraries to renew their claim to being the heart of the university, even if the university is widely dispersed. As universities talk about distance learning and the need for campus services at remote locations, the Johnson Center, combining library services, student services, auxiliary services, and food, is a model that merits attention.

References

1. Commonwealth of Virginia Council of Higher Education. *Academic Library Facility Needs in Virginia's Public System of Higher Education: A Report in Response to House Joint*

Resolution No 32 of the 1986 General Assembly (Virginia: State Council of Higher Education, 1986), 6.

2. George Mason University. *Toward a University of the 21st Century: A Report by the George Mason University Library Task Force* (George Mason University: GMU Library Task Force, 1989).

3. George Mason University. *Proposal for a University Center* (George Mason University: University Life Taskforce, 1990).

4. Charlene S. Hurt, *et al.* "Collection Development Strategies for a University Center Library." *College and Research Libraries*, 56 (1995): 487–495.

Phoenix Central Library—"Crystal canyon" from fifth floor. (Credit William P. Bruder, Architect; photograph by Bill Timmerman.)

Top: San Antonio Central Library—Aerial view showing the use of simple geometrical forms expressed on a large scale, and two of the four outdoor terraces. (Credit San Antonio Public Library; photographer Celine Casillas Thomasson.) *Bottom:* IUPUI Main Library—Aerial photograph. (Copyright Trustees of Indiana University.)

Bibliothèque François Mitterrand in Paris. The great shapes of the BFM are lit at night, both from within and from without, bringing nightlife to an old industrial quarter that was entirely darkened before. (Credit Bibliothèque Nationale de France François Mitterrand; Dominique Perrault, Architect; photograph by Alain Goustard.)

Above: British Public Library—The piazza in front of the main entrance combines brick and stone to relate to the St Pancras Chambers building behind and will be used for public events of various kinds. The clock tower is the only one to have been built in Britain since the Second World War and houses the main flues for the building. (Copyright British Library Board.)

Opposite, top: The Walsh Library—An interior shot of the fourth floor rotunda, the Peterson Reading Room. (Photograph by Seton Hall Public Relations.) *Opposite, bottom:* The new Peking University Library. (Credit PKU Library.)

Above: British Public Library—The main entrance hall of the library. The tapestry on the wall was made by the Edinburgh Tapestry Company and is the largest hand-woven tapestry to have been made in this century in the UK and is based on Ron Kitaj's painting, *If Not, Not.* (Copyright British Library Board.)

Opposite, top: The Kapiolani Library entrance at dusk. (Credit Augie Salbosa.) *Opposite, bottom:* Shanghai Library—The Catalog Room. (Credit the Shanghai Library; photographer Yu Li.)

Phoenix Central Library—Fifth floor, looking south at dusk. (Credit William P. Bruder, architect; photograph by Bill Timmerman.)

6. NewsWare: Integrating Mass Communications and Library Resources*

T. D. Webb
Library Director

Construction of the new Kapiolani Library was part of the relocation of Kapiolani Community College, which is part of the University of Hawaii, from downtown Honolulu to a new master-planned campus at the foot of Diamond Head Crater. Construction of buildings at the new campus site began in 1983. The new library was finished in 1992, and the last building of the campus master plan was completed in 1994. Now Kapiolani College nestles on the slopes of Diamond Head, with a commanding view of the Waikiki skyline and the limitless ocean on one side, and Oahu's wall of mountains and valleys on the other. Its situation suggests an openness to the community and the world that the Library staff want to capture in our approach to information delivery.

The main planning team for the new library consisted of the library director, the provost, the architects, and assorted technical consultants. Throughout the planning, however, input was sought from the library staff, college administrators, faculty, students, and even community members, since Kapiolani maintains a close relationship with local businesses and the non-student community.

The planning team identified two basic criteria that would greatly affect the design of the new library facility. One factor was architectural, the other administrative. First, the team believed that the Library's shape should itself contribute to the learning that would take place there by positioning the information resources in a way that was engaging and meaningful to our students. To us, functionality did not necessarily equate to convenience. Instead, the planners believed that the arrangement of library resources should reflect the way students study and enhance the characteristics of the information resources we intended to use.

*Earlier versions of some of this material appeared in The Electronic Library and American Libraries.

The Kapiolani Library. (Courtesy Augie Salbosa Photography.)

The second design factor was the realization that even with the 100,000-volume collection we intended to build, the Library would never hold the size of collection we wanted for our students. This meant that electronic information delivery would be crucially important in the Library's acquisition plan, and that these other information formats must be utilized to their optimum level of effectiveness to complement, update, and extend the print collections.

The Footprint

As part of the master-planned construction, the Library's location and its basic shape, or "footprint," were determined in the early 1980s by the architectural firm retained to develop the master plan. Because of height restrictions, the placement of adjacent buildings, and other considerations, a two-story, elongated shape was chosen for the Library. Among other features, this would produce an imposing facade and a visual sense of largeness by displaying more of the exterior treatment from the front than would be possible with some other plan. So when actual planning for the library building began about 1987, there was no opportunity to alter the footprint. This presented two interrelated problems, namely, what arrangements of materials and internal spaces were practical within a long, narrow facility? and, where was the best location for the entrance?

The task confronting library planners, then, was to determine the interior space allocations and functional arrangements within the given footprint. Librarians began this process by composing the Educational Specifications (Ed. Specs.) that would identify the needed spaces along with their size, electrical specifications, and functional, but at that point not spatial, relationships.

Once the Ed. Specs. were devised, the planning team began in earnest to arrange those spaces on a working floor plan. Although the footprint was already established, the planning team was determined to devise a method to take maximum advantage of the building's shape to make the interior space reflect a logical arrangement of functions and materials within the Library.

Situating the entrance was the crucial issue in this discussion. With a footprint that made the Library longer than a football field, the first thought was to place the entrance at the center of the building for the sake of convenience. Splitting the building in two, perhaps with the book collection on one side and the media and electronic services on the other, was considered, so that students could more easily and quickly reach the service areas they needed without having to travel the whole length of the building. This, however, would have made it necessary to increase the size of the staff to cover the two halves of the building. Furthermore, students might spend most of their time in one side of the building, and never see what services were in the other half.

The final decision, therefore, was to locate the entrance at one end, and cluster many of the electronic and non-print technologies and special services near the entrance so that students would encounter them immediately after entering.

As a result, students would be drawn into the center of the building, past numerous intriguing services, activities, and technologies that they might not expect to see in a library. To obtain information from the print sources students were most accustomed to using, they could not simply dash in and dash out as they would at a convenience store or a fast-food restaurant. Once they entered, they could not avoid being exposed to and held by the Library's full range of services.

Channels of Information

The planning team's second design factor emphasized the role of electronic access to information to give a small library the resource capacity of a large library. Access to computerized catalogs, databases, and indexes were envisioned, of course. But the planning team felt very strongly that while early "electronic" libraries assembled an assortment of technologies to modernize library services, the Kapiolani Library must select the best information technologies, and integrate them into a single learning system so that the technologies complement each other. For the Kapiolani planning team, this involved more than simply gathering a variety of information delivery formats in a single location; it involved managing the best information formats so they could be most effectively utilized by library users.

The team also believed modern mass communication channels, especially television news and educational programming, to be the best technology to link current events information to the Library's conventional collections. But while libraries have done an admirable job of adopting computerized resources in various formats — online, CD-ROM, and interactive multimedia — they have not been quick to adopt television as a valid electronic information technology, despite its relatively inexpensive implementation costs and its prominence as an information provider in modern society.

The last few years have produced momentous, world-changing events. These occurrences vividly demonstrate that libraries need to monitor television newscasts to add their immediacy to the standard information sources of libraries. Events such as the bloodshed that has followed the reformation of Eastern Europe and the dissolution of the Soviet Union, the War in the Gulf and the turbulent search for peace in the Middle East, numerous natural and human-made disasters, nuclear intrigues in Korea, China, and elsewhere, and many other events revise global affairs every day, and influence local conditions internationally.

The Kapiolani planning team believed that unless libraries adopt this medium and integrate it effectively into their complement of services, they will not be able to fill their social function in the 21st century.

Integrating Divergent Technologies

Society's two predominant information technologies have developed independently of each other, such that two separate electronic information domains now exist simultaneously — the computerized and the televised. This split stems not only from the differences of the two technologies, but also from the different way each technology handles information. The bifurcation may even foster an undesirable social outcome to which libraries are unknowingly contributing.

Computerized resources deliver information only when queried, and are designed to respond to highly focused searches constructed from controlled vocabularies made up of keywords, delimiters, locators, and other search parameters. The information stored in computerized resources, therefore, is extensively indexed, tagged, and linked. Managers of online databases select information from highly segregated, specialized fields of study for storage in computerized files based on its current value and on their anticipation of the future needs of those who are expected to access the resources.

The type of information usually delivered by computer is most useful to researchers, professionals, and specialists who know how to manipulate the machines and other electronic technologies in order to locate and extract the desired information. They know how to formulate the sophisticated logic statements, using delimiters to increase the precision of the search, all arranged in a semantic fashion appropriate to the specific system being queried, since different systems require different structures for their search arguments.

In contrast, the information in televised newscasts and other news programs is disseminated immediately with little concern for later retrieval. It is not tagged, indexed, or linked. No special training is needed to receive this information. No query is required. Because of television's remarkable ease of access, it is almost universally viewed at one time or another. In fact, information is selected for broadcast according to the broadcaster's preassessment of the immediate, not future, interests of a popular, general audience.

Where computerized information is focused, video information is ambient. It permeates the airwaves and, therefore, society. It is almost inescapable. And all societal sectors, including scientists, professionals, and engineers, keep current on local and world conditions not through computerized resources, but through televised newscasts and the proliferation of television news "magazines." Even intelligence agencies monitor television newscasts for up-to-the-minute, on-the-scene coverage of events in international hot spots.

Computers require an active interaction from the user. Television, however, requires only passive interaction, namely, watching and listening. Yet information from both these sources is very susceptible to incompleteness. Television news can be sketchy and inaccurate because it is immediately broadcast. And because computer resources are normally queried using quite specific subject keywords, interdisciplinary breadth is often lost. Furthermore, because computer databases are composed mainly of materials from print publications, they may be dynamic, but they may be no more timely than print.

A concomitant splitting of society could be occurring along the lines of the two technologies, one specialized and costly, the other popular and practically free. Computerized information, by virtue of its content and its method of access, is the realm of the information literate, the information rich. They are that portion of society that receives early introduction to computers, and they have a continuing personal need to interact with them. And although this sector of society also draws regularly on the information available through televised broadcasts, for a very large segment of society — the information poor — television is the only source of electronic information they have access to.

The purpose of this essay is not to discuss ways of preventing the very real possibility of social stratification according to the information sources we possess. But it is pertinent to point out here that libraries are playing favorites by integrating computerized resources into their services without a comparable effort to incorporate mass communication channels into their information collections. The argument that everyone has a television in his or her home does not justify the neglect of video information sources by libraries. In the first place, no such argument is made to discourage library subscriptions to local newspapers.

Furthermore, the fact that almost every home has at least one television does not mean the viewers know how to use the information they see there, nor that they can relate current events properly to historical conditions, future possibilities, and personal well-being; nor does it mean that they can properly interpret the implications of the events they see transpiring before their very eyes, nor that they know where and how to find the additional information that will make current events more meaningful.

Librarians, however, are adept at making these information connections, and the Kapiolani planning team proposed to connect the most potent mass communication channel with the organized, stored knowledge contained in the Library collections. Jorge Schement observed that in today's information deluge,

> Information arrives as mutually exclusive bits without organic unity, so
> that individuals attempting to optimize their lives face a formidable
> challenge. The deluge of fragmented messages hinders the ability to
> meaningfully interpret the swell of information [34].

He added, however, that "librarians who have been organizing information for centuries," can

> help the public think critically, [and] help them learn to prioritize and
> judge the quality of information they receive in torrents. The evaluation
> of information is an old and persistent need that will never go away.
> Librarians should service that need, wherever it exists [35].

Schement even advises the profession to "embrace" television to help accomplish these tasks, and to help librarianship find a new niche in the information field (36).

In libraries more than anywhere else, the links between current local and international events, and the effect these events will have on the public, can be made apparent by incorporating television information into an engaging information mosaic. Furthermore, despite a continuing overabundance of drivel on television, it is not the "vast wasteland" it once was. There are more channels, many of which are dedicated to information and education. Much of the news coverage broadcast today is high quality journalism, and certain television magazines regularly address quite sophisticated scientific, medical, governmental, and social topics that are of interest to general and specialized audiences alike.

A library's function is to provide information to all sections of its user group, specialized and popular. Yet because libraries have been less energetic about incorporating televised information into their complement of services than they have been about computerized information technologies, they provide access to electronically delivered technical data, but ignore the very important dynamic, popular information broadcast continuously by the mass media. And this is despite the fact that the immediacy of televised news coverage acts to update the library's other, less timely resources, including the computerized.

The impending convergence of computer, television, and telephone technologies will only increase the presence and value of televised information. It also means that soon both types of electronic information will be accessible through the same electronic device. The problem of the separation between focused and ambient electronic information, however, will persist because the problem involves two disparate information storage and dissemination philosophies and access techniques, and is deep enough that it cannot be solved by simply merging the industries into a single conglomerate. Users of the two technologies need to be taught to use both effectively and integrate them with other, more traditional information and knowledge sources. This was precisely the scheme behind the layout of resources in the new Kapiolani Library.

Form Follows Information

The best learning combines the most current available information with thorough background knowledge. In the past, printed books, journals, and newspapers were a library's major means of supplying the combination of background knowledge and current information that distinguishes quality learning and research. But the changing nature of information delivery, especially the televised newscast, has established electronic, visual immediacy as the new basis for learning about current events.

The television newscast is the only place to obtain information about fast-breaking events, and for several reasons. The technology itself provides instantaneous information transfer from the eyewitness to the viewing audience; the infrastructure of broadcasting stations, satellites, and TV receivers is vast; the economic infrastructure of advertisers, ad agencies, promoters, and consumers is also well-established; and, perhaps most importantly, the planet is flooded with journalists, reporters, commentators, anchor-persons, editors, stringers, and other human resources who do the research, investigation, and reporting, often risking their lives to get the stories upon which society has become dependent.

Yet the Kapiolani Library planning team was acutely aware that despite abundant ambient information and mass communications on pressing issues that demand intelligent action, student research often lacks the comprehensiveness provided by up-to-the-minute data combined with a good grounding in the existing documentation of an issue. Demonstrating the co-relevance of world events and classroom instruction remains a problem for academic institutions and for their libraries.

In an attempt to address this problem, a number of libraries have already introduced television newscasts into their information delivery services by installing monitors in their buildings. But often these efforts are less effective than they could be because this type of service was not envisioned in the design of the library facility. Monitors tuned to CNN or network news may have to be located in areas that are less than accommodating to the large numbers of students who want to know, who need to know, the fast-breaking events that affect us all. The monitors are often stuck in a corner out of the main traffic flow because the building was not designed for video information delivery, and a corner may be the only place a video line could be installed or dropped from the ceiling, after the fact.

The Kapiolani planning team, however, designed the new Library's interior space with a visually prominent video information delivery system in mind. The new facility was spatially arranged to integrate the two divergent information technologies — computerized and televised — with the more traditional information formats of books, periodicals, microforms, etc. that have been common in libraries for most of the 20th century. The design positions the several information formats in a physical arrangement that accentuates and takes advantage of the best features of each, and places them in a logical relationship to each other to integrate those characteristics.

The ground floor is the "noisy zone" (see floorplans). It's like an information buffet. Here interaction between students and the Library staff is intense, and it is the setting for many of the Library's activities. Students entering the building encounter two computer labs, the audio-visual alcove, the "NewsWare" alcove with the large-screen television, display cases and museum-quality exhibits, programming, conference rooms, and other features before they even see any of the book collections, which on the first floor are located at the far end of the building.

The audio-visual alcove surrounds the NewsWare area, and includes mediated carrels that can be linked to the campus cable TV system and data network. Many of the other study carrels throughout the Library can also be linked to the campus data network for users who wish to bring their own portable computers to work in the Library.

Work stations for the Library's online catalog are also located in this area. The Kapiolani Library uses the CARL system, which is located at the Hamilton Library on the University of Hawaii–Manoa campus. Using CARL terminals in the Kapiolani Library, students can access the holdings of the University's twelve libraries around the state, numerous other resources in Hawaii, dozens of online databases available through CARL, and the catalogs of more than 200 other libraries across the United States. Students can also access "Uncover," CARL's very popular online index to millions of journal and magazine articles, and then place an online request for a FAX full-text copy of any article they find indexed.

These work stations also provide access to the Internet and World Wide Web, the Library's multi-user CD-ROM server, and the Library's own locally developed full-text, Web-based online databases (see Webb). These various resources are accessed via the Library's home page (http://library.kcc.hawaii.edu). In this area are also located equipment for the visually impaired, the multi-media library instruction room, and the microform collections with reader-printers.

The reference collection occupies the ground floor beyond the NewsWare, catalog/Internet, audiovisual, and periodical areas. The general and special collections are located on the second floor, which is the Library's "quiet zone." The Library's special collections include materials on Japan, China, and Korea, the majority of which were donated by private individuals and corporate donors such as the Japan Foundation, the Japan Forum, the Sun Yat-Sen Peace Foundation, and various Asian universities with which the College and the Library have cooperative agreements, such as Beijing University and Inha (Korea) University.

NewsWare

The NewsWare alcove is the means the Kapiolani Library uses to incorporate mass communications into its information delivery strategy. It is intended to be visually riveting to emphasize the presence of a new library information technology integrated into the Library's more familiar resources. Continuous cable news is carried on a 61"-screen television installed in the alcove in full view of all who enter the Library. Four additional 27" monitors will be stacked alongside the large-screen TV create a multiscreen device that allows the Library to provide simultaneous multichannel news coverage. The major screen is normally dedicated to cable news. The other monitors will display network and local news broadcasts, educational programming, or video bulletin boards. Because of Hawaii's multinational population, local stations broadcast many foreign-language news programs, which the Library will also regularly carry.

The sound portions of the broadcasts will be selectively available through directional speakers and earphones. The NewsWare alcove is sunken three feet to help control the sound from the speakers, and to create a comfortable setting while students keep current with international and local news. The steps down to the alcove also serve as seating, and contain the wiring and controls for the audio channel selectors.

The control station for the NewsWare display is located behind the circulation desk in the electronic distribution center, or "head end," of the Library's cable TV network. From there the staff can coordinate broadcasts to the NewsWare alcove, media carrels, conference rooms, and offices. The head end was designed by the College's Educational Media Center, and is equipped with VCRs for videotape

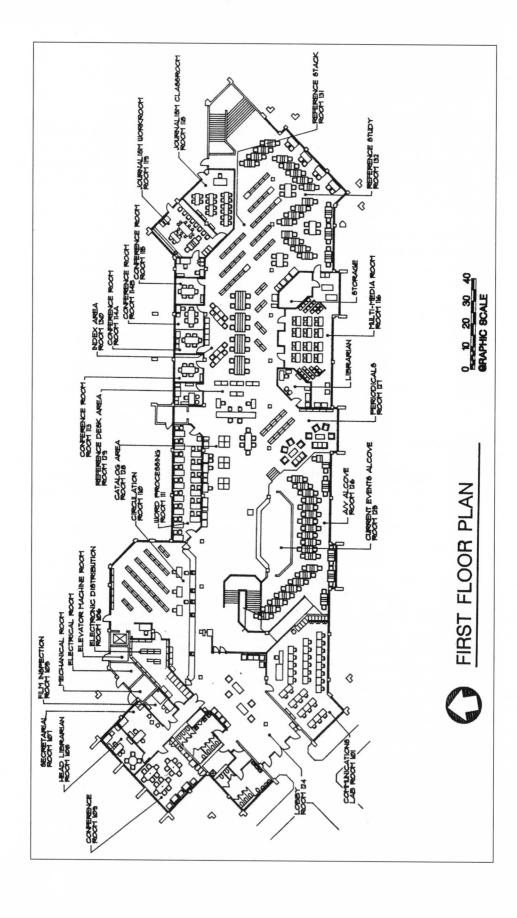

FIRST FLOOR PLAN

0 10 20 30 40
GRAPHIC SCALE

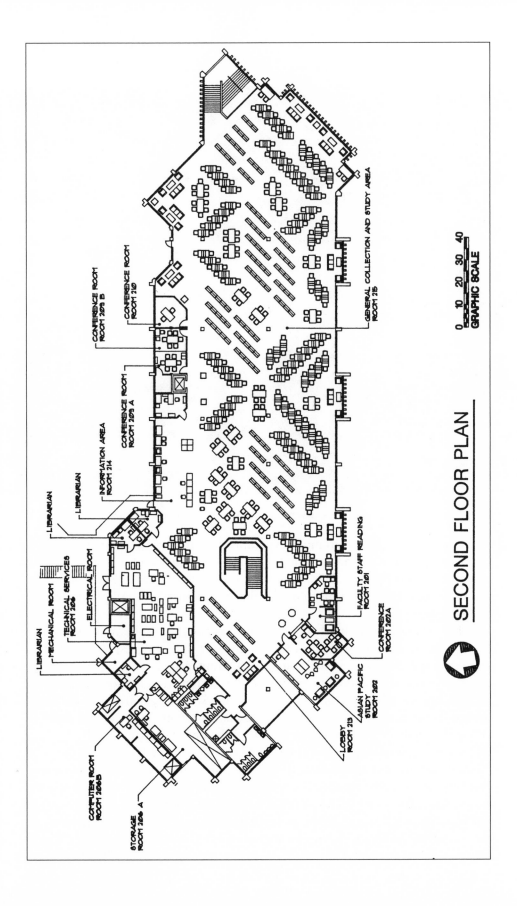

SECOND FLOOR PLAN

0 10 20 30 40
GRAPHIC SCALE

NewsWare and the Current Events Alcove. (Courtesy of *Kapio*.)

playout, channel selectors to move programs from one screen to another, and a character generator for a scrolling bulletin board. This way, a college-related broadcast or a breaking local news story can be switched to the large-screen device, and cable news can be output to one of the smaller monitors. All programming is closed-captioned.

The NewsWare and head end equipment is not cheap. The student government, however, provided most of the funding for the TVs presently located in the NewsWare alcove. Originally, an old 74" front-projection TV was installed in the alcove, and the students quickly grew accustomed to the service. The old TV was retired when it began to dim, and the student government willingly funded its replacement and supported the plans to upgrade the alcove by providing the multiscreen capability for which it had been designed.

Locating NewsWare near the entrance and adjacent to the current periodicals, catalog/Internet, and reference areas permits students to follow important events or crises, such as political developments, military conflicts, space flights, earthquakes, and other topics of interest, from their most current stages in the newscasts, through recent, more in-depth treatments of the events in news magazines and newspapers, which are located next to the NewsWare alcove, and which may be accessed in print, CD-ROM, online, or microfilm formats. Students then can proceed to the Library's reference, general, and special collections to get detailed background information on the events and the issues they entail.

During the 1992 and 1996 U.S. presidential campaigns, for example, students were stacked in front of the television to witness the debates, take notes for their classes, and generally become informed on the issues of the highly animated political happenings. Often there was standing room only. Many students brought news magazines from the periodical alcove to refer to while watching, using the facility exactly as the Library planners had intended.

Information Ergonomics

The Library's design places several information services in a spatial arrangement that is logical and intriguing to our students. Awareness of the continuity between historical conditions and current events yields the richest type of learning, and is essential for intelligent modern living. But the planning team had observed that students often fail to grasp the full importance of local and world developments because they do not associate current affairs with the knowledge contained in library collections, or with the learning that takes place in their classrooms. The new Kapiolani Library was designed to integrate these various learning formats in a single, structured whole.

This required an attitudinal change among the staff. Television has been anathema to the library profession for two generations because of its shallowness, its obvious catering to broad public entertainment tastes, and its displacement of reading as a common pastime. Yet over the last decade, the growing public awareness of the need to keep current with a changing world has produced a wealth of good programming on television.

The presence of television in the Kapiolani Library was never intended to provide entertainment, diversion, or respite from studies. It was designed to be an information device to complement the Library's other resources. It was intended to satisfy the students' desire that the happenings of the outside world be brought into the college environment. While the Library was still under construction, for example, the president of the student government voiced this desire with great sincerity when she stated that she was tired of waiting until she went home in the evening, after a long day of school and work, to find out the latest developments in the U.S. Senate hearings on the nomination of Judge Clarence Thomas and the testimony of Dr. Anita Hill.

Events like this that attract the viewership of millions and galvanize public opinion have a place on the campus and in the Library. These are the very issues that students need to incorporate into their studies to give relevance to the classroom instruction they receive and to the research and writing they produce. Six years of providing televised news in the Kapiolani Library have made the service a part of the instructional process and an integral component of the Library's information delivery program. Besides political events, the most-watched telecasts have included coverage of the Oklahoma City bombing, the Million Man March, and the Simpson verdict, not surprisingly. For some reason, former President Nixon's funeral also drew a large viewership. Coverage of a lengthy hostage-taking situation in Honolulu, in which the gunman was shot and killed by police after a day-long standoff, was the most-watched and most gripping local newscast.

Some instructors have assigned their students to watch certain programs in the NewsWare alcove, and even accompany them while doing so. In one unfortunate instance shortly after the new Library opened, one college administrator, unconvinced of the importance of NewsWare, insisted that the service be temporarily disconnected so the visually striking sunken alcove could be used to exhibit several paintings by an internationally renowned artist from China. He did not take the protests and warnings of the Library staff seriously. Within a few hours of removing the television and installing the paintings, however, an instructor appeared in the alcove with her entire class to watch a special news program on the subject of juvenile gangs, unaware that the television had been unplugged and removed.

The teaching exercise failed, of course, prompting the instructor to complain vigorously to the administration for interrupting the NewsWare service. The television was quickly restored to its place, the exhibit was relocated, and the administration agreed not to tamper with the service again.

The Kapiolani Library staff did not create this need for televised news in the Library. It was there all the time, as we had suspected. The success of the project has been gratifying, and it indicates that more needs to be done to exploit the vast field of televised information and make it even more integral to the Library's information services.

Although not intended for entertainment, NewsWare certainly attracts many "browsers" who have time between classes or who are intrigued by the news stories they see as they pass by. This reaction of the students, however, is like that of readers who discover an interesting article in a magazine or newspaper by happenstance.

Some students, however, have been displeased by the presence of television in their library. A few have even expressed the view that television is inappropriate for a library. But usually, it was because the audio distracted them while they were trying to study. Yet most were placated by staff members who explained the reason for the television and that the ground floor was intended to be noisy, and directed the students to quiet study areas on the second floor.

Converging Technologies

The Kapiolani Library had the opportunity to develop its integrated technologies plan because a new facility was in the works. It is at just such times that mission, services, and methods are most closely scrutinized as specifications for the building are being developed. Input from various sources is essential in such instances. The NewsWare project especially was the result of ideas contributed by several individuals, including the Library staff and the college's media specialists, administration, students, and faculty. Its location and orientation were designed by the planning team in consultation with the architects and builders.

Not many libraries, of course, have the opportunity to plan new facilities or renovate existing ones that would permit the type of thematic restructuring of information services designed into the Kapiolani Library. But it is not necessary, of course, to build a new structure to integrate television news into a library. The integration of television should be carefully planned, however, and any appropriate reorganization of interior space and services should be conducted to make this type of information readily accessible to the library's users. And certainly, any new library facility should be planned with effective video information delivery in mind.

The merging of the video, data, and telephone industries will only increase the importance of video information delivery. It will refashion the way research is conducted and disseminated because all formats will be accessible through the same device. For instance, researchers and students will conduct research over video-compatible networks and transmit their findings over the Internet as multimedia documents, even using newscast footage when data from the realm of popular information is relevant, and all this while working from a single work station. The advent of interactive television suggests even more possibilities for discovering and communicating new knowledge and information.

Along with bringing more information into a library, video-data convergence also has enormous implications for a library's community responsiveness because it will allow information and education to be delivered to faraway homes, classrooms, and offices so that users can utilize a library's resources right at their desks or in their living rooms. Libraries must take a leading role in developing these video research and information networks. As Schement stated, the modern library "will need to transform itself from a territorial institution to a functional institution, delivering its services wherever virtual communities coalesce — no mean feat" (36).

Video News Collections

The new Kapiolani Library was configured with a reverse chronological concept of information delivery in mind. That is, students can move progressively in steps from televised newscasts through the Library's current periodicals area, catalog and Internet resources, reference materials, and general and special collections. Following this information path, students will see more clearly the relevance of events in today's fast-changing world to the subjects of their classroom studies and to the wealth of knowledge held in the Library's print collections.

The NewsWare alcove is the source and the symbol of the Library's innovative vision of integrated information that will help students see the relevance of the past to today's fast-changing world. Installing an emphatic video information system in the Library is a departure from traditional library services. But it is a strategy that will improve our students' grasp of current world and local events, while also providing the resources for students to gain a familiarity with the scholarship that will add depth to their understanding of important world happenings. With NewsWare, the Kapiolani Library links electronic information channels to the accumulated, organized knowledge of our book collections. This greatly enhances learning in the Library.

But merely incorporating televised newscasts into a library is no more efficient for acquiring information than subscribing to the *New York Times*, *Newsweek*, or a local newspaper, and then discarding every issue when a new one is delivered. Just as back issues of periodicals have a place in library collections, video presentations of information also need conscientious collection development. Despite the fact that they have TVs in their homes, most people cannot or do not know how to select and collect video information for later use. But librarians are quite familiar with collection strategies, and we should develop one for televised information just as we have for information we collect in other formats. At this moment, in fact, the profession is grappling with ways to "collect" and "catalog" Internet/WWW sites. Why are we neglecting to do the same for televised news programming?

Unlike computerized catalogs, online databases, CD-ROM materials, and other electronic resources that simply have replaced paper equivalents, television newscasts are a new information source for libraries that remains entirely untapped. Yet the value of television journalism for information and research has not entirely escaped scholarly attention. The Television News Archive at Vanderbilt University hopes eventually to have all its abstracts of television newscasts on the Internet, all the way back to 1968. Users can search the Archive by various access points, and request a videotape of any broadcast. The Archive may even digitize its videotape collection for computerized distribution (Wilson, A16). And while sources like Vanderbilt's provide access to nationally televised newscasts, local libraries can develop similar access to local newscasts to make them part of the public's information banks as well.

To control this information, libraries need to assign staff to "gather" video information just as they assign others to develop print, media, and electronic collections in many subjects. And just as a library's system manager controls the content and operation of its computer resources, a television information manager must engineer an intelligent program to perform such tasks as: 1) scheduling broadcasts for reception and display on the system and publicizing that schedule so that library users can plan to watch appropriate broadcasts; 2) selecting broadcasts to be taped for later playout and or permanent addition to the library's video collection; 3) publicizing this collection and its availability to users; and 4) obtaining transcripts of these programs in print or computerized formats, or perhaps subscribing to a service such as Journal Graphics.

Local television stations could become important partners in these activities by providing monetary or technical assistance, or by permitting the library to assume a depository role for local news stories. In Honolulu, for instance, the local cable television provider "loaned" three technicians to the Kapiolani Library to help design the NewsWare service, develop the specifications for the equipment, and recommend the best manufacturers.

Television is such a pervasive and varied medium that it has been the target for a great deal of criticism for many years. Its power to spread information, however, and its value as a communication device are now beyond dispute. The advice often given to concerned parents that they control what their children watch on TV, or that they watch TV with their children, bespeaks a selectivity that librarians also need to adopt to make the best use of television for their users. It is a selectivity that librarians have been well trained to perform.

References

Schement, Jorge Reina. "A 21st-Century Strategy for Librarians." *Library Journal* 121.8 (1 May 1996): 34–36.

Webb, T. D. "Stuck Between E-Mail and the E-Library." *American Libraries* 27.9 (Oct. 1996): 39–40; "Exploiting Online Potential: Information, National Development, and Libraries." *IFLA Journal* 22.4 (Nov. 1996): 285–291.

Wilson, David L. "Vanderbilt Archive Puts Abstracts of TV Broadcasts on the Internet." *Chronicle of Higher Education* 40.40 (8 June 1994): A16.

7. Library Services at California State University, Monterey Bay

John Ober
Assistant Director, Education and Applied Research
California Digital Library, University of California

A New Library

The Library Learning Complex at the newest campus of California State University at Monterey Bay has been in operation for nearly two years at this writing in mid–1997. The campus is billed as the "21st Campus (of the CSU system) for the 21st century." Its location on the former Army base at Fort Ord, very short planning and implementation time frame, focus on reinventing education with a focus to the future, and concentration on the application of high technology to education are all characteristics which have accrued to the Library and focused attention, both internal and external, on what the library of the 21st century might look like.

The attention has been keener because of widespread reports that this Library might be the first to eschew print materials altogether and to rely upon electronic resources and document delivery; that is, to rely completely upon access to information resources rather than upon ownership. While those reports, which sprang from under-informed, publicly stated hopes of University administrators, have not proven accurate, the Library has found a middle ground between the traditional collection-intensive physical place and the completely virtual.

The Library likes to consider itself a transformational library and this chapter hopes not only to give some evidence of those transformative qualities, but to reveal some of the conditions that led to them. A short section at the end of the chapter will also discuss the ongoing challenges to keep the momentum aimed toward the transformative. Which is to suggest that, not surprisingly, the social, economic and political landscape in many ways conspire against innovation even as they publicly required it over the past several years while the University became reality.

A New University

California State University, Monterey Bay (CSUMB) celebrated its opening on August 24, 1995. Built on Fort Ord, one of the largest of the closed military bases in the country, the University's 1,500 acres were home to 1,400 students in the Spring of 1997. The eventual on-site student population of approximately 10,000 is to be augmented by an almost equal number of distance learners. The University is focusing on undergraduate programs which are innovative reconfigurations of traditional disciplines.

Many individuals and institutions were attracted to the relatively simple idea of turning the former Army base — or more accurately, a portion of it; there are many other plans for the thousands of acres on the 40–square mile base not being used by CSUMB — into a college campus. Local congressmen, then Presidential Chief of Staff Leon Panetta, city governments and other regional organizations which were concerned about the economic effects of the base closure, and the California Legislature all rallied to the cause of what has become the first — and to date the only — post–Cold War conversion of a military base into a university anywhere in the United States.

The planning horizon under which this work was done was unusually brief. From the time the necessary federal and state approvals were in place until the University was mandated to have students in seats was approximately 14 months. This contrasts sharply with a more usual planning phase of four to six years for a new university.[1] CSUMB was to be the 21st Campus of the CSU system "for the 21st century," which is to say it had the additional burden of redefining key educational precepts and structures while carrying on the work of hiring faculty and staff, attracting students, and converting old army buildings into contemporary homes for education. At one point first-year administrators and faculty were afraid that classes would have to be held in tents, and while that did not come to pass, it is an appropriate metaphor for the moment-by-moment decisions and pioneering or homesteading ethos that pervaded that time and, to a large extent, still exists today after two full years of operation. That the original members of the campus were simultaneously proud and nervous about their task is reflected in this excerpt from the first year catalog:

> A Work in Progress means...
> In less than one year, the U.S. Army transferred land and buildings from Fort Ord to the CSU, and the CSUMB campus became "a work in progress." We have formed a new community of teachers and learners, and have done so effectively, in the public's interest, within one year. By design, and in some cases by default, we are in the midst of change. We are committed to constant metamorphosis reflecting the evolving needs of our society and its rapid growth in knowledge and technology.
>
> Our students will experience our evolution, in our academic offerings, rules, regulations, policies, requirements, and day-to-day life. This inaugural campus Catalog reflects some of the evolving framework which has guided the initial development of CSUMB. The information contained

in this Catalog will also evolve, as the fabric of our campus is woven into the cloth of our community. Each new development is a milestone in the personal and institutional growth which we have all come together to nurture here at CSUMB.[2]

There is no better description of the University's attempts to define a 21st-century education and the processes by which to achieve it than in its Vision Statement. The Vision Statement is a real guiding document and is referred to often in campus planning efforts, including the development of campus-wide academic services such as information services provided from the Library. The Vision Statement emphasizes disciplinary integration, appropriate use of technology, service learning, entrepreneurship, multiculturalism, and community outreach. As will be discussed below, all of these principles have guided the development of library and information services, often suggesting, and sometimes requiring, a non-traditional approach to the Library's own goals and objectives, its organization, operations, and the staff who are drawn to it.

CSUMB Vision Statement

California State University at Monterey Bay (CSUMB) is envisioned as a comprehensive State University which values service through high-quality education. The campus will be distinctive in serving the diverse people of California, especially the working class and historically under-educated and low income populations. It will feature an enriched living and learning environment and year-round operation. The identity of the university will be framed by a substantive commitment to multilingual, multicultural, gender-equitable learning. The university will be a collaborative, intellectual community distinguished by partnerships with existing institutions both public and private, cooperative agreements which enable students, faculty, and staff to cross institutional boundaries for innovative instruction, broadly defined scholarly and creative activity, and coordinated community service.

The university will invest in preparation for the future through integrated and experimental use of technologies as resources to people, catalysts for learning, and providers of increased access and enriched quality of learning. The curriculum of CSUMB will be student and society centered and of sufficient breadth and depth to meet statewide and regional needs, specifically those involving both inner city and isolated rural populations and needs relevant to communities in the immediate tri-county region (Monterey, Santa Cruz and San Benito). The programs of instruction will strive for distinction, building on regional assets in developing specialty clusters in such areas as the sciences (marine, atmospheric, and environmental); visual and performing arts and related humanities; languages, cultures, and international studies; education, business, studies of human behavior, information, and communication studies, within broad curricular areas and professional study.

The university will develop a culture of innovation in its overall conceptual design and organization, utilize new and varied pedagogical and instructional approaches, including distance learning. Institutional programs will value and cultivate creative and productive talents of student, faculty, and staff and seek ways of contributing to the economy of the state, the well-being of our communities, and to the quality of life and development of its students, faculty, and service areas.

The education programs at Monterey Bay:
- will integrate the sciences and the arts and humanities, liberal studies, and professional training;
- will integrate modern learning technology and pedagogy to create a liberal education adequate for the contemporary world;
- will integrate work and learning, service and reflection;
- will recognize the importance of global interdependence;
- will invest in languages and cross-cultural competence;
- will emphasize those topics most central to the local area's economy and ecology, and California's long-term needs; and
- will offer a multicultural, gender-equitable, intergenerational and accessible residential learning environment.

The university will provide a new model of organizing, managing, and financing higher education.

- The university will be integrated with other institutions; essentially collaborative in its orientation, and active in seeking partnerships across institutional boundaries. It will develop and implement various arrangements for sharing courses, curriculum, faculty, students, and facilities with other institutions;
- The organizational structure of the university will reflect a belief in the importance of each administrative staff and faculty member working to integrate the university community across "staff" and "faculty" lines;
- The financial aid system will emphasize a fundamental commitment to equity and access;
- The budget and financial systems, including student fees, will provide for efficient and effective operation of the university;
- University governance will be exercised with a substantial amount of autonomy and independence within a very broad CSU system-wide policy context; and
- Accountability will emphasize careful evaluation and assessment of results and outcomes.

Our vision of the outcomes of California State University Monterey Bay includes: a model pluralistic academic community where all learn from and teach one another in an atmosphere of mutual respect and pursuit of excellence; a faculty and staff motivated to excel in their respective fields as well as contributing to the broadly defined university environment; our graduates will have an understanding of interdependence and global competence, distinctive technical and educational skills, the experience and abilities to contribute to California's future high quality work force, the critical thinking abilities to be productive citizens, and the social responsibility and skills to be community builders. Monterey Bay will dynamically link the past, present, and future by responding to historical and changing conditions, experimenting with strategies which increase access, improve quality, and lower costs through education in a distinctive CSU environment. University students and personnel will attempt, analytically and creatively, to meet critical State and regional needs, and provide California with responsible and creative leadership for the global, twenty-first century.

Do You Need a Library?

The extent of the willingness to innovate at CSUMB is perhaps epitomized by the widely reported initial intent of the California State University Chancellor, Barry Munitz, to avoid building a physical library at all. As quoted in a *Newsweek* article that appeared in January 1995 — eight months before the campus was to open — resources would be devoted to computers for access to electronic resources rather than a library per se. "You simply don't have to build a traditional library these days,"[3] Munitz was quoted as saying. As it turns out, he was right, if the focus of the remark is put on "traditional." In fact, library services and alternative ways to deliver them were high on the list of activities for the "planning faculty" and the first academic provost. While they consulted with other California academic librarians about alternative schemes, such as "cluster libraries" in academic centers, they also filled the position of Dean of Science, Technology and Information Resources with an academic who had been serving as Vice Provost for Information Resources at the California State University campus at Chico. In that position Dr. James May had responsibility for the Chico Library. Early in his new position at CSUMB he spent much of his energy convincing administrators, including Chancellor Munitz, that a physical library with a collection of print materials was necessary at CSUMB; the appropriate use of technology to provide access to undergraduate level resources could and should be a cornerstone of library services but would not be sufficient in and of itself.

The audience for this debate was larger than the group of original campus planners, or even of the administration for the now 21-campus CSU system. As early as 1992, when the San Jose campus was trying to convince the system to consider Fort Ord as the site for an extensive branch, a library planning document suggested that the "collections developed for the Monterey [branch] Campus will be very different from the traditional primarily print collections."[4] That report, trying to strike a middle ground, went on to describe the need for a "core collection" of print materials and the importance of that collection not only in serving the branch campus community, but said it was also necessary to make "mutual resource sharing agreements" viable. "Cooperation and mutual resource sharing are only effective when each party has something (in this instance, collection resources) to contribute."[5] A later report recommending that the CSU system move forward with CSUMB as an independent 21st campus was performed by the California Postsecondary Education Commission.[6] Among the ten specific recommendations leading up to their conclusion to proceed, only the following covers a specific programmatic challenge for the plans:

> 6. The creation of a modern, technologically oriented library will represent a major challenge as planning for the new campus proceeds. While a core collection of books and periodicals is probably essential, ways should be found to distribute and diversify library access throughout the campus, including in the residence halls.[7]

The debate carried to the local regional press as well, and was apparently decided in favor of establishing a physical library with a core collection of print resources very soon after the widely quoted *Newsweek* article. A commentary written by the campus' new president, Peter Smith, for the *Monterey County Herald* newspaper on February 12, 1995, in reaction to an editorial lamenting the fact that the region's new University apparently was going to be absent a library, made the opposite promise explicit:

> Of course we're going to have a library on the campus where, along with books, periodicals and other on-hand information, we'll also have a burgeoning array of technological connections that connect our faculty and learners to other, more distant information resources. Surely, being able to stroll the aisles of the Library of Congress via technology is not a step backward for any of us.[8]

The First Two Years

President Smith's rhetoric of the technologically sublime side of library services was in full keeping with the high ambitions of the campus in general. To support those aspirations a huge planning and implementation effort had to be undertaken in a very short time frame. Securing, redesigning, and converting a former army building (as was the case for all campus physical spaces), hiring library faculty and staff, acquiring an initial and core collection of monographs, selecting electronic resources, selecting and implementing integrated library systems software, to name a few of the tasks, were accomplished between March 1995 and the opening of the Library in mid–October of that year.

As the following section describes, a set of services and resources has been constructed which occupies an interesting middle ground between the traditional and the completely virtual. It is interesting to consider whether the success of the Library — where success is measured not only by a solid reputation on campus for providing high-level service but also by transaction counts, foot traffic, etc. — was achieved despite the time frame or to some degree because of the time-induced pressure. It is possible, for example, that the relative lack of library expertise in the physical building conversion — a local Community College Librarian was called in to consult very late in the design process — resulted, in effect, in organizational innovation. A lack of office and processing space contributes to pressure on the Library to constantly re-examine work flows and job descriptions to keep staffing low and efficient. Shelving that is fixed, limited, and widely spread limits open areas. It is already encouraging a mingling of the electronic library with the physical, through an incursion of full-featured net-based work stations into the stacks, while also making it obvious that the print collection has definite and not too distant bounds. It also helps encourage patrons to use library resources, at least electronic ones, from anywhere on campus where there is a work station that will be authenticated as having access privileges to the many full-text and abstract and citation databases to which the Library subscribes.

Although the campus was officially sanctioned by statutory legislation in 1994, and a decision to include a physical library had been made by February 1995, the founding date of library services is somewhat arbitrary. The following time-line indicates the milestones of the first two years, using the hiring date of the first full-time faculty librarian as the starting point.

Table 1
Milestones of the First Two Years at the CSUMB Library

1995

1 July	Starting date of First Library faculty member
July	Offers made to two Library Co-Directors who contribute to decisions before their start dates in August; Book vendor chosen (Yankee Book Peddler); core collection ordered; first electronic resource subscriptions; ILL & reference services for extant faculty & staff established
7 August	Co-Directors start
August	Budget for equipment and initial collection approved (approx. $1.5 million); Select Endeavor as integrated system vendor; Book acquisition profile established with Yankee; Initial serial subscriptions established with Ebsco; Assume responsibility for campus Audio-Visual services; Establish course reserve service; Establish Memoranda of Understanding with local institutions for cooperative borrowing; Draft library assistant job positions and start recruitment
mid–August	Co-Director for Library Resources assumes Campus Web responsibilities (until mid–1996)
28 August	Instruction begins; Co-Directors teach sections of Communications Science & Technology 102, "The Internet"; Web-based Document Delivery forms made available; reference by e-mail established
4 September	President Clinton helps dedicate CSUMB
early October	Hire 4 temp. library assistants and 6 part-time reference librarians
10 October	Move from temporary quarters into Library Learning Complex
16 October	Library Learning Complex opens for business; space includes 19 public access computers, 90 study seats, 4 group study rooms, 2 computer labs
early November	First public photocopier on campus installed in the Library
mid–November	Shelving and security gate installed; first shipment of books from acquisitions profile arrives
22 December	First semester ends

1996

mid–January	Encyclopædia Britannica trial; hits-per-student 6 times higher than any other CSU campus
20 February	Official Opening Celebration of Library Learning Complex; keynote speaker is Brian Lamb, founder of C-SPAN
late February	Instructional services program starts with workshops for students and faculty
5 March	Endeavor system goes online with MARC records received from Yankee Book Peddler
mid–April	Advertisements for 4 librarians, 6 library assistants, 1 instructional support technician, and 1 administrative assistant posted
May	CSUMB academic year 1 ends
Summer	Library remains open for small summer class and conference schedule;

	Library Assistants and Admin. Asst. are hired; "Serials List" of full-text online journal titles created
August 28	Year two begins; Catalog description of Library includes 25,000 volumes, 3,000 electronic full-text journals; community on-site use policy est.
early October	Development Librarian for Electronic Resources arrives
October	Course-integrated instruction in 43 classes; 1200 student contact hours
early November	Electronic Reference Services Librarian arrives
November	Library faculty chair three Faculty Senate Committees and are members of three other committees
December	Instructional development plan for Information Resources submitted with emphasis on information competency, co-teaching of regular discipline curriculum, 7-course information science curriculum

1997

March	Library faculty receive 2 out of 8 campus Instructional innovation grants; Packard Foundation grant awarded to CSUMB-led consortium to distribute the collection formerly at the California Department of Fish and Game Marine Resources Division
May	Library faculty member is co-author of $69K CSU Academic Opportunity Fund grant
May	Academic Press' IDEAL electronic journals becomes 16th full-text subscription boosting elect. journal holdings to ~4000 titles; 41 citation/abstract databases also available
23 May	Spring semester ends; gate count of approximately 70,000 visits during semester; 1st University Commencement; Leon Panetta speaks; 130 graduates
1 June	Collection Processes and Access Librarian arrives bringing full staffing to 7 librarians, 7 Library Assistants, 8 FTE student assistants
July	Library faculty make 4 presentations covering CSUMB philosophies and technologies at American Library Association annual conference

Philosophies, Collections, and Services

The Library does have a small print collection and a set of services that resembles, in function, that at most other academic libraries. What sets it apart is the explicit declaration of a preference for the electronic over print, and the virtual access that allows access to library resources from anywhere on campus or from an authenticated campus member's work station. The current mission statement says that "to the extent possible and economically feasible, the library acquires and provides access to resources in electronic format rather than print."[9] We have also stated this philosophy as an intent to make maximum use of new technologies targeted at providing information resources to meet known needs of faculty and students "just in time," rather than building collections "just in case." There is an interesting, though subtle, difference in the two statements of philosophy, one that the library faculty has discussed at length. The difference is one between preferring electronic sources per se and preferring to use technology appropriately to provide the right kind of access at the right time. The current mission statement seems to suggest that a preference for technology for technology's sake is a calculated if somewhat internally controversial decision. Given the vision of the University, the embrace of technology is not only prudent politically, but dramatic enough to influence the day-to-day approach to providing services, preparing budgets and staffing plans, and creating expectations in clientele.

So the Library believes it is "transformative" in information formats, access, and base technologies. In choosing to collect primarily electronic resources and assuming a fairly low cap on print collections, it has moved beyond the transitional stage in which most libraries find themselves adding electronic resources to a large and growing print collection. While many libraries feel that electronic resources are an ever more valuable supplement to print, CSUMB feels that print resources supplement electronic access, and that they probably will become a less important supplement as time goes by. Echoing the distinction made above, this focus on format only thinly disguises the "real" focus on access and on the economies to be had when there is a drastic reduction of handling, storing, and caring for physical objects. In this regard the Library realizes that its intentions are not at all novel, but that the extent to which they can be followed and the situation under which they can be implemented — creating a library from scratch — are nearly unprecedented.

At this point a few indicators of the effect this core principle has on the Library and its use should be instructive. Using a cohort comparison group of the other 20 campuses in the California State University system,[10] the following figures show a dramatic difference in user behavior between CSUMB and more typical academic library users at primarily undergraduate institutions.

The relatively low ratio of transactions involving physical items allows the Library to avoid, for the most part, the large number of paraprofessionals devoted to processing those acquisitions, cataloging, or circulation transactions. CSUMB hopes to maintain a balance of roughly 50 percent professional staff, as opposed to the more usual 32 percent at cohort institutions revealed in Figures 3 and 4.

To further complete a view of the differences, as well as similarities, between CSUMB and its cohorts the following summary (Table 2) is offered. Interestingly, the similarities include the relative size of the Library as a cost center of its campus. Assuming that costs of electronic access continue to be lower, on average, than print, the size of the CSUMB Library as a cost center should drop, because the figures in Table 2 include the high initial expense of the core print collection of approximately 25,000 volumes. A wild card of sorts in the equation is the cost associated with the relatively high number of interlibrary loans and document delivery. Note that the figures reported here are from a period of total subsidization of nearly unlimited ILL and document delivery. Mechanisms for adjusting demand, such as a threshold above which requests are made on a cost-recovery basis rather than subsidized, are probably in the future for CSUMB. The challenge of predicting and influencing the economics of electronic access to materials is named as one of the larger ones facing the Library's future in the next section of this chapter.

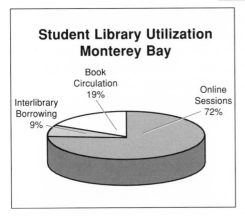

Figure 1. CSUMB Library Utilization

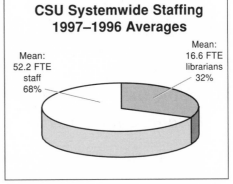

Figure 2. CSU average Library Utilization[11]

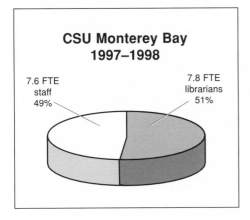

Figure 3. CSUMB Library Staffing

Figure 4. CSU average Library Staffing[12]

Table 2
Summary Statistics CSUMB and CSU Cohorts[13]

Statistical Category	*CSU Avg.*	*CSUMB*
Total library budget	$4.4 million	$1.5 million
Percent of Campus Budget	4.5%	4.3%
Library Faculty & Staff	54	16.5
Bound Volumes	714,000	29,000
New Books Purchased	11,000	4,500
Print Journals	2,750	325
Electronic Journals	N/A	3,600
Interlibrary Loan Activity	19,500	10,700

The opportunity for the Library to invent itself as the campus starts up, and with a primarily electronic collection, also allows it to be transformative in other dimensions. Organizationally it is a member of an academic unit, the Center for Science, Technology, & Information Resources, and thus finds itself tightly coupled to a large unit of the academic program. This coupling presents some challenges, discussed later, in creating connections to other instructional programs. On the other hand, the small team-based work flow also has allowed the Library, from the outset, to avoid some of the traditional internal compartmentalization, for example between technical and public services.

Ongoing Challenges

A summary of the lessons learned and the lessons that are still to be learned is best given in a discussion of the certain challenges that this library of and for the "21st century campus" faces. These challenges include:

- Assessing whether electronic "just in time" resources and services match patron needs
- Creating user self-sufficiency and competence
- Predicting and influencing the economic context
- Aligning with the 21st century Campus context

Assessing the Match Between Services, Resources and Needs

To some extent the Library benefits from the often chaotic and stressful conditions of a start-up campus with the short planning period described above. Because library services and resources were in place very early on and have grown substantially over the first two years while many other services were lacking, there has been "automatic" institutional support and good will toward the Library. Responding to early unanticipated needs of the campus, such as providing the campus Webmaster and instructional audio/visual services, enhanced the reputation of the Library as a responsive campus-wide service.

This reputation combines with the strong campus advice, given to faculty, staff, and students that they must be flexible and adaptive during the start-up of the University, to produce very few criticisms of the services and approaches of the Library. Indeed, there is little feedback at all, and the Library has created very few feedback mechanisms. The lack of feedback mechanisms is due in part to the start-up of the Library itself and a focus on creating services rather than measuring their effectiveness. But it is also due to the large challenge of finding or creating output measures and patron evaluation mechanisms that will work in this environment. The library evaluation literature, while replete with descriptions of output measures and instruments for relatively traditional libraries, is lacking in reports that will aid the development of measures for non-traditional, distributed services provided to high populations of multi-cultural and "disadvantaged" students enrolled in academic departments that have few counterparts elsewhere. Satisfaction measures can surely be developed, but deeper measures, for example of baseline information competencies of incoming students and the enhancement of those competencies as a result of learning about and using library services and resources, are more difficult to construct.

It is crucial for accountability, ongoing institutional support, and simple peace of mind that the Library find ways to determine the constellation of needs of campus members and measure how and whether they are being met. At least one library faculty grant, an internally sponsored "instructional innovation" grant, is directed toward that end, with a focus on creating an assessment tool for information discovery skills in library patrons. That study should enable the construction and tuning of tutorials, pathfinders, quick guides, and other instruction to create stronger, deeper, more applicable information discovery and synthesis skills. But it is only one small contribution toward the question, "do we know the needs of our patrons and are we meeting them with the services, resources, and instruction on hand?"

Creating User Self-Sufficiency and Competency

If matching needs to resources is an ongoing challenge (for any library, of course), so too is creating user self-sufficiency. Declaring that electronic resources allow use of "the library" remotely and independently ups the ante in making sure that the interfaces to those resources do not get in the way of their use (or to put it another way, that inhibitors to patron self-sufficiency are predicted and mitigated by modifying interfaces, providing contextual help, etc.). The Library has a strong preference for providing electronic resources via the web. Content vendors are feeling this demand strongly in the overall market and are responding. The web is approaching the stature of panacea as a delivery mechanism (though some might argue that it is more accurate to say that tcp/ip and client/server computer architecture is the real panacea). But it is not a panacea for the problem of the large variety of interfaces between users and information sources. The web as unifying interface fades into the background quickly across vendors of content who have all ported to the web not only the look and feel of their search and retrieval interfaces but in most cases the underlying logic as well. It is difficult to construct the same search in a predictable way when using web-based products from different vendors.

Metadata standards and the standardization of language that categorizes query types, query fields, result sets, etc., such as the Z39.50 protocol and the Government Information Locator Service (GILS), hold great promise. But the promise is little realized for institutions such as CSUMB which are faced with little choice but to bewilder their patrons with access to thousands of titles through dozens of different looking "databases" from many different vendors. To date, and certainly with the approach at CSUMB, the burden to sort through the variety and create a successful query still falls in greatest measure to the patron. Just as it has always been with print-based tools, the ongoing challenge is to relieve that burden as much as possible. In addition to effective and timely instruction, sometimes relatively simple engineering at the local level can help, as with the case of the CSUMB Serials list which allows an alphabetic search of full-text journal titles and a click, through an explanatory gateway page, to the electronic source of a journal.

Predicting and Influencing the Economic Context

The challenge of a dependence upon electronic resources does not end with the bewildering array of search and retrieval interfaces that inhibits user self-sufficiency. In the short run it may not even begin there. CSUMB expects financial resources devoted to electronic subscriptions and document delivery to equal those spent on print within a year or two and to grow predictably. But that expectation is based upon uncertain estimates of the costs of electronic resources and with little confidence that the change in costs will be predictable. It is no secret that publishers seem not to have figured out the pricing structures of their electronic products. They present convincing arguments that it is difficult to determine "first copy" and marginal costs of digital resources, and that the transition from selling objects to selling access is a difficult one. In the meantime libraries have to struggle with little standardization in pricing models, in license agreements, and in who shoulders the burden of authenticating remote users, the library or the vendor.

CSUMB has two natural advantages in this arena. First, it is able to get discounts and to indirectly influence the economics by participating in the 21-campus purchasing consortium of the CSU system as a whole. Secondly, an advantage which will erode over time is that many purchasing agreements, including relative share of consortial purchases, are based upon campus population. It is unclear whether the disappearance of this significant advantage, as the campus grows toward its eventual target of 20,000 to 25,000 students, will be offset by the enhancements to the library budget from campus economies of scale and absolute growth in income from fees and tuition.

Another sensitive piece of the economic context, and one of which the Library is acutely aware, is the reliance on document delivery and interlibrary loan. While the Library promises to become very skilled at purchasing high-use items for local use, directing the bulk of document delivery requests to for-profit vendors such as CARL UnCover, and spreading interlibrary loan requests among partner institutions, there is still justifiable concern among its partners about the "balance of trade." Under conditions where CSUMB is a net borrowing library and larger and older partners fear the costs of being net lenders, the challenge will be to create real collection development agreements and other innovative exchanges in which CSUMB has something substantial to offer.

Aligning with the "21st Century Campus" Context

The final challenge to mention for the CSUMB Library is actually a set of challenges connected to the University trying to invent itself as a learning institution for the next century. The University, for example, has an academic structure based upon "Centers" and "Institutes" whose academic integration and alignment is unusual. Programs in Earth Systems Science & Policy, Teledramatic Arts & Technology, and Management & International Entrepreneurship, while they are exciting reconfigurations of the academic enterprise, create challenges in nearly every facet of library services and resources. This is true from constructing course-integrated instruction to assessing the relevancy of a journal title, to predicting what reference materials will be in high demand. Some of the working tools of the profession are ill-suited to face this challenge; consider, for example, basing collection development and acquisition profiles on the LC classification scheme while simultaneously trying to provide resources to a program in "Geospatial Applications in the Social Sciences."

On a similar note, CSUMB has incorporated "entrepreneurship" into its vision and has a stated goal of meeting 30 percent of its operating costs through entrepreneurial activities. Quite aside from the campus challenges in defining those terms and activities or distributing the goal among campus units, the Library, in good company, is faced with figuring out which of its activities can be valued, priced, and marketed to generate income. If the core activities seem unlikely sources of revenue, there will be pressure to create revenue-generating activities while not eroding those very core activities. Conceivably the Library can develop products and become expert at raising money in a traditional development sense. Conceding that possibility, the challenge between here and there will be to create a library culture that accepts that facet of the mission and to time well the partitioning of attention and resources among services to the University and services and products for sale.

Conclusion

The Library at CSUMB was founded, as was the University itself, under difficult and ambitious circumstances that included a mandate to do things differently and to prepare students for the next century. The short time for planning and creating programs and services was the result of the conditions placed upon the opportunity to receive land and facilities from the closure of the large Army base at Fort Ord. Library planning proceeded in the face of mixed messages, including, at one point, a claim that a physical library was not necessary at all. Two years into the "experiment," as some still call it, the Library has walls, staff, a small core collection of print materials and a mission to concentrate on the provision of digital resources in preference to print where feasible. Successful services have been created based upon that mission, but challenges remain to keep the services integrated and sustainable in light of the ambitions of the University vision and the uncertain economics of the digital resources themselves.

References

1. Planning for Evergreen State College in Washington took four years and planning for Florida Gulf Coast University, due to open in 1997, has been under way since 1993 according to "A Vision in Progress: The Decision to Establish a Public University at Monterey Bay," by William Chance. Prepared for the California Higher Education Policy Center, June 1997.

2. California State University, Monterey Bay 1995/1996 Catalog, pg. 4.

3. "Wiring the Ivory Tower," *Newsweek*, January 30, 1995, pg. 62.

4. "Monterey Campus Library and Instructional Resource Center: Collections, Space, and Staffing." Report produced by Jo Bell Whitlach, Interim Library Director at San Jose State University. May 4, 1992, pg. 1.

5. *Ibid.*, pg. 2.

6. California Post-Secondary Education Commission. "Creating a Campus for the 21st Century." September 1993.

7. As quoted in "The 21st Campus for the 21st Century: A Needs Assessment Conducted for the California State University System, for the Proposed Campus at Fort Ord, California." The Tomas Rivera Center, February 1994, pg. 135. Other recommendations were much broader and connected to the current vision statement. For example:

> 3. In planning for the Monterey Bay campus, the State University should take the probable realities of life in the twenty-first century into account. Those realities will include the facts that the United States will be a technologically oriented, knowledge-based society; there will be an overwhelming emphasis on manufacturing and service quality (including educational services); multiculturalism and international-ism will dominate social, political, and economic life; and in the midst of rapid change and an increasing demand for higher education services, resources for higher education will be limited as never before, and higher education will be asked to do far more with less.
>
> 4. Planning for Fort Ord should not advance along traditional pedagogical and managerial lines. The new campus should devise a highly flexible and administratively "flat" organizational structure that will not only encourage educational innovation and a multidisciplinary curriculum, but will also discourage the establishment of academic fiefdoms.

8. Smith, Peter. "Campus will indeed have a library." *Monterey County Herald*. February 12, 1995.

9. The entire Library mission statement reads as follows:

> The Library Learning Complex of the California State University, Monterey Bay supports the University's innovative and interdisciplinary curriculum by providing the diversity of information resources essential for learning and teaching. To the extent possible and economically feasible, the library acquires and provides access to resources in electronic format rather than print. The Library's instructional programs promote information competency and critical thinking, contributing to lifelong learning skills among our primary clientele of students, faculty, and staff of the University.
>
> The Library fulfills its mission by:
>
> - Providing access for our students, faculty and staff to print and electronic library resources regardless of their location;
> - Providing a range of promptly accessible library collections and electronic resources that will support the curriculum;

- Providing timely document delivery and interlibrary loan services to fulfill specific requests of students, faculty and staff;
- Providing in-person and online reference assistance and instruction to students, faculty, staff, and the local community;
- Offering course-integrated instruction in library research;
- Teaching how to evaluate and appropriately use information technology;
- Teaching a core curriculum on technology and information studies, and discipline-specific research methodologies;
- Creating cooperative partnerships with local libraries, organizations and agencies to augment our own resources and to provide reciprocal support;
- Supporting distance learning and instructional media needs campus-wide;
- Promoting the use of innovative technologies to provide rapid access to information.

10. The CSU system enrolled approximately 336,800 students (261,000 full-time equivalents) and employed 18,142 faculty (10,625 full-time) in Fall 1996, according to the Public Affairs office of the Office of the Chancellor.

11. Analysis performed by Director for Library Resources, Steve Watkins. Circulation and interlibrary borrowing/document delivery figures are from *1995–96 Library Statistics* of the California State University, Division of Information Resources and Technology and 1996–97 CSU Monterey Bay statistics. Online sessions are based only on preliminary, partial data for several network-accessible databases and vendors for which systemwide usage data is available and are presented here for purposes of illustration only.

12. *Ibid.*

13. *Ibid.*

8. IUPUI University Library: A Library for the 21st Century

Barbara B. Fischler
President, DAR BAR Consultants

The IUPUI University Library is one of the most technologically advanced public university libraries in the United States. The stunning exterior of the square-shaped building is native Indiana limestone and glass. The building sits at a 45-degree angle to adjacent buildings and has lovingly been referred to the "baseball diamond tied back to the campus by an umbilical cord." This "cord" is a corridor that overlooks a plaza with a pyramid-shaped fountain, green spaces, trees, and benches — an oasis amid the concrete paths and blacktop streets that frame and intersect this urban campus.

Building Facts

Architects: Edward Larrabee Barnes and Gajinder Singh — Design; Howard, Needles, Tammen, and Bergendoff— Design/Engineers

Project Representatives: Raymond W. Casati, Assistant Vice President and University Architect; Barbara B. Fischler, Director, IUPUI University Libraries

Size: 256,800 assignable square feet; 273,200 gross square feet

Floors: Five — lower level and four above ground levels

Volume Capacity: 1,000,000

Seating: 1,740

Public Computers: 275 Scholar's Workstations; 52 OPACs with Scholar's Workstation capabilities

121.5 miles of wiring — single and multimode fiber and Category 3 copper to every data connection. Under-floor cable tray grid and floor-embedded sleeves that permit wires to be pulled though every 4'6" × 5'

1760 data connections

641 networked individual study carrels

42 networked group study rooms

40 networked faculty study rooms

3 networked classrooms

2 networked rooms for Adaptive Educational Services

8 public computer clusters integrated into the stacks with 20 Scholar's workstations and 4 laser printers to each cluster. PC to MAC ratio: 4 to 1

Auditorium with full Scholar's workstation capabilities, seats 100 people

Individual Learning Center which provides students with capability of producing multimedia presentations

Center for Teaching and Learning

Server Room with Network Operating Center for campus

Campus Video Distribution System

Compact shelving capability throughout the building

The Library Information System (LIS) and the Scholar's Workstation

The learning environment is dependent upon the successful integration of voice, video and data technologies, and the delivery of these technologies through a telecommunications network. These resources are:

60 CD-ROM and locally mounted databases

56 full-text electronic journals

14 application software packages

50 online databases

50 online card catalogs

Literally hundreds of links to other Internet resources

The Interactive Multimedia Distribution System (IMDS) which supplies television channels, videotapes, and laser discs technologies to the desktop.

Some background about the university, its goals, the philosophical approach, and the financial atmosphere will help in understanding the directions taken in designing this library.

Indiana University–Purdue University Indianapolis (IUPUI) is an urban university established in the state capitol in 1969. The 285-acre campus, located on the west side of downtown Indianapolis, enrolls more than 27,000 students, employs 1,894 FTE administrators, faculty, and lecturers and 6,824 staff, offers 184 authorized Indiana University and Purdue University degrees but none of its own (*Indiana University Fact Book, 1996-97*). IUPUI is classified as "Doctoral II." The average age of our students is 27; 58 percent women, 13 percent minority; 19 percent married; 50 percent full-time.

The university has very close ties to the Indianapolis and surrounding communities and an historical commitment to cooperation and collaboration both within and without the campus. The three buildings that housed IUPUI initially were meant for a junior college.

The original 56,415–square foot University Library was designed to accommodate not only the library collections garnered from two decaying downtown locations, but also a cafeteria, School of Social Work offices, and instructional media services. The academic school and instructional media were relocated before occupancy, but it was obvious within five years that the building could not serve as the library for the astonishingly rapidly growing university. By 1976 efforts were begun to have a new library building become part of the capital plan for IUPUI.

The efforts for not only a new library building, but also a general upgrading of library resources and staffing, were enhanced through the IUPUI University Libraries Development Task Force report (May 15, 1984). Among the recommendations were the following:

> ...the new main campus library should reflect urban campus needs, incorporate the best features of present and future library automation...

> ...incorporate the highest levels of automation possible.

Finally, in 1987, through the combined efforts of the director of libraries and the dean of the School of Law, permission to begin programming was given by the IUPUI Administration. An advisory committee made up of representatives of every school on campus, students, staff, and technologies was formed, as well as a working committee comprising librarians and computer and systems experts. There was heavy input from all campus constituencies and the Indianapolis community as to what functions should be in the new building. Unfortunately for some, such requests as a child care center, saunas, and parking facilities could not be honored. As the building program was being written to serve the needs of the users, the campus goals of Continuation, Completion, Consolidation, and Cooperation were also being reflected (*IUPUI Development Plan: 1988–2000*, Indiana University–Purdue University at Indianapolis, February 1, 1988).

Full state funding for public university capital projects had not proven successful beginning in the mid-1980s. The president of Indiana University, Thomas Ehrlich, decided to initiate a fund-raising campaign to raise $18,000,000 toward the proposed $32,000,000 new library building, the "gem" of the campus.

The Indiana University Foundation at IUPUI, working in conjunction with

President Thomas Ehrlich, Vice President (Indianapolis) Indiana University Gerald L. Bepko, and Director of Libraries Barbara B. Fischler, developed the "*Vision for Excellence*" campaign. "The Committee on the Library" was established. William H. Hudnut, III (mayor of Indianapolis), Glenn W. Irwin, Jr., M.D. (Retired Vice President [Indianapolis]), and Richard D. Wood (CEO, Eli Lilly and Company) were the three co-chairs of a 29-person committee of prominent Indianapolis business and civic leaders. The official campaign was launched June 23, 1988, on the IUPUI campus with the announcement of a $12,000,000 donation from the Lilly Endowment, Inc. The remaining $6,000,000 was raised in the Indianapolis community in less than two years, making the campaign one of the most successful public university library fund-raising campaigns in the United States.

When the new library was being conceived, a number of factors came into consideration:

- The IUPUI campus had few expansion possibilities since it was surrounded by water on three sides, and the city on the fourth.
- There were exceptionally strong research collections located at Indiana University and Purdue University, each within 50 miles of Indianapolis.
- Cooperation and collaboration among all libraries in Indianapolis and the surrounding counties were strong.
- Computers were playing an ever-increasing role in libraries.
- An excellent relationship and understanding of the future possibilities of the use of technology existed between the libraries, computing services, and learning resources on the campus.
- The IUPUI Administration was fully supportive of a technology environment for the campus with the library wiring and its proposed Scholar's Workstation setting the direction.

Decisions were made and programming begun to create a new library building which would integrate the finest aspects of the traditional print-based sources with the most advanced technologies available. Emphasis in the programming was placed upon flexibility, functionality, and space-saving interior design. The technology vision was the development of a workstation which would have the capability to provide the users, in as seamless an architecture as possible, bibliographic and full-text information, data, video (still and live), voice, application tools, and graphics. This workstation was to be the foundation of the library's evolution into the "virtual" or "library without walls" concept.

The university contracted with Ameritech Information Systems to analyze where we were with our technologies and to produce a plan which would enable us to realize our vision. The project was frequently referred to as the "Enterprise" as we boldly, and sometimes fearfully, moved ahead. Thirteen projects were recommended, analyzed for personnel requirements, time frames, and one-time and ongoing costs. This information systems plan, completed January 31, 1990, was presented to the IUPUI Administration and approval was given to move forward immediately with three of the projects: the workstation, the gateway, and the multimedia system (*IUPUI University Library. Information Systems Plan Project.*

Systems Integration Master Plan: Realizing the Vision. Ameritech Information Systems, January 31, 1990).

A Request for Information (RFI) was issued later in 1990 and then followed by a Request for Proposal (RFP) in 1991. IBM was awarded the contract in 1992 to work with University Libraries and Integrated Technologies personnel as co-project managers and developers. Just as with the building design, numerous committees were established. Joint Application Design (JAD) sessions were held, each of considerable significance in shaping the development of the technologies.

The first JAD session involved faculty and students, with the technologies staff simply listening to the needs that were expressed. Fifty-six hours were spent brainstorming ideas for the design and application content of the workstation. The expected 65 requirements became 265, necessitating a reevaluation of the scope of the project and some eventual down scaling.

The second JAD session was for the library staff. Their session, 10 hours in length, provided the developers with yet another set of needs.

The third JAD session was with the project's Steering Committee, a group of high-level administrators, library directors, and technology directors from both the IUPUI and Indiana University–Bloomington campuses. This committee produced the goals and was the oversight committee throughout the development of the LIS (IUPUI/IBM *Library Information System Project,* 1992). These goals were:

The library system and its applications will:

- Use technology to develop information skills in our students and to reshape the learning environment by providing enhanced access to knowledge and tools.
- Become the centerpiece of a coordinated support system for scholars.
- Become a major information resource for Indiana residents.
- Become the center for specific information resources vital to economic development in Indiana.
- Play a role in Indiana's economic growth.
- Become a center for information services throughout Indiana.
- Become a paradigm for learning centers of the 21st century
- Become a visible symbol of unity and excellence for the University.
- Position IUPUI as a national leader in information technology.
- Work technically and functionally.
- Provide access to and retrieval of more information in a wider variety of formats more rapidly and completely than through traditional services.
- Be as technically uncomplicated as possible. This means that the design, which is developed, will lead the novice users from a lower-level of expertise to the complex scholarly functions in a systematic incremental manner.

The committee's system design requirements were:

- The system must be designed with open and forward-thinking architecture. (The University is in a unique position to drive standards for like systems throughout the world.)
- The system must incorporate the list of University standards published in the RFP.
- The system must incorporate established national and international standards.
- The system must interface to existing and new applications.
- The system must be intrinsically easy to use.
- The system must have adequate capacity. (Prudent consideration during design must be directed towards connectivity, dependability, reliability, and auditability.)
- There must be seamless movement from one system to another.
- The system must be responsive to the requirements of the ADA.
- The system must provide a consistent approach to system assistance functions.
- The system must provide automated assistance for scholar functions.
- The system must be designed to facilitate scholar functions. (Administrative functions will be a secondary target.)
- The system must accommodate use outside of the library from campus and off-campus locations through Internet technology and local networks.
- The system must provide an initial screen, which will attract users' attention, inviting use.
- The system design must consider the direction toward selective charge back fees.

These Steering Committee requirements, though simple in their statement, were to prove challenging to all involved, both technically and emotionally. Acquiring and testing a wide variety of hardware and software was not easy. Disparate staffs had to learn to work together, and this element of development proved to be one of the most difficult aspects of the entire building and technology projects.

The interior of the IUPUI University Library is as striking as the exterior. Concrete, oak, dolomite marble, slate, and stainless steel are blended to create a warm and comfortable atmosphere that is conducive to formal and leisure study. The use of natural light, with careful shielding of ultraviolet rays, enhances this environment.

Although constructed before the Americans with Disabilities Act (ADA) was enacted, the library meets all ADA requirements. Special design accommodations were made with the furnishings in the open areas so that persons using the standard wheelchair could study in the individual carrels or at the Scholar's workstations. All service desks were designed for both the users and staff who had disabilities.

One of the most important areas in the library is the Adaptive Educational Services learning center rooms. The furnishings in this area, supplied by Human Factors, are completely adjustable for any type of wheelchair. The equipment

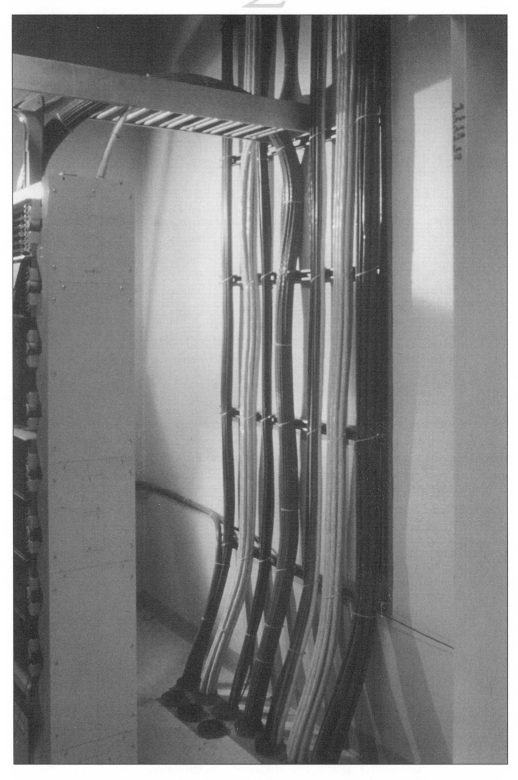

An intermediate distribution frame. (Courtesy of Barbara Fischler.)

installed in these rooms initially included a Kurzweil machine, soundproof booths, several special computer keyboards, scanners, tape recorders, voice synthesis for IBM computers, brailler and braille printer, page enlarger, and calculators. As technologies have advanced, more sophisticated equipment has been made available for those students with visual, hearing, mobility, and learning impairments.

At the time the IUPUI University Library was conceived and built, the combination of fiber, copper, and other electrical wiring to the desktop had not been a consideration in library furniture. The majority of the furniture in the public areas was custom designed and supplied by Worden. The staff furniture was from Steelcase, and several conference rooms by Thomas Moser. These companies were challenged by the need to accommodate the number of wiring strands, the connection box, the need to protect the fiber, and the requirement of flexibility. They met these challenges and produced some of the finest wiring accommodations in furniture to date.

The decision was made early in the library's design stage to place computing clusters as close to the circulating collection as possible, eventually interspersing them into the shelving areas. Convenience for the users to the majority of the collection materials was paramount over providing easy access for assistance by the librarians. When the electronic reserve system was developed, this stack location of the computers and their printers proved advantageous. This open location proved to be less of an acoustical problem than had been originally envisioned. The volumes on the shelves absorbed the keyboard noise and laser printer sound was almost undetectable.

Another programming element of the building which has been highly successful is the group study rooms. With the growing popularity of group and or team assignments, or simply because students enjoy or need to work together, these rooms are heavily used. Some of these rooms are now equipped with computers, making it unnecessary for students to bring their own laptops or to take advantage of the library's circulating laptop project.

The faculty study rooms have been less successful. Although needs for these rooms was expressed frequently by faculty during the programming stage, few faculty members have taken advantage of them. Progressively, groups such as our Senior Academy, a short-term institute, and a writing clinic have been located in these rooms. With the ever-increasing availability of electronic information, it seems that faculty prefer to work in their own offices or homes, coming to the library only when monographic materials or research assistance are needed.

One of the most beautiful sections of the library is the Special Collections and Archives, furnished by Thomas Moser. Young universities such as IUPUI's are not expected to hold significant primary source materials, but ours is an exception. We maintain the strongest collections in the United States of documents on German-American Turnverein societies, and philanthropic societies and fundraising organizations. Preservation and sharing of these resources is strongly electronic-based.

The auditorium and the display areas have all proven to be highly attractive

Computer clusters at the IUPUI University Library. (Courtesy of Rick Baughn, Manager/ Photographer, IUPUI Photographic Services.)

to both campus and community organizations. The auditorium is used for instruction, lecture and film series, training sessions, intimate recitals, and conferences. The first Dinofest Conference was held in the building shortly after it opened in 1993 and, in addition to lectures, the three lobbies were filled with dinosaur replicas, fossils, and other numerous visitors. The full traveling King Arthur exhibition was also displayed in the library.

There is a study room where food and drink are permitted. We decided it was easier "to join them" rather than to continue to try to deter bringing food and drink into the building. The popularity of this area is great and public relations with the students have been greatly improved.

Buildings of this size and filled with high-level electronic equipment can present a security challenge. The IUPUI University Library has employed a number of sophisticated electronic systems as well as providing a monitoring station near one of the public entrances. Whether it is the nature of our location, users, or the variety of deterrent systems, theft and other disturbances have been minimal.

The Center for Teaching and Learning, viewed originally as cooperative operation between the library staff and Integrated Technologies, has continued to evolve in its operations and purposes. At present its emphasis is upon developing faculty and graduate students skills in their use of high end technologies.

The requirement for flexibility in interior design, as few permanent walls as possible, and open spaces has already proven to be correct. Rooms envisioned for specific operations changed their purposes before we ever moved into the building. Other areas have been reconfigured, an action made easier because of the considerable use of paneled (landscaped) offices for support staff rather than the use of walls. Monumental built-in furniture may be attractive, but it is a deterrent to flexibility. However, when fiber to the desktop is employed, extreme care must be taken to prevent damage to or breaking of it. In such areas, heavier furniture that cannot be easily moved or other damage-prevention devices must be employed.

Computers certainly were not new to the library profession when the design and technology emphasis of the IUPUI University Library was envisioned. Nevertheless, what the full impact of the capabilities of the Scholar's workstation was to have upon the staff initially was somewhat surprising. Reactions ranged from fear to happy excitement. One interesting comment was that "Reference is fun again." What was absolutely necessary throughout both the building process and the technology development was keeping the staff well-informed and involved. Training was and will continue to be of the highest importance as the virtual/digital library continues to evolve. Also, within academe, working with the faculty to integrate the library's capabilities into their teaching and research is a necessity. The library profession is changing rapidly because of information technologies and with our deep involvement in this area, we have the opportunity to become a far more vibrant and indispensable profession than at anytime in our history.

Another necessity in such an endeavor as this library building is a close and friendly relationship between the library project director, the architects, the construction personnel, and vendors. The library project director needs to be very familiar with the blue-line drawings and to attend all construction progress meetings. This attention to development is also required where the technologies are involved although on a less day-to-day basis. An expert systems integrator is a mandatory employee when large and complicated systems are employed. Support teams are also necessary.

The IUPUI University Library has and will continue to have many of the traditional functions of an academic library. Its emphasis has and will continue to shift toward the digital or virtual library.

If the success of the IUPUI University Library can be judged by its use (students, faculty, staff, and the Indianapolis community), the number of presentations at national conferences about it, and the interest expressed in it from around the world, this library and its LIS have been a major achievement. During the first two years of operation, more than 200 groups visited. Their visits were for a few hours to several days in length. A number of directors working toward new library buildings, additions, and/or restorations have patterned their programming after some or all of the design of the IUPUI University Library. The library has fulfilled the goal of positioning itself and IUPUI as a national leader in information technology.

Visit our web sites: http://www.iupui.edu and http://www-lib.iupui.edu

References

Indiana University–Purdue University at Indianapolis. University Library. Project No.: IUPUI 866-257. Program. May 3, 1988.

Indiana University Fact Book, 1996–97.

IUPUI University Libraries Development Task Force Report, May 15, 1984.

Vision for Excellence, brochure. n.d.

Ameritech Information Systems. IUPUI University Library. Information Systems Plan Project. *Systems Integration Master Plan: Realizing the Vision.* January 31, 1990.

IUPUI/IBM Library Information Systems Project. *IUPUI University Library,* 1992.

Paul Tarricone, "A Library for the 21st Century," *Facilities Design & Management,* September 1995.

William M. Plater, "A labyrinth of the Wide World," *Educom Review,* March/April 1995.

"Limited Only by the Imagination: Information Technology at IUPUI," *Partnerships,* IUPUI Alumni Newsletter, Autumn, 1995.

Unit 3
STYLE
Architects and Builder-Librarians

Unit Background

Architect Will Bruder, who designed the new central facility for the Phoenix Public Library system (PPL), has labeled the new main library in Chicago "high theater." Of this and other major library projects completed in the last few years, he said, "The architecture is about civic image, about exterior imagery rather than specific function" (quoted in Wiley, 112). In other words, at least where libraries are concerned, the lure of form and symbolism tends to spirit the designer away from the building's function and toward its beauty and significance.

The Harold Washington Library Center, Chicago's new main library, is not included as a chapter in this book, but the story of its design and construction provides instructive insights into how some architects look at libraries, how the library design process unfolds, and how factors outside the library can influence that process and to what degree. Most of the following details of the new main building of the Chicago Public Library (CPL) are from *Design Wars*, a thought-provoking video documentary about the CPL architectural competition. It was written, edited, and produced by Marian Marzynski in 1989.

Chicago's Hopes

Regarding its love affair with architecture, Chicago has been called passionate, obsessive, and insecure. Although modernism is well represented in Chicago as a result of its mania for new building technologies, imitations of earlier styles abound as well. The "bastard Gothic" Chicago Tribune tower and the buildings of the University of Chicago are examples. These edifices and others like them, according to Marzynski's video, echo past greatness in an attempt to establish Chicago's claim to a grand heritage, much the way the *Aeneid* forged

149

royal, Trojan antecedents for ancient Rome. History repeats itself again and again in Chicago, just as it does almost everywhere else.

While the style of most of the libraries in this book is decidedly modern, the style of the new CPL facility is not. Quite the contrary. In fact, according to Thomas Beeby, the building's architect, it is part of a "lineage of libraries" that, he says, started with the 19th-century Bibliothèque Ste.-Geneviève in Paris, which he acknowledges as the inspiration for the new CPL facility. Surprised by the modernism of the designs submitted by the four other architects in the CPL competition, Beeby believed that the new building should translate traditional library values into a "cultural institution … which everyone would understand," and not present a futuristic notion of what the library should be (Marzynski, n.p.).

The result of Beeby's estimation of what is architecturally understandable and accessible to everyone is a reiteration of a lovely but bygone style that was itself a reverberation of even more distant antiquity. That he tapped a dated motif as the most appropriate style for a major urban 21st-century library is, on the one hand, his tribute to the "traditional values" of libraries. On the other hand, it is a troubling association, if the public thinks such distant virtues are too remote to be of real value to modern individuals. If citizens of the next century believe it is necessary to retreat to an earlier millennium to enter and deal with a "cultural institution," and that library values are inherently of that era, libraries will have little to do with modernity.

That the eleven-person jury who selected the winning CPL entry made their choice based on the same perceptions Beeby used to formulate his design is also a little troubling, because Marzynski's video captures the contradictions in their reasoning. Jury chairman Norman Ross said the Beeby design was "pure architecture … solid, gentle, with noble spaces…. This is a building that you can trust…. The windows have a genuine feeling of grandeur…. This looks like a library." The examples in this book, along with virtually every other library constructed since the time of the Carnegie libraries, demonstrate that there is no single "look" for a library.

Ross also said that he and the jury

> decided we shouldn't exploit the concept of the hero-architect, the man who reinvents with every project…. We knew that there should be architectural dialogue between the past and the future … that our building should relate to architectural masterpieces, and should be functional, and should be flexible, and should be architecturally handsome [Marzynski, n.p.].

It sounds as if the jury, in trying to protect themselves from what they perceived as the pomposity of "hero-architects," may have achieved an even higher level of pretentiousness. For in Marzynski's documentary, Ross reveals that the jury admitted that the design favored in a poll of librarians was "precise, utilitarian, functional"; nevertheless, the jury eliminated it early because it was not "exciting." One of the jury members said it was "the kind of building no one would walk across the street to see" (Marzynski, n.p.). But on the subject of redesigning library services amid technological change, Michael Buckland states that "steadfast attention to what is needed can provide a plausible basis for effective planning.... If form should follow function, then concentration on the function should help us anticipate future forms" (16). In other words, and the CPL is a good example of this, striking style should not be made the hallmark of librarianship. To use Ross's own words, architectural handsomeness ought to be quite sufficient.

It is seldom sufficient, however. Custom expects something grand and imposing to house books, and this is not a belief peculiar to Chicagoans building civic pride and power on revivals of past greatness. It is the same expectation held almost everywhere. And whether it be due to a bout of municipal boasting, as Marzynski's documentary suggests, or to a deep respect for books and libraries, or to both at once, the feeling has to do with what I call "symbolic librarianship," which is an aspect of library and user interaction that librarians must know how to manage right along with all the library's other resources (see Unit 4).

Rising Phoenix

Before designing the new PPL central library, architect Will Bruder had designed other libraries for the PPL branch system. So he already had a good working relationship with the library administrators and was familiar with the building priorities of Ralph Edwards, then the Phoenix City librarian. As Edwards' chapter relates, those priorities boiled down to simplicity, flexibility, and economy. The result was, in Edwards' words, "a five-level precast concrete box," with the main circulating collection in one room and one classification to make materials easy to find; an absence of subject collections to make better use of the staff; rectangular public areas with no intruding irregular spaces to create illogical floor plans or inefficient staffing needs; open spaces with few load-bearing walls and lots of reconfigurable area; and a very expandable and economical facility.

Edwards credits Bruder with making a highly functional building also very attractive and "architecturally significant." The building's distinctive "saddle-bags" provide the exterior with aesthetic interest, and also hide the mechanical services, restrooms, stairways, and other necessities, which have been transferred to the facility's perimeters, away from the rectangular integrity of the central service space. The point of highest architectural significance inside the building is the acre-size Great Reading Room on the top floor with its panoramic views and an ingenious "floating" ceiling penetrated by gem-like skylights that project moving light patterns on the floor 30 feet below. At noon on the summer solstice, crowds gather to watch for the moment when the sunlight falls straight down through the skylights and appears to "ignite" the tops of the columns that reach toward but do not quite touch the ceiling.

Library Immeasurables

In his chapter, Geoffrey Freeman of Shepley Bulfinch Richardson and Abbott (SBRA), the architectural firm that designed the Johnson Center Library at George Mason University (see Unit 2), paints a different and thought-provoking picture of the 21st-century library than do some of the other chapters in this book. He speaks of the need to relieve the physical burden of overly large print collections, and of designing libraries for zero-growth, remote storage, and arrangements of materials by their level of usage. In his chapter, "a library without walls" becomes an organizational metaphor for the merging of library, computer center, and classroom. And, as might be expected from an architect, he insists that there will always be a demand for physical libraries to provide collaborative inquiry, socialization, and independent research and learning. But he backs up this claim by pointing out that SBRA now plans for a much higher and much more consistent rate of building occupancy when they design academic libraries, because library usage, he says, has tripled.

Freeman also speaks of library "immeasurables," and says that users' desire for these features has increased right along with their increased desire for technology. These immeasurables are the intangible emotional and symbolic values of libraries: the expectations users have for their libraries; the trust that libraries induce; the inspiration for learning they instill; and the pleasure they bring by providing what Freeman calls "memorable space." These reassuring features, not just the information itself, are the qualities that attract users to a library and make them return to be refreshed and uplifted.

Design/Build

In conventional public construction projects, architects submit their plans for a building that meets the client's specifications. Then, when a plan is selected, the low bid from competing contractors determines the cost of construction. Cost overruns are common with this technique because the architect while planning the facility, may care little about the cost of realizing the design. The Walsh Library at Seton Hall University, however, made use of a building technique called "design/build," which holds the architects to a prescribed cost by keeping them in close contact with their chosen construction companies during the planning phases.

In design/build, the client sets the cost first. Then the architects, teamed with their respective builders, produce plans that commit them to complete their proposed facilities at the client's cost and according to the client's schedule. This way, the architect is prevented from designing a facility the developer cannot construct within the time and funding limits. This can help prevent cost overruns, and collaboration with the builders can also enable architects to incorporate the most current construction technologies and economies in their design.

Though it has often been used in commercial construction projects, design/build was somewhat new among educational institutions when Seton Hall adopted it for the Walsh Library. But it allowed Seton Hall to get more library for its money because the design/build team worked closely with suppliers and subcontractors to minimize costs by eliminating unnecessary steps and duplication during construction and by utilizing the newest and most economical construction techniques. According to Roger Morton,

> Indeed, the final 150,000-square-foot building is 25,000 square feet larger than the university had requested. The extra space — and the copper dome — came without additional cost to the university because of Seton Hall's decision to create the library using design/build techniques [25].

And invoking his own version of Freeman's "immeasurables," architect David M. Childs observed,

> The most striking feature of the building is the dome, with its reading room immediately below it. That part of the building carries the sense of fusion of knowledge and light, which is an ancient symbol. Here, at the heart of the entrance into the place of learning — the storage of knowledge — is where light pierces down through the entire dome [quoted in Morton, 26].

While the architect and the builder consult very closely in the design/build process, critics of the technique point out that the client often has very little input, except for composing the technical specifications at the outset of the competition. This, however, is a danger in the more conventional low-bid process, too. In her excellent article, Sarah Michalak warns, "Architects and other consultants can offer the technical knowledge and design concepts; the library planners must bring to the process the deep understanding and appreciation of the function" (106). She elaborates:

> Architects, interior designers, structural and mechanical engineers, and telecommunications consultants sometimes consider human needs in their work, but it is the librarian who has the best opportunity to interact with the user and who must continually refocus the design process onto end-user requirements. In other words, the library staff members on the planning or design team must be the chief advocate for the library users, and indeed, the library staff who will occupy the space. They are also "customers" in the process [110].

Design/Build in Chicago

The new CPL also was constructed using the design/build method. The Chicago city government had suffered from cost overruns on previous building projects, and hoped to escape the same outcome on the CPL project by using the design/build method. The City wanted a number of benefits from the project: 1) a highly functional library, 2) a public space to add civic importance to the building, and 3) the best value for its money.

According to Marzynski, the City wanted the selection jury to evaluate the entries on 1) building design, 2) how the building would meet the technical specifications, and 3) how it would fulfill the library program. Her video says that these specifications could well have been met by a square box, which sounds a lot like the PPL project, IUPUI, and others in this book, and recalls Kaser's endorsement of simple rectangles (300). And after all the heroic architectural, municipal, civic, and professional struggles, the new CPL does in fact look like a big ornate box.

But more was in the CPL works than just cubic footage, architectural grandeur, and library technology; another struggle was underway on an entirely separate image echelon. According to Elizabeth Hollander, Chicago's Commissioner of Planning during the architectural competition, "The message to the world is loud and clear: the City of Chicago has the will and the ability to complete large projects" (Marzynski, n.p.). And perhaps in keeping with that "will," City planners had their day with the jury before the deliberations began, just as each of the five architects did. The City planners shared with the jury their own professional evaluations of the five submissions before the jury retired behind closed doors to reach its verdict.

Foremen, Consultants, and Inspectors

Unfortunately, however, bringing Michalak's "deep understanding and appreciation of [library] function" to the library design process often dead-ends with the architects and technical consultants. Building a new library is a complex undertaking that involves many, many more individuals than just the architects and consultants on one side of the table and the librarians on the other. As previous chapters have shown, the process of designing a library is always a group project. The library planning team may include administrators, selection panels, and others. In Chicago, a jury of eleven citizens selected the winning design; only one of them was a librarian. And the design favored by Chicago's librarians was eliminated early by the jury because, despite its functionality, it was unexciting compared with 19th-century Paris. And as Unit 4 will show, a library construction project may even be influenced by politics, as well as the press.

But it gets worse. In between the selection of a design and the opening of the new library, hundreds and maybe thousands of workers, technicians, foremen, suppliers, subcontractors, and inspectors must perform the actual labor and produce the structure. And here, the librarian-builders are even farther removed from the process.

Envisioning the final building by studying 80 pounds of specifications and architectural blueprints is not easy; locating design flaws in the schematics is even more difficult. There are those who can help, such as planning consultants, but even they have their weaknesses. For instance, while the KCC library was under construction, we discovered an error in the blueprints that indicated the conduits leading to a certain room might be too small for the video cabling that was necessary. But the state's electrical consultant insisted the conduits were adequate, so he declined to submit our change order. And of course, when the building was completed, the conduit proved to be much too small, even after the video contractor substituted finer cable for the run.

And some design features, such as ceiling treatment, might not even be rendered in the blueprints. And since the ceiling holds the lighting fixtures, this can lead to unexpected problems. For example, the lighting above the circulation desk of the KCC library consists of large round fixtures that were discussed in the planning and drawn as circles on the electrical drawings. We approved the design, and beyond that took little thought, assured that the architect and builder would see to the proper installation of the fixtures. Walk-throughs during the construction revealed no problem. The first time it became necessary to replace a light tube, however, the College's maintenance staff encountered a problem. The KCC library ceiling is textured, but the circular light fixtures above the circulation and other public service desks were designed to fit flush against a flat ceiling. As a result, light apparently leaked between the ceiling texture and the large round fixture housing. So the installers simply caulked the opening around the metal housing to seal the light leaks. Unfortunately, they also sealed shut the housing, which must be pulled downward to access and replace the light tubes.

When the KCC maintenance crew tried to pull on the housing, it would not budge because of the caulking. Forcing it would have damaged the ceiling. When they told me the problem, I realized that because these fixtures were also used above the library's other two public service desks, all the circular lights in the library undoubtedly were installed incorrectly. I angrily called the architect, who blamed the contractor, who blamed the subcontractor, who blamed the inspector. Meanwhile, I told the maintenance crew to slice gingerly through the caulking to replace the light tubes, and to do the same on the remaining fixtures when tube replacement became necessary. The light leaks are hardly noticeable.

A lot depends on the construction crews at the scene. Even when the technical specifications are accurate, when the design is outstanding, and when the form and function harmonize, it is hard to visualize every possible misfit and problem when working in a blueprint dreamscape of floor plans and elevations that render thousands of construction and furnishing components. Some matters come down to poor workmanship, poor equipment, and poor building materials. And walk-through inspections, payment delays, and lawsuits are hardly adequate remedies when the building is already finished and it's time to move in.

9. A New Central Library for Phoenix

Ralph M. Edwards
Retired City Librarian

In the mid–1980s the decision was made in Phoenix, Arizona, to build a new central library. The need was obvious. The city had been growing rapidly since World War II, and library facilities had not been able to keep us with that growth. A central library of about 77,000 square feet was built in the early 1950s, and it was expanded to 146,000-square feet in 1976. But by 1985 the city's population had grown to nearly 900,000, and the existing 146,000 square-foot building was far short of what was needed to serve a city of that size.

The central library's collections could no longer be contained within the existing building, and over 150,000 volumes were being housed in a remote storage warehouse. Seating and study-table space were not adequate to meet the public's needs at busy times. And, as is usually the case in overcrowded library buildings, it was no longer possible to organize collections and services in a logical way that the library users could easily recognize and understand.

There was an additional factor that stimulated the city's leaders to promote a new library building. The city's art museum had been built in the same block as the central library, and the museum also desperately needed more space. It was obvious to all that more additions to both the art museum and the central library were not feasible within that one city block.

The mid–1980s in Phoenix was a time of optimism and expansive thinking. The city's leaders concluded that the economy and the city's continuing growth warranted major capital expansion, and they launched the process leading to an election at which the voters could approve the sale of city bonds to finance a large number of capital projects — including both a new central library building and a major expansion of the art museum.

The library staff's first opportunity for involvement came prior to the bond election in the form of a request for a statement of the central library's facilities needs for the future. The staff submitted a document to the city fathers and the citizens' bond committee in the fall of 1986. This document pointed out that the central public library of a major city is rightly expected to maintain a comprehensive and balanced materials collection of significant breadth and genuine depth to support and sustain the intellectual, cultural, business, and educational needs of a large and diverse population. The central library in Phoenix, as in other large cities, is a cultural resource for the whole city and beyond. As the largest public library in Arizona, the Phoenix central library is a resource for people throughout the state when they have gone beyond the resources of their local libraries.

The library staff's best prediction, based on the evidence available in 1986, was that around the beginning of 1992, the existing central library would be overcrowded to the point that the quality of service would be seriously affected, and the public would have become highly critical of the way things would look and of the way things would work in the building. By that time, it was predicted, people would frequently have to stand or sit on the floor to read in the library, and it would have become much harder to find a book on overcrowded shelves, especially when about one-third of all the central library books would be in remote storage. (These predictions proved correct, except for the one about public criticisms. Most people are amazingly forgiving of library failings, and when they do complain, it is usually only to each other rather than to the officials who could do something about the situations.)

The 1986 facilities needs statement provided the first opportunity to define what Phoenix's central library should be, and the following was included in that statement:

> *The Importance of Planning for the Future*
> There are two characteristics of large city central libraries that are surprisingly consistent. One is that the book collections grow steadily. They typically outgrow the space provided for them within twenty years of the time a new building is built. This growth is continuing to occur in American public libraries in spite of microforms and even though electronic storage of data has entered the picture in a major way. The other observable characteristic is that a central library is such a large investment for a city that it cannot easily be discarded and a new building built. In other words, once a central library is built, it must last a long time. Library buildings that are one hundred years old or more, and are still in use as libraries, are not at all uncommon. The logical implication of these two conflicting characteristics is that major library buildings should always be planned from the beginning to grow. Additions should be planned as part of the original building conception, for if this is done, they can accommodate logical expansions of the library's collections and services.
>
> *The Configuration of the Building*
> The building and all its phased additions must be planned so that at any point in its development, it can be efficiently staffed and operated. A frequent mistake in library building additions has been that staffing and operations compromises were made as buildings grew with poorly planned add-ons, and continuing costs soon surpassed the savings the city thought it had achieved in its building project.

There are two major factors in library building efficiency. One is the efficiency of staff deployment and utilization; the other, and even more important consideration, is the ease with which the public are able to find and make use of the library materials they need. The keys to achieving optimal conditions for both of these factors are open space and simple arrangements. Logical planning both for the first phase of a new building and for its ultimate expansions can achieve great savings in staffing costs over the many years that the building will be used and can increase the public's success and satisfaction immeasurably.

The ideal characteristics of a new Phoenix Public Library library building are as follows:

(1) It will be six floors above ground and one basement level. Six floors and a basement provide a good fit for the way a large library is best organized.

(2) The building should be rectangular with the long side of the rectangle not more than 1.5 times the length of the short side. The shape of a library building is very important to efficiency of collection arrangement and operation, and the nearer a building approaches a square, the better. The interior spaces of the building should be completely open and flexible with no load-bearing walls. The ideal shape of the building can not be achieved in the first construction phase, but it should be planned so that future additions will bring it near the ideal.

(3) It is very important to emphasize that the alternative of adapting almost any existing building for use as the central library would be highly undesirable. The arrangement of space in most buildings built for other purposes would force illogical arrangements of the library's collections and would not permit efficient use of staff. This would annoy the users of the library and, in only a few years, would cost more in staffing than was saved in building costs. [This last point was added and emphasized because the suggestions, of course, surfaced that the city could save money if it converted the old city hall or an old high school building into a new central library. Fortunately, none of these suggestions was taken seriously by city officials.]

In retrospect it is clear that the most important point made in this first staff document was the point about building configuration as it relates to simplicity of space and efficiency of operation. It was clear even before the bond program goals were set, that the Phoenix central library would need to be an economical building project — both in its construction costs and in its future operations. Subsequent experience has borne that out. The building had to be planned to be built at a very low cost to come anywhere near providing the square footage needed, and adequate staffing to operate it has yet to be provided.

But at the time the bond program allocations were set in 1987 and the election was held in 1988, citizen and official optimism was still running high. The central library project was allocated $43 million for total project costs, including land acquisition. It and nearly all of the other bond projects passed. The voters approved the library bonds with a comfortable margin, thanks to the optimism of the time and to a well-orchestrated support campaign by the Citizens Bond Committee and the Friends of the Library.

Once the bonds were approved and everyone became genuinely convinced that a new building could be a reality, serious planning began. As an early step a preliminary program document was developed by the staff to define the basic assumptions and requirements to be addressed in building planning. Key points in that 1988 document were about building organization and configuration and about flexibility of the uses of the building's interior spaces. The document noted that square footage represents only the simplest of measures and cannot alone determine the success or failure of a building. Whether or not the space is usable for the functions intended is a critical factor. Another is the flexibility of the space so that it can be put to other uses in the future. The preliminary program document stated that:

> The ideal library facility is a large, open block of space without permanent internal constraints, expandable in any direction. Materials and services can be grouped as needed for the particular time. As needs change, sections can grow or contract, or be completely redistributed. With minimum barriers between areas, personnel can be used to optimum efficiency.
>
> Fixed-size rooms, particularly for public service functions, are to be avoided, as are narrow or odd-shaped spaces that limit the relationships between the activities housed. Large interior courts, grand stairways and odd building shapes frequently require additional people and additional circulation space, they force large areas to be broken up into smaller units, and they impose limitations on the possible relationships between library collections and services. A square building is usually the most practical shape for a library, minimizing the movement of people and books and making the uses of the space most flexible.
>
> Permanent elements such as elevators, stairways, toilet facilities, and mechanical equipment should be located in areas where they are least likely to interfere with changes in space and library use, ideally at the periphery of the building, rather than in the interior. All the major spaces should be designed to a structural floor load suitable for book stack use. Structural bay dimensions should be carefully selected to ensure column spacing appropriate for both shelving and work stations without space waste.

This flexibility requirement was emphasized throughout the project, and it became one of the primary determinants of what was built.

The preliminary program document also reemphasized the importance of planning from the beginning for the future expansions of the building.

> The library building that is to be designed at this time is only phase one of a much larger building of up to 700,000 square feet that will be needed by Phoenix in the future. Bond funding limitations dictate a building of only about 250,000 to 300,000 square feet at this time. A building of this size will be adequate for only a few years, and then it will need to be enlarged. But the same principles of rectangular shape and interior space flexibility will apply just as strongly to the building of the future as they do to the building that is to be built now. It is essential, therefore, that the first-phase building be designed to that it can be easily

South elevation of the Phoenix Central Library at night. (Courtesy of William P. Bruder, Architect. Photograph by Bill Timmerman.)

added to on all of its levels in a way that will retain the rectangular shape of the entire building.

Another important element of the 1988 preliminary program document was its definitions of the organization of the library that the building was to contain when it opened. For three quarters of a century large American public libraries have been organized in variations of the subject divisional arrangement first conceived for the Enoch Pratt Free Library in Baltimore. The rationale of this arrangement was that dividing the library's collections into several large categories of similar subjects grouped together would help the public find what they need and would enable the reference staff to specialize to some degree and be able better to help the public. This subject divisional arrangement was certainly a major improvement over the old, largely closed stack libraries of the 19th century.

But we in Phoenix felt that it was time for a change — that the traditional subject divisional arrangement had outlived its effectiveness and that a better arrangement was possible. What we were seeking was an arrangement that would

Northeast elevation of the Phoenix Central Library. (Courtesy of William P. Bruder, Architect. Photograph by Bill Timmerman.)

be easier for the public to understand and would also permit more efficient use of staff. We believed that we had such an arrangement in the following:

> Functional considerations call for a building of seven levels. One of these levels should be below ground and the other six at ground level and above. The functions that are to be located on each of the seven levels are as follows:
>
> 1. The first or basement level will contain the following functions:
>   Business Library
>   Government Documents
>   Sort Area
>   Loading Dock and Shipping and Receiving
>   Supplies Room
>
> 2. The second level will be the ground floor and will have the public entrances to the building. Library functions to be located on this level are:
>   Browsing Library
>   Audio-Visual Center

Special Needs Center (services to the handicapped)
Children's Room
Circulation Services

3. The third level will be the principal reference and information center of the library. The functions located here will be as follows:
General Information (Reference) Center
Interlibrary Loan Services
Magazines and Newspapers

4. The fourth level will be used primarily for open shelving of books and for public seating. There will also be several small staff offices and small conference rooms for public use.

5. The fifth level will be used primarily for open shelving of books and for public seating.

6. The sixth level (or fifth floor) of the building will contain special collection areas, some of which will require high security provisions. The areas are as follows:
Arizona Collection Reading Room and Storage Area
Rare Book Reading Room and Vault Storage
Music Library and Listening Area
Map Room
Exhibit Area

7. The seventh level (or sixth floor) of the building will contain the following library functions:
Library Administration
Technical Services
Computer Room
Book storage space
Exhibits office and workshop
Staff lounge and lunch room.

The essential characteristics of this arrangement are that the collections are divided into fewer and simpler categories than had been the case in the typical subject divisional libraries. The special types of materials — audio-visual, periodicals, government documents, reference materials — are separated from the circulating books because the public's approach to each of them is different from its approach to circulating books, and because most people think of these types of material as different and have no trouble understanding the distinction. Most of the circulating book collection is housed in one open stack area in one classified arrangement. At first we thought we would have to divide this collection between two floors because one floor would not be large enough to hold it all. Our plan was simply to put the first half of the Dewey classification-numbered books on the fourth floor and the second half on the third floor of the building. Fortunately, we did not have to make that split.

In addition to the separate collections of different types of material (AV, periodicals, etc.) we recognized the justification for special libraries within the central library. These were determined and justified primarily by special user characteristics — the Children's Library, the Special Needs Center providing service to the handicapped, and the Browsing Library for those looking for recreational reading — or by special subjects that could easily be understood by the public but that demanded extra protection, handling, or special help in their use. These latter included the Business Library, The Arizona Collection, the Map Collection, the Music Library, and the Rare Book Collection.

To summarize, the special requirements emphasized by the library for its new building from the beginning of the planning were:

1. Simplicity of building arrangement and floor plate layout, including planning for future expansion of the building that would maintain the rectangular shape and simplicity of each floor as the building grows.

2. Flexibility of the use of all interior spaces in the building so that it will be feasible to change the use of any part of the building in the future.

3. An organization of the library and an arrangement of library collections that will be easy for the public to understand and efficient for staff to operate.

These were basic requirements that Phoenix was determined to insist upon, and thanks to the selection of a great architect and to cooperation from the city and project staff, we were able to achieve them.

As in any building project, the architect's abilities and the client's relations with the architect were of crucial importance to the final success of the Phoenix Central Library. The architectural association of Bruder/DWL, both local Phoenix architectural firms, was chosen for the project, and the lead design architect was William P. Bruder. Bruder's ability to work with the library staff was unusually good throughout the project. He quickly understood and accepted our priorities and basic requirements. But he also applied remarkable creativity to achieving them in a building that is interesting and attractive.

Many architects would balk at the requirements we presented. Bruder himself described what we said we wanted as a book "warehouse." A lesser architect would probably have responded to what we were demanding in one of the following ways:

A. "They are demanding a boring building. O.K., I will follow their instructions and give them a boring building."

B. "I will not design a boring building; therefore, I will ignore what they are demanding and present them with what I believe to be an architecturally significant building, and then talk them into accepting my ideas."

The latter is, of course, what most self-respecting but misguided architects do, and this results in a great many library buildings that are functionally poor.

Will Bruder is not that kind of architect. He listened to our statements of our library needs, he made the effort to understand exactly why we were asking for them, and he then set out to give us what we needed — but also to make it significant architecture. It wasn't easy, but the result is a great building, both functionally and aesthetically.

The basic structure is a five-level precast concrete box, simple and rectangular, flanked on the long sides of the rectangle by steel-framed "saddlebags" (as befits the Southwest) that contain the fixed services: stairways, restrooms, freight elevators, mechanical equipment, and electrical power and communication sources. These steel-framed saddlebags are clad with copper panels with variations in texture and areas of perforation to give them visual variety and interest.

A small atrium cuts through the middle of the building from top to bottom, and vertical public transportation — glass elevators and a staircase — runs through this atrium. The top floor of the building is a spectacular room with a thirty-two–foot ceiling, with more than thirty skylights, that appears to float on a system of cable supports. The result is visually stunning.

But the concern of this article is not with the architectural success of the Phoenix Central Library but with its success as a functioning library. The final organization of the library is similar to what was requested in the preliminary program document quoted above, but it is different in some significant ways — most of which are improvements on the preliminary conceptions. The building ended up on five levels instead of seven, with the five floors each larger than had originally been anticipated. This had the great advantage of enabling all of the non-fiction circulating books to be in one simple arrangement on one floor rather than two. This became the great room at the top of the building, and it has ample space for reading tables and as many Dewey classified books as the library will probably want to display on open shelving for the foreseeable future.

Because of a site oddity — part of the building had to be built over an underground freeway — two floors of the building are larger than the other three. Only two floors could be built over the freeway because of a weight limitation. But this worked out satisfactorily because the contents of the first two floors needed more space than the others.

The first floor, about an acre and a half in size, is organized very much as was called for in the preliminary program. It contains circulation services, the Special Needs Center providing services to the handicapped, the Children's Room, and an audio-visual collection. But the original idea of a browsing room was expanded into all of the library's fiction collection, the biographies collection, and a foreign languages collection. The definitions of the contents of these collections are easy for the public to understand and, as anticipated for the browsing library, much of their use is for recreational reading.

The second floor, like the first about an acre and a half in size, is probably the most problematic floor in the building, but also surprisingly, probably the most gracious and pleasant of the floors. Its problem is that it has so much on it and will almost certainly be the first of the floors to become overcrowded. All of the public services that had originally been conceived of as going onto the basement level and second floor ended up on the second floor. This floor is the principal "information center" of the central library, with a major reference collection in each of the four quadrants of the floor: general reference, the business library, government documents, and periodicals. In addition, in the central part of the floor, there are areas that provide backup for all of these major collections with computer information, microforms, and a photocopy center. The interlibrary loan service and a map library are also on the second floor.

The other major rearrangement of the building from the original plan was the moving of the administrative and technical services functions from the top floor of the building to its middle floor. This was advocated by the architect, and agreed to by the staff as an architectural improvement that would not negatively impact library functioning. The third floor contains the staff offices, the computer room, all of the technical services, and library administrative functions. Thanks to the glass elevators, this has not proved to be a problem for the public. People who are unfamiliar with the building can easily see from the elevators that the third floor is office space without library materials.

The fourth floor became what had been planned originally as the fifth floor "special libraries": the Arizona History Collection, the Music Library, and the Rare Books Room.

This arrangement left the fifth and top floor available to become the architecturally spectacular Great Reading Room with its large open-stack collection of books and seating for 240 readers. This room is more than one acre in size and, as noted above, can contain all of the non-fiction collection that had originally been planned for the third and fourth floors of a seven-level building.

The need for providing for future expandability, which had been emphasized by the library staff from the earliest planning, was addressed by making the entire north face of the building removable. This north glass wall can be taken off without having any impact on the structure of the building. All five floors can then be extended northward. There is enough space reserved on the north end of the site to permit the building to be more than doubled in total size. Bruder even had the foresight to retain the steel forms that were used to cast the building's columns. He had them installed as "sculptural elements" in the parking median so they will be available in the future to cast more columns for the building's expansion.

As in every building, and especially every economical building, compromises had to be made in the construction and final realization of the Phoenix Central Library. We had hoped to provide the public with escalators. But the escalators had to be given up early in the planning process because there wasn't enough money. An atrium was not wanted by library purists, but the atrium we got has a minimal impact on functional flexibility, and it adds spectacularly to the excitement of the building and to the visibility of the means of vertical transportation. No one who enters the building has to ask, "How do I get upstairs?" The glass elevators are the first thing people see, and they are visually exciting and get attention. But the compromises became minor, almost insignificant, in the overall success of the building.

From the librarian's point of view it is already clear that the most significant achievements of this new central library building that Phoenix opened in May of 1995 are its success in determinedly following the best principles of good library design while also providing 280,000 square feet of space at a very low cost (less than $100 per square foot) and putting it all together in an architecturally exciting

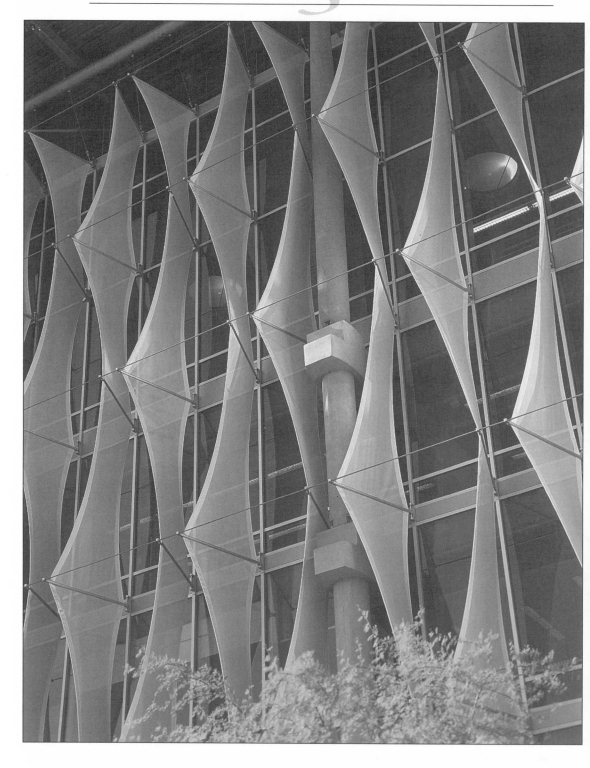

Detail of shade sails at north elevation. (Courtesy of William P. Bruder, Architect. Photograph by Bill Timmerman.)

structure. The library staff is very happy with the building, and the public of Phoenix is delighted with it.

From the beginning we believed that the real test of the success of the central library would be the public's ability to understand and use it effectively. Simplicity and functional visibility were what we sought from the beginning, and they were achieved even beyond our hopes. Much of the credit for the excellent functional visibility must be given to the unusual attention the architect paid to graphics and signage. People can easily understand the basic organization of the collections and services, and once they get to the floor that contains what they are seeking, the highly visible signage is easy for them to understand and follow.

The total success of the building is, finally, amply demonstrated in the way the people of Phoenix use the library, in the fact that they love the building, and in the observable rates of success they have in finding the library material or information they are seeking. The Phoenix Central Library has a great deal of value to say to planners who will be planning the world's large public library buildings for the twenty-first century.

10. The Academic Library in the 21st Century: Partner in Education

Geoffrey T. Freeman

AIA, Principal, Shepley Bulfinch Richardson and Abbott

One student reads at an individual study carrel; another scans digitized images using full multimedia capabilities. One researcher browses the shelves on a journey to self-discovery; another searches a database linked to a worldwide network.

Each comes to the academic library with a unique need. All come to share the common, rejuvenating, and enriching experience of intellectual pursuit. The library is a pathway — enhancing, extending, and supporting the academic life of an institution. It is a catalyst in the learning process, the essential link to scholarship and information of endless variety.

As we move into the next century, we face the unprecedented demands of technology and an explosion of information. In designing and planning our libraries, we know that an equal, if not greater, proportion of technology and space needs will change within five years. We are asked to plan for the inevitable and the unforeseeable. What lessons are we learning now, and what do we take into the future? How do we — as architects, librarians, and administrators — collectively join to shape the academic library so that it emerges as a true partner in education?

How Do We Learn in the Information Age?
Understanding the User of the Library

To respond to the challenges before us, we must first look at the person for whom we are designing — the user. How do people learn? How do they use information? People come to a library not only to have access to knowledge, but also to socialize, interact, and collaborate. While there will always be a singular effort of concentrated research, we are finding that people also need to learn in a social environment. The constant invigoration, tempering, and exchange of ideas that happens in the library extends the process of learning beyond the classroom walls.

We are, in fact, placing the classrooms which we took out of the library years ago back into the library. Today, the library is the classroom. We are designing library space that is fully wired, adaptable, and changeable — space that provides everything imaginable for teaching, including access to video projection and digital displays. Librarians are working hand in hand with faculty to develop curriculum. Dynamic and evolving, the library is the information enabler, the partner furthering the pedagogical mission of an institution, and carrying forth that vision for education and research.

Our experience at Shepley Bulfinch Richardson and Abbott, Architects with a full range of libraries — professional, undergraduate, and research facilities — has confirmed that there will always be a demand for the physical embodiment of the library. Early predictions that technology would create a "virtual" library, with students and researchers networked from residence halls, have proven wrong. In fact, as electronic media has increasingly been introduced on college and university campuses, and paper has made way for electronic data, the usage of libraries has actually increased in staggering proportions.

In our projections for new and renovated facilities five years ago, we anticipated a doubling of occupancy for the library, and still we have underestimated. Usage has tripled. Technology is neither replacing collections nor, with remote access available, discouraging people from the facilities. Technology is actually serving to encourage individuals to come into the library where there is activity — where people are coming together to access, use, and turn information into knowledge.

Where we once assessed typical seat occupancies ranging from 35 percent off peak to 90 percent at exam times, we now look at buildings occupied at a consistent rate of at least 65 percent as the greater investment. We are designing carrels and stations for collaborative use, areas for small group study for four to six, small seminar spaces for over eight people.

Why are people being drawn back to the library, when technology once suggested otherwise? What in the environment fosters learning and the exchange of information? How do we plan for and integrally design for the different uses the library must serve? What place should the library have on the campus? What makes people comfortable in and attracted to a particular place? Although we are beginning to assess and plan for the impact of technology, it is the user and the dimension of the user that remains of greatest importance to us in answering these questions and giving the library new form.

How Do We Collect in the Information Age? Understanding the Stewardship of the Library

As we reinvent the library for the future, we must recognize the distinctions between how people use the library now, with the constancy of paper-based collections, and how they will use the library in the future, as the impact of paperless information is felt.

Today's library user ranges from a technologically sophisticated researcher conversant with publication in different formats, to a more traditionally focused scholar whose interest is in a relatively narrow yet important part of the library collection. The library has traditionally been the provider of collections and the primary resources the faculty needs to support academic research. But the library's role is shifting to providing services and assistance in navigating the vast amounts of information available to us. The greatest percentage of library space, once dedicated to spiraling collections, is now being allocated to more seats for readers and interactive spaces for users. And, as institutions increasingly develop specialties and share resources, the issue of identifying and assessing core collections becomes even more critical.

What is the size and nature of the collection necessary to support the level of quality of research and instruction? Understanding the mission of the institution and how the library is a partner in achieving that is essential in understanding the nature of the collection. Yale, Columbia, Harvard and other major research institutions bear the tremendous responsibility of maintaining and preserving the priceless collections with which they are endowed. Smaller institutions are less burdened by materials and are more free to concentrate on accessing and dispersing information than on acquiring it.

As we reorganize the library, we must address the diminishing resources for housing and caring for collections. How much of the collection needs to be physically maintained in the library building or on the campus? Are there other ways to handle the collections — compaction, remote storage, robotically accessed warehousing — that can free an institution to focus on the new demands for services? For a number of years, it has been a rather straightforward exercise to organize libraries and integrate books and readers into the space. Today we are using space differently and finding inventive ways to house collections, distribute documents, and deliver information to users wherever they may be.

Just five years ago, typically 15 percent of the collection could be housed in a remote location. Today there are examples where it is as high as 50 percent. Access techniques, from document delivery to electronic cataloging and translation, have made it possible to browse and to distribute collections beyond the walls of the library and beyond the bounds of the campus.

We are revising our planning methodology to acknowledge the impact of electronic data storage. Where we once looked at a 20-year projection of rising collections, we now turn to a 12-year model aimed at zero-growth collections. Major academic institutions such as Duke University, Harvard University, and Dartmouth College are all involved in the examination of their collections and how they can control and maintain them in a feasible approach.

Renovating the existing 400,000–square foot Butler Library at Columbia University allowed us the opportunity to look at collections and the nature of scholarship in order to create an environment aimed at the user. With the university leadership, we worked long and hard to understand the different levels of research and the potential impact of technology on those research patterns. As a result, we are reorganizing the collections and access to them: breaking down the collection, and bringing portions of it into identifiable reading spaces dedicated to periods of scholarship, similar to an older European version of a library. The intent is to place newer information formats with some of the most used paper-based materials, where they are most easily accessible to the people who come into the library for hours and hours — spaces to celebrate researchers and the scholarship they pursue. Taking the library into the future, Columbia has made the momentous decision to move to zero growth, preserving other parts of its collection in remote storage.

Over the years, the Regenstein Library of the University of Chicago had developed as a subject specific model of a research library. Its collection, too, had exceeded the bounds of its support. In a similar process, we began to address how people used information before we could understand what consolidation could take place. We created a hierarchy of zones moving up the building, allowing a more effective level of service and efficient use of staff without sacrificing the collections that remain the essence of the institution's research focus.

Collections will continue to evolve, but not at the expense of providing services and an environment for learning. While the library remains a preserver of information, it is assuming the greater role of generator, exchanger, and server of information.

How Do We Access in the Information Age? Understanding the Services and Functions of the Library

Basic statistics used in planning libraries have changed dramatically. In a commercial building, space planners estimate 160 work stations for every 10,000 square feet of space. In a library, 10,000 square feet can accommodate many more than 160 — each requiring a communication closet measuring 110–120 square feet on the floor. We must provide the support space and build in the flexibility to accommodate the functions and services we are just beginning to envision. Today we are trying to diagram what takes place in the library, what goes into the library. Can we identify the distinct functions and services within a library for the future and design according to what those functions are?

We are assembling the pieces of libraries in different ways. In designing the Leavey Library for the University of Southern California, we first sought to understand how people learned, accessed information, and exchanged it. Working with Peter Lyman, whose thesis is that the library is really a very large classroom, we created 90,000 square feet, housing approximately 125,000 volumes and 1,200 seats. Designed around the use of electronic information, it includes a technology center with related classrooms as a base; from there, the building rises up into the air.

In planning USC, we looked at the existing research library in an attempt to distinguish the reference area and the computing area and to staff them independently. We found that users asked library questions at the computing area and computing questions at the reference area. Thus, in the new library, we have combined these two functions in the lower level and made them the heart of the building — a radical cultural shift with significant implications.

The new library at USC fundamentally serves as a gateway. It brings students and faculty from all the disciplines into an introductory medium which then distributes them to the research collections and professional libraries within and beyond the walls of the university. The USC Library exemplifies a new type of partnership: academic computing consultants and media technicians converging and collaborating with library staff— an integration of technology, computing, and library science that will be essential to the future.

How is it working? Students wait in the aisles, rooms for group study are often booked until after midnight, the information commons is staffed and operating 24 hours, and walls are lined with how-to instructions and log-on sheets.

Partially as an experiment in outreach, the library at USC also includes an element called the Center for Scholarly Technology, designed to entice the faculty, especially those who are more traditionally oriented, to come to the library and explore the use of newer information and media technologies in the privacy of a more exclusive environment. Hence, the Center provides secure spaces specially designed for faculty, to allow them to proceed on technology's learning curve without fear of interruption or scrutiny.

At Emory University, we have perhaps gone one step further in addressing the service functions of the library. The challenge was to bring two separate buildings, a newer research library built in the 1960s and an older library housing a major reserve reading space and a 200,000-volume collection, together with the introduction of academic computing and media. The initial proposal was simply to build an addition to one of the two buildings. We then worked with Emory to determine how information was handled and accessed, not just within the library, but throughout the university on all levels. The process led to the conclusion that a simple addition would not suffice. We had to provide a new center — located between the two existing library buildings — to serve as the gateway. This new center combines all of the information technology and physically connects the two existing buildings. All services and functions come together as one facility. The cultures of library science, academic computing and multimedia are totally merged, with technology-based supercarrels and 100 staff members from academic computing, reference and multimedia all located together on the principal reference floor. In this partnership, the "walls" between individual staff disciplines have come down and new cross-disciplinary definitions are being made.

How Do We Inspire in the Information Age?
Understanding the Immeasurables of the Library

While the expectations for service have increased with technology, the expectations for the immeasurables that only a library provides have also increased. As we create a more supportive environment that functions as a 24-hour center of activity, we address aesthetic issues that have no boundaries of time: what the spaces feel like, how they attract the user, how they stimulate and inspire as well as give pause for reflection and focus. How do we integrate technology and yet humanize the environment so that technology does not dominate, but serves as a tool for people and for critical examination and study?

By design, we can affect the behavior, use and security of library buildings. The more we know about how people use libraries, the better we can protect and maintain the people, space, and collections within those libraries. We can achieve this by bringing in light and creating the comfortable spaces that people want. By finding space for carrels under the eaves of a building, for example, we not only increase the utilization of the building and improve efficiency, but create a memorable space to which people are attracted and want to return.

We are involved in returning the library to its rightful place at the heart of the institution. For a while, as campuses grew in the 1960s, elements of the library were pushed to the periphery. Now, released from the physical burden of collections, we see a renewed commitment to the centrality of the library. We are finding new ways to revitalize and invigorate the library as the magnet core. We are placing the library at the crossroads to the academic and residential experience. The library form expresses its importance, yet is visually penetrable and welcoming, gesturing to the excitement and activity taking place within. It is a destination place — a place to go for growth, intellectually and emotionally.

At Fordham University in New York, the user arrives at the very center of the new library. Light becomes the pathway connecting spaces in a fairly grand space — the organizing element both horizontally and vertically that allows the user to understand the building and feel secure. In a traditional way, Fordham exemplifies how critical the use of light and human scale continue to be to the library experience in creating a sense of awe and spiritual uplifting, as well as comfort and security.

Housing special collections and rare books, the Kroch Library at Cornell University is a wonderfully successful building, thanks to natural light carefully brought into its center space. An open well, with very small skylights, introduces light into a building placed totally underground. Connected to the existing central library, the new "invisible" 100,000–square foot expansion preserves the historical site and venerated path for the academic processional from the president's house — an extreme example of the suppression of architecture for the sake of tradition.

In a dramatically contrasting experiment, we have placed the new 350,000–square foot Library/Campus Center for George Mason University in Virginia at the campus center as a colorful and inviting intellectual marketplace. Designed as a central space fostering the vital intellectual interchange in an academic environment for 20,000 commuting students, the library becomes an enticing, living space, providing students access to both software and soft drinks. Breaking down the library walls, George Mason has made a daring commitment to responding to user demand and education that meets the user halfway. They have a 100,000-volume disposable collection — a collection that can go anywhere within the building and be replaced if necessary. Unlike the traditional library, the building has many entrances. The collection is housed on upper floors, along with food services, student activities, a movie theater — everything imaginable. The open library is sited on one of the upper levels next to student activity space: books and computers sit alongside the billiard and pool rooms. The library is where the user wants to be.

Where Do We Go from Here? Understanding the Opportunities of the Library

Truly, the academic library is at a crossroads. Information, communication, and library resources are all coming together in the library building for the purpose of education and knowledge. The library of the 21st century is being reinvented in real time as people use information that has both a current application and a future.

Right now we are working intensively with representatives of the entire membership of Dartmouth College to move their Berry and Baker libraries into the next century and merge new information technologies with more traditional formats. We are addressing all of the issues that relate to the user: the size of the collection, the levels of service, the nature and culture of the academic village, and the library's place in the center of it. In creating the library as a gateway to information of all kinds, we are building a new community — faculty, students, librarians, computing and media consultants joined in partnership.

As facilitators, we are helping institutions across the country engage in dialogue, challenge ideas, and see change as opportunity. We are asking them to look at their libraries in a demanding and dynamic way, and to see how the library can support and service its education mission. In our discussions, we acknowledge the extraordinary impact of technology on our lives. But despite the commitment to new and emerging information formats, people still hold on to the comforting notion of books. Our challenge is to make the imposing, physical aspects of technology disappear, while concentrating on the individual user. We are reworking the conventional 4'-carrel into a flexible station, where everything is moveable and equipment can be dismounted or reconfigured to meet the user's changing needs. We are examining the ergonometrics of the learning station. How long does a person sit there? What are the levels of use?

We are learning from bookstore cafés, just as we are learning from monuments of the past. We are injecting new energy, just as we are holding on to strong traditions. Ultimately, our libraries will only be as good as the intensity with which they are used. As we continue to integrate new technologies and different formats of information, we will always come back to the human dimension of people meeting and talking, discussing and accessing, sharing and exchanging ideas. This is both the magic of learning, and the magic of the library.

11. The Walsh Library, Seton Hall University

Anita L. Talar
Librarian and Professor

"Seton Hall needs a new library and she needs it now. It must be her star, the jewel of her campus. This beacon of intellectual commitment needed to guide us as lovers of learning must be built — and it shall be."[1] With these words spoken by Father Thomas R. Peterson (1992), University Chancellor, in his inaugural address on October 13, 1990, planning for a new library moved into the forefront of university activity.

This was not the first time that a new library had been discussed. Twice before, planning had begun to replace the overcrowded McLaughlin Library, built in 1954 to serve a smaller student body and now overcrowded and technologically inadequate. A university development program announced as far back as December of 1979 stated that "the library is a number one priority." Ten years later, Seton Hall took the first real steps toward that goal when it built a much-needed parking deck, thereby "freeing-up" another parking lot as the site of the proposed new library. On earlier occasions, other projects had been prioritized — additional residence halls had been built, and a new recreation facility had been added. Letters written to the Seton Hall community just before the beginning of Fall semester 1989 announced Seton Hall's first major capital campaign and an ambitious building plan for the university. Now, finally, a new library was about to become an actuality.

In reality, libraries had figured in various plans over the years. The university's Strategic Plan 1991–1996 had as its Goal #3: To make the libraries a special academic priority. Including the university library, the libraries of the School of Law and the School of Theology, as well as the University Archives and the Media Center, Seton Hall's library resources are considerable. McLaughlin Library, the central university library building on the South Orange campus, needed to be replaced by a new building which would be large enough to accommodate operations and resources housed in at least three separate facilities. Faced with the inability to meet requirements for new library technologies and services, and a desire to meet accrediting boards' recommendations for space for our changing student body, the university moved to prioritize the major improvement of library facilities, collections, technology, services, and funding. The construction of a new library building became the cornerstone for the newly announced Capital Campaign.

Other library initiatives were taking place simultaneously. McLaughlin Library installed its first computerized catalog in 1987, Library Corporation's Bibliofile CD-ROM catalog. At just about the same time, the library applied for and received a state technology grant which provided seed money for its first CD-ROM installation. Then, in 1989, a large National Endowment for the Humanities grant was awarded to assist in collection development for books in the arts and humanities.

Meanwhile, other campus initiatives were changing the structure of our student body. Four new residence halls had nearly doubled the on-campus student population. Additional demands for resources were unable to be met in the now overcrowded and inadequate McLaughlin Library.

The first of what was to be an endless series of planning meetings was held. The new library project was announced, and preliminary ideas were shared. From the earliest "recommended program" proposed in 1988, a comprehensive plan for a state-of-the-art library that would meet present and future needs of the Seton Hall University community evolved.

Planning then began in earnest. The University's Planning Office was involved at all stages, as were the other constituencies of the University. Dr. Robert Jones, Dean of University Libraries, provided extensive opportunities for dialogue with representatives of all of the schools of the University during the years 1988 and 1989. The initial site plan for the new library was approved in the winter of 1989.

The services of an architectural firm, Rothe-Johnson of Edison, New Jersey, were obtained to assist the university's Planning Office and the library personnel in expanding these plans. The new library would be designed to meet the needs of the new Seton Hall. Better prepared students, many of them residents on campus, preparing for careers in an information-centered society, put heavier demands on library services. Librarians, teaching faculty, students, staff, and administrators all joined in verbalizing their needs and wish lists for their ideal library. The meetings to shape these requirements, needs, ideas into actual plans were many, and at times overwhelming. Yet these meetings were essential to the process and continued all during the construction.

In planning the building, architects Rothe-Johnson Associates and the Dean of University Libraries predicted and incorporated rapid advances in library technology, to design a functional, flexible, and image-enhancing "laboratory for learning." The daily operation of the library was the primary consideration in its design. Original notes included information on size of collections, volumes added annually, future (desired) size, campus population (commuter vs. resident, undergraduate vs. graduate student), special areas, meeting/study rooms, technology requirements, ADA requirements, library hours, security issues, processing areas adjacent to a loading dock, to mention just a few! To address proximity issues, library staff completed (individually) a comprehensive grid listing where services/facilities needed to be located for greatest functionality and service.

From a preliminary draft of an "85,000ASF/132,000GSF" scheme, various designs were proposed, discussed at frequent meetings, and sent back to the drawing board. The fax machine became an essential piece of technology as revisions went back and forth between South Orange and Edison. Wish lists and ideas took shape over the many weeks of planning (and meetings). These then formed the basis for the specifications which then shaped the Request for Proposals (RFP) which went out.

The architectural firm of Rothe-Johnson, asked to expand preliminary plans into more detailed schematics for the new library, submitted these in July of 1990. At this time, the Committee on Buildings and Grounds of the Board of Regents of Seton Hall confirmed the decision to proceed with a "design/build" concept in the construction of the new library. Rothe-Johnson then assisted in the preparation of the bid package.

In February of 1991 a list of design/build teams was prepared and the bid packages were finalized. The bid packages were sent out to these companies in August of 1991 with a required return date in mid–October. Initially, seven companies agreed to present bids. When the final date arrived, five major companies had submitted bids. The process agreed upon was that all bids should be sealed bids. All of the design/build teams received exactly the same information. Any additional information sought by any team was automatically provided to all the teams.

In preparation for the opening of the bids, the University hired two architectural consultants to assist in the analysis of the bid proposals. One consultant was Mr. Robert Heintz, an architect who had previously done work for Seton Hall. The second architect was Mr. Jamil Faridy, who had been involved in the building of more than 40 libraries in this country and abroad. Mr. Faridy was not previously involved as a consultant here at the University. The one architect (Heintz) familiar with the University would bring a sense of continuity to the project; the second architect (Faridy) would provide the objectivity of a new approach to the evaluation.

The main work of the consultants was to see to it that all bids were complete and that each of the bidders addressed the same scope of work implied in the project. The five sealed bids were opened by the Chancellor, Father Thomas Peterson, with the assistance of Monsignor Dennis Mahon of the Planning Office, and turned over to the architectural consultants for analysis.

While the bid proposals were being reviewed, the accompanying materials were on display in Presidents Hall. Members of the University community viewed the plans and models and were not shy in offering their opinions and suggestions.

When analysis of the five bids had been completed, a meeting was called by Mr. Frank Farinella, the Chairman of the Buildings and Grounds Committee of the Board of Regents. Present at the October 22, 1991, meeting were Chancellor

Peterson, Monsignor Mahon, Dr. Bernhard Scholz (Provost of the University), Mr. James Allison (Executive Vice Chancellor for Finance), and Dr. Robert Jones (Dean of University Libraries). Each of the design/build teams was given one hour to make a presentation and then to answer questions posed by those present. Each team, as one would expect, took care to present what it anticipated to be the strengths their companies would bring to the design/build plan. One team emphasized the functionality and flexibility of the design; another, how the architecture fit into the existing campus structures; and another, placement of the entrance to the library and its appeal. A main feature of the design/build plan is cost containment. The architectural firm works closely with and is really subordinate to the head of the construction firm charged with execution of the design. This elaborate system of checks and balances demands close cooperation and communication between and among all members of the "team."

At the end of the day of presentations, members of the Buildings and Grounds Committee unanimously chose the model for the new library which was considered to be the most impressive (Figure 1). This model met not only the financial requirements but also the aesthetic components that would truly make the new library the "Jewel of the Campus." The Buildings and Grounds Committee then passed a resolution recommending to the Board of Regents that Seton Hall University begin to negotiate a contract with the design/build team which had been tentatively designated for the construction of the new library. The Committee recognized that there were certain design changes that would have to be accommodated, but had the assurance of the design/build architect that all of these modifications could be incorporated into the final plan. Indeed, one of the key phrases that was repeated many times was that "any of the walls can move — just tell us where you want them!"

The recommendation of the Buildings and Grounds Committee was approved by the Executive and Finance Committees of the Board of Regents at their meeting on October 31, 1991. The University was authorized to negotiate the contract with the design/build team, subject to final approval of the full Board. Construction on the library was scheduled to begin sometime in the early spring of 1992, with a completion and occupancy date for September, 1993. The project was scheduled to be completed in eighteen months.

It was at this time that a new member was added to the project team. Michael Otto, a civil engineer, was appointed Project Manager for Walsh Library. Employed by Seton Hall to coordinate the overall project, he had just completed a similar assignment for the Seton Hall School of Law in Newark.

The model of the proposed new library was placed in the McManus (Special Collection) Room of McLaughlin Library and all members of the University community were invited to view it at their leisure. A special open meeting was held on November 20, 1991, with key personnel present to answer questions concerning the design, construction, and financing of the new building.

One of the next steps was to take the approved final design to the South Orange Planning Board for approval, a prerequisite for any campus construction. The Board had already seen a preliminary design prior to the design/build "competition."

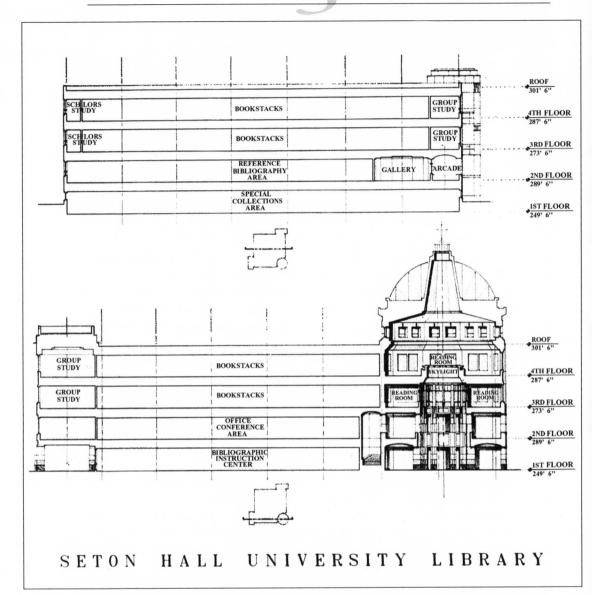

Figure 1. Building sections, part of the original presentation by the design/build team. (Courtesy of Skidmore, Owings & Merrill.)

The new design called for a larger (1,300–square foot increase in the "footprint") library, with a tower that exceeded the village height limit. After much discussion, which included a promise that the upper portion of the dome (104 feet from the ground at its highest point) would not be lit at night, as well as a requirement for "plant foliage buffers" so that nearby residents would not find the new library excessively intrusive, the design was approved. University representatives also promised that South Orange residents would have access to the new library, as they did to McLaughlin Library, and would be able to borrow books using a cooperative county-wide borrowing card.[2]

In March 1992, the University Board of Regents authorized construction, and the University moved quickly to begin making the dream of a new library a reality. Markers appeared on the building site, and construction equipment multiplied overnight. Fencing went up, and the groundbreaking ceremony took place on June 28, 1992. The foundation was excavated, with several delays due to the necessary removal of some materials (from an earlier science laboratory) from the site. Finally, construction began in earnest, and the building took shape before our eyes.

While planning for construction was progressing, the financing of this project was also a major concern. The Department of Public Relations developed a handsome brochure or "library case statement" to describe the library project and to help in the solicitation of funds. The brochure detailed the history of libraries at Seton Hall, their importance, and their requirements for the future. In laying out this document, Seton Hall gave testimony to the careful and thoughtful planning that had been so much a part of the process. The brochure clearly stated the mission of the library, highlighting its main features and its importance on campus. Subsequent pages gave "special gift opportunities in the new library," listing various possibilities ranging in price from $5,000 to $5,000,000, the latter for the naming opportunity. As part of the ongoing capital campaign, Dean Robert Jones chaired the on-campus effort. Each unit on campus was invited to a presentation and encouraged to make a contribution toward this building project. This facet of the campaign was highly successful, if not in actual dollars contributed as much as the percentage of the donor pool, with the staff of the library coming in at the top!

As the campaign progressed, so did the library. After looking at the large hole in the ground with not much visible progress (while pipes were put in place), the foundation was finally complete. The steel girders quickly gave shape and form to the library (Figure 2), rising quickly until the final one was "topped" with the traditional ceremony. The next phase of construction was probably the fastest and most carefully orchestrated. The walls of the library were to be constructed of pre-cast concrete, which began to arrive on large trucks, a few pieces at a time, carefully marked so that they could be slotted into their proper place, all while the regular life of the university campus continued through the semester (Figure 3). Progress could be measured daily. It was at this stage, before the building was completely enclosed, that the worst snowfalls in recent decades intervened. The winter of 1992-1993 was marked with an abundance of snow in the Northeast, resulting in an unheard of (and unplanned for) delay of twenty snow days before the building was enclosed for work to begin on the interior.

Progress continued, however, with minimal delays. Changes were made as construction continued, another feature of the design/build process. In one instance, the location of the processing area (acquisitions, cataloging) was moved to place it on the perimeter of the building, with windows, as a concession to the large number of staff concentrated there. (Many of them had worked in the basement of the "old" library, and expressed the desire to be "aboveground.") As it turned out, the design/build team was able to use the fifteen-foot slope of the

Figure 2. Steel girders soon gave shape and form to what had been vision and plans. (Courtesy of Seton Hall Public Relations.)

construction site to have most of the building aboveground, with just a few areas, some of them media studios and storage, windowless.

Another substantial modification from the original plan involved the design of the rotunda area. The main focal point of Walsh Library is a large rotunda at the northeast corner of the building (Figure 4). Visible from the main entrance to the campus, it is topped by a copper dome and a cross (see Figure 2). This rotunda area was originally designed to feature a large circular staircase, but this proved to be a problem both with library access and security and the building codes. Walsh Library consists of four floors, the first of which is devoted to the Media Center with its attendant preparation rooms, photography darkroom, studios, and offices, as well as multimedia rooms, Archives and Special Collections, and a gallery. The "library proper" begins on level two with the Circulation Desk and reference and browsing areas. The third floor houses periodicals and government documents, while most of the books in the circulating collection are found in the stacks located on the fourth floor. This access problem was solved by putting in enclosed sets of stairs between the entrance and the bank of elevators and shifting entrances to several of the first-floor facilities.

Figure 3. Daily progress was easy to watch at this point. (Courtesy of New Jersey News-photos.)

Yet another substantive alteration to the original design occurred while the copper dome over the fourth floor rotunda room was being finished. The room was open to the top of the dome during the work, and university officials liked the spaciousness provided (see color insert). Originally intended to have a traditional ceiling, the design for this area was put on hold until a fiberglass lining could be constructed for the interior of the dome. This change made the room into a two-story area and resulted in one of the nicest pieces of real estate and most definitely the greatest view on campus.

While the construction continued, the design/build team and university officials began to work with an interior design firm. Winecoff/Stathis Associates of New York organized an experienced team to work with the Walsh Library project, and plans for the shelving and furniture began to take shape. As had been the custom, members of the university community were consulted for suggestions with regard to chairs. Charged with making suggestions for furniture, the librarians were busy visiting (and taking countless photographs) of new or newly renovated libraries and using these as a basis of what would be best for Walsh Library. In addition, McLaughlin Library became the repository for an extensive collection of furniture catalogs. The librarians also spent time at library conferences visiting exhibits to check out the latest furniture and equipment displays.

Figure 4. A view from the first floor of the rotunda showing the entrance to the first floor and the stairs to the second floor entrance, also accessed from the arcade. (Courtesy of Seton Hall Public Relations.)

It was at one of these library conference exhibits that a certain furniture company became aware of Seton Hall's new library project. A Seton Hall librarian had seen and admired the beautiful wood designs and craftsmanship of the Thomas Moser Company of Maine. Consequently, Moser heard for the first time of our new library and expressed an interest in furnishing it. They contacted our interior design firm and the rest, as they say, is history.

A slight complication arose when, as a result of input from the campus community, a preference was stated for three-position study chairs. Samples were displayed prominently in the lobby of the "old" library, with signs posted asking people to try them out for comfort. Most of our clientele expressed a liking for the three-position chairs that are becoming more popular, the library or study chairs with sled-like bottoms that can be tilted forward or leaned back without causing the legs to break off or separate.

When it became known that our desire was for the three-position study chairs to go with their cherrywood study carrels, Moser acknowledged that they had none in their current inventory, but designed and executed one just for us. Known as the Seton Hall study chair, this piece of furniture is comfortable, attractive, and well used by all our patrons.

The completed Walsh Library is a $20 million learning center that reflects the stature of Seton Hall itself. Carefully planned to integrate the existing campus buildings while creating a commanding architectural presence of its own, Walsh Library is truly a presence on the South Orange campus. Its copper dome is a campus landmark, as well as a point of orientation for students and visitors alike. Located at the heart of the campus, opposite the Brennan Recreation Center and the multi-level parking deck, the library is highly visible and accessible to campus visitors, as well as to students and faculty.

Walsh Library is more than twice the size of McLaughlin Library, the facility it replaced, and is designed with the user in mind. Taking advantage of its sloping site, there are entrances at both the first and second floors. The first floor houses the Media Center, complete with audio, video, and computer graphics studios as well as a photography lab and other production facilities. Because the Media Center personnel are responsible for delivering audiovisual equipment across campus, their first floor location, with ready access to the loading dock and a small parking area for their delivery vehicles, is ideal.

In addition to the Media Center, the first floor also features a Special Collections Center housing University archives and other special collections. This state-of-the-art facility has a large climate-controlled vault, preservation facilities, a conference room, and a research area, in addition to offices and a large gallery. The gallery, with extensive windows open to the arcade and adjacent to additional large window display cases, hosts many varied and elaborate exhibits throughout the year, and is responsible for bringing many visitors to campus for workshops and receptions. Another feature of the first floor is a large multimedia room equipped with projection and network capabilities. Used for large-group instruction, the area has folding walls and can be subdivided into three smaller rooms, each similarly equipped. There are also four computer labs on the floor, built with modular walls. One of these is the Bibliographic Instruction (BI) Lab. Equipped with eighteen Pentium computers, it is used primarily by the library faculty to teach basic CD-ROM search techniques, how to use the online catalog, and how to find information on the Internet. (Large classes are taught in the Multimedia room, demonstration style, but the BI Lab gives us the luxury of hands-on experience with smaller classes.)

We have just celebrated the third anniversary of Walsh Library, and there

have been changes and space reallocations. The remaining three computer labs
are in the process of being reconfigured! The opening of a new academic building in the Fall of 1997 gave us additional electronic classrooms and brought about
some major shifting of rooms. The two computer labs run by the English department were relocated to the building where the English Department faculty have
their offices and classes, while the third, the former MAC Lab, will be phased out
as the campus concentrates on IBMs. The space vacated by the three computer
labs will house the Teaching, Learning, and Technology Center, where faculty
learn to use new technologies in their teaching. Adjacent to the Media Center,
this TLTC is conveniently located for one-stop shopping at the information mall.

The three remaining floors more closely resemble a university library, one
that is designed with user ease and comfort considerations. The second floor features two large service desks, the larger one for Circulation (including Reserve
and Interlibrary Loan) functions, while the smaller one is for Reference. Surrounding the two desks are pods of computers and the reference collection. Right
now there are four different configurations of computers, but even this will change
in the near future as we migrate to a new online library system and additional
electronic journals and texts. A large room adjacent to the Circulation Desk holds
the microform collection, complete with the latest digital reader-printers and a
public fax machine. A beautifully furnished Browsing Room, featuring a collection of current newspapers and magazines, and an adjacent Curriculum Library
round off the "public areas" of the second floor. The office areas for library administration and librarians are concentrated along the east side of the second floor,
with a large connecting area that is used for Collection Development. This area
has bookshelves for display of approval books, a large work table, and a comfortable seating area, where faculty frequently meet with librarians to discuss acquisitions in their particular disciplines. A conference room and a large and airy staff
room with attached kitchenette are adjacent to the Collection Development area
and the Dean's Office, while an internal corridor leads to the cataloging and processing area adjacent to the loading dock.

The third floor of Walsh Library houses periodicals, the entire non-micro-
form collection, that is, and the documents collection. To the relief of everyone
concerned, the periodicals are shelved in this one area. In our former (overcrowded)
McLaughlin Library, because of several collections shifts and lack of space, periodicals had been divided by date and science or non-science, with large runs of
older journals stored in an off-campus facility (with next-day retrieval). Much
assistance was required to actually locate specific issues, and the librarians had a
spiel that included "current five years are in the reference room, unless the title
is science or nursing; all science and nursing journals are downstairs with older
issues. If the list says 'storage,' you need to fill out a pink card and come back
tomorrow." What a relief to have everything in one building! Most of the books
in the circulating collection are on the fourth floor, with some on one wing of
the third floor.

Lining the perimeter of the building on the third and fourth floors are 64
individual scholars' studies and, in the corners of these floors, 42 group-study

rooms. The scholars' studies are assigned for the semester or the year to faculty or students who apply for them with a specific project (research, thesis-writing, book publication, etc.). There is usually a waiting list for these rooms, to the dismay of some occupants who would like "squatter's rights!" The group study rooms, holding from four to eight people, are available on a daily, first-come, first-served basis. These have also been extremely popular and were, in fact, one of the items on many wish lists — places for group work. All of these rooms have network connections.

All told, Walsh Library has seating for more than 1,100 and housing for up to one million volumes. Four hundred cherrywood open carrels provide comfortable work/study areas for the individual scholars. Walsh Library is indeed a library that will serve Seton Hall well into the 21st century. It has demonstrated its technological capabilities, yet is flexible and ready to adapt to ever-changing requirements. The building features large open areas and the capability for adding compact shelving if needed in the future.

We continue to plan for technology. As the result of a strategic alliance between the university and IBM, several initiatives have been or are being implemented. Several of them have library implications, among them the mobile computing project and the digital library. The introduction of laptop computers to students and faculty in certain programs (with rollout to all Freshmen beginning in the Fall of 1998) has involved the library and its staff more intimately in training and uses of technology in instruction. The digital library will further enhance the ways in which we make information available to our users.

Fortunately, the new Walsh Library facility greatly enhances our ability to offer the best possible service and access to our university community, with the promise of being able to adapt to future technologies yet unknown to us. Walsh Library is a building that is warm, inviting, and inspiring, a true "jewel of the campus" and a technological treasure of information both for today and the next century.

References

1. Peterson, Thomas R. (1992). "Inaugural Address," *Current Issues in Catholic Higher Education*, 12 (2), Winter 1992, p. 52.
2. *News Record*, February 6, 1992.

Unit 4
SIGNIFICANCE
Symbols and Emblems

Unit Background

All the world over, people find it ennobling to be associated with libraries. Celebrities pose for ALA posters. Mayors appear at library openings. Donors bequeath their estates to build libraries named after them. Even so, libraries around the world have found themselves in some unusually illustrious company in the 1990s. In 1994, for instance, the government of Singapore mobilized to undertake the Library 2000 project, which is no less than a reinvention of Singapore's public library system. In a letter to the Library 2000 study committee, Minister George Yeo of the Ministry of Information and the Arts, wrote,

> If we do not keep up with the revolution in information technology
> sweeping the world, we will be left behind.... It is knowledge which will
> determine the wealth of nations in the next century. We must therefore
> concentrate on two important things. First, we must educate our people
> to their maximum potential and throughout life. Public libraries help us
> to do this. Second, we must be plugged into the world's information net-
> work. We have always been a hub for goods, services, people, culture,
> languages, and ideas. Really, what we are and what we should always be
> is a hub for knowledge. Thus, the public library system should strengthen
> our ability to access and trade in knowledge [*Library 2000*, iii].

Far to the north, China arrived at the same conclusion. In 1996, China's premier Li Peng addressed the opening session of the 62nd annual IFLA conference in Beijing with a revolutionary fervor. He said that libraries were treasure houses of knowledge, and that the government of China would support the building up of libraries and librarianship in order to hasten the nation's social and economic development (see "Beijing," 306). Premier Li's appearance at IFLA, and indeed Beijing's hosting the conference, provided an important opportunity to attract international attention to China's ambitious campaign to have a library in every town in China. Of course, instead of actually building a library facility in every hamlet, the project may eventually be realized by simply making every village a

189

node with access to an online library network. By using advanced technology in this way as an alternative to costly building crusades, developing nations are leap-frogging over their lagging communication infrastructures, and saving them-selves decades and maybe even centuries of technological evolution. And still, as this book has shown, there is a massive amount of library construction occur-ring in China.

Before that IFLA session, in any case, I never expected to be addressed by a sitting national leader of any country under any circumstances, certainly not at any library or information technology conference I happened to be attending. Nor had I ever seen a national television network cover a library conference as Chinese television did the IFLA conference, and with great relish. Few librari-ans are accustomed to such elevated attention.

A Library for the Next Millennium

Meanwhile, in Paris, the new edifice of the Bibliothèque Nationale de France (BNF) was christened with the name of François Mitterrand, France's former president who, in 1988, as the following chapters relate, conceived the idea to build a library that would include knowledge in all fields, be available to every-one, utilize the most modern data technologies to support remote access, and cooperate with other great libraries. Mitterrand's statement called for nothing short of a reinvention of the French national library, not unlike the reinventions taking place in Singapore and China. Is it possible that the current explosion in information technology is turning all countries into developing nations, reset-ting the clocks of social evolution, and leveling the global playing field of infor-mation access and delivery?

The new BNF is actually a new generation of the centuries-old Bibliothèque Nationale, with a new flagship facility in the Tolbiac section of Paris on the bank of the Seine. This site will be the new location for most of the book collections currently held at the historic rue de Richelieu site, which will retain the special collections.

But the reinvention of the Bibliothèque Nationale does not consist simply of a redistribution of its collections. The venerable institution has traditionally been seen as the repository of France's complete cultural history, and in the past its collections were strictly reserved for researchers. The new BNF, however, will also serve the general public, thus combining preservation with more open acces-sibility. And going one giant-step even farther, the BNF has committed itself to an ambitious full-text digitization project that promises to turn passive accessi-bility into the active dissemination of an entire national culture.

This activity recalls the missions articulated earlier in this study in which the Shanghai Library stepped into the role of the people's university, using elec-tronic technologies and even television, and the Beijing University Library adopted as part of its mission the intention to make the culture of China more widely known around the world. Could it be that libraries of the future might assume the task of actively broadcasting culture in addition to preserving it?

The Library of Congress ventured into digitization in 1989 with the American Memory project, the pilot forerunner of the massive National Digital Library Program (NDLP), which Associate Librarian Suzanne Thorin calls LC's "first major move toward creation of a library of the twenty-first century" (quoted in Lamolinara, 31). NDLP aspires to digitize five million items by the end of this century, making it one of the world's most ambitious digitization projects. It is also one of the most prominent examples of partnering. LC will turn to the private sector for as much as 75 percent of NDLP funding, and will outsource some of the conversion to private companies. LC also uses "advisors" and educators to help determine which of its many collections to digitize (32).

Despite the rich holdings of NDLP and similar projects at many other large libraries, they may rely too much on their advisors and librarians to select materials for digitization. In the future, more than ever before, users will determine the legitimacy of libraries based on how well the users' information needs are met, not on how well the librarians have employed technology to achieve their own curatorial purposes. Projects to digitize library collections, therefore, must be well-dosed with an awareness of users' preferences and information needs. Otherwise, digitization might become another costly technological misjudgment, like the comprehensive catalog retrocon projects that granted complete accessibility to library collections, but heaped users with multitudes of records for books they never wanted to retrieve anyway.

The BNF digitization project will eventually include millions of volumes and will begin with an initial batch of 100,000 titles that are either requested by library users for their research, or that are in an unsuitable condition for reading in the original (Muratori-Philip, 11). According to Serge Salomon, the initial collection will focus on works that are patrimonial and encyclopedic in nature, rare or otherwise of limited accessibility, and of historical or critical reference value (15). Alain Giffard prophesied that the collection would be the "grand texts of reference, those which will be the 'classics' of the 21st century, and rare and precious works" (quoted in Kessler, n.p.).

The conversion project, then, will not be random, and will be selective, not universal. It will also rely to a great extent on user demand and input. This sounds very different from and much more level-headed than the costly, comprehensive retrocon projects that libraries undertook a generation ago to computerize their entire catalogs despite the fact that many of the books in their collections were of little value or interest to users anyway.

Nor by any means is the purpose of the BNF digitization process to replace the book. According to Jean Favier, head of the BNF, "The day has not come when you will read a large, difficult work on a screen." Instead, he says, there is little reason or economic justification to convert popular books and classics that are available in inexpensive print editions; or pleasure books such as novels and poetry collections; or works that are deeply or philosophically engaging. For instance, he disputes any notion that the new technologies will make it reasonable to read

Kant in the middle of the Sahara. This suggests that the outcome of the first pass of the digitization project will be an online, full-text collection of high-quality, relatively recent titles that are in sufficient demand for conversion, but not easily available in inexpensive print editions, along with some older titles in great need of preservation (Muratori-Philip, 11; translated by TDW).

The BNF conversion project is in fact well underway, with many thousands of books already digitized. And whatever the digitized collection finally looks like, the redirection of the French national library to serve the needs of the general public and even to diffuse the materials that are themselves the source of much of French culture, treasures the BNF once guarded inside its walls, sounds like the French Revolution all over again. In its interview with Favier, *Le Figaro* suggested that the new BNF was the embodiment of the mythic universal library, and called it the library for the next millennium (Muratori-Philip, 11).

Controversy, Again

But the new Tolbiac facility has had its detractors and naysayers right from the beginning, as the chapters in this unit amply document. And they continued right up to December 1996, when, only days before the new facility opened, the new building was officially named the Bibliothèque François Mitterrand by decision of Jacques Chirac, Mitterrand's successor and the current President of France.

I happened to be in Paris at the time, and saw first-hand the immediate outrage sparked by the announcement. It was decried as a scandal; disparaged as the politicizing of the arts and letters; portrayed as a political grand gesture or outright subterfuge on the part of Chirac; denounced as an assault against tradition since the Bibliothèque Nationale had never taken the name of any of the kings and statesmen who had a hand in its development over the centuries. The naming incident was compared to the British Library and the Library of Congress, the point being that the British and the Americans would never dream of renaming their national libraries after a politician, and a living one at that (see Rouart, Moinet).

Author Philippe Sollers said, "Gaullism had a writer [Victor Hugo]. His tomb is the Pantheon. The Socialists will have the Library. In the one case, you have a tomb without books. In the other case, you have books backed by a dead man who is still with us." Another writer, Jean Lacouture, doubted that Mitterrand wanted the honor, and with all the controversy that had surrounded the library's construction, speculated that one of the other monumental public works initiated by Mitterrand might be a better choice to bear his name. On the other hand, Jean-Edern Hallier, yet another writer, railed that French culture had collapsed under Mitterrand: "His architectural projects, which are crumbling one after another, cannot cover-up the unbelievable decline of French literature … and the intellectual corruption that prevailed during his 14 years in office" (see Moinet; translated by TDW).

Naming theaters, public buildings, and spacecraft launching sites after a fallen statesman is one thing. But it is unlikely that clear-thinking leaders in the U.S., England, Germany, Japan, China, and most other nations would presume to name their national libraries after an individual whose reputation was still vulnerable to tarnish. All the notoriety over the BNF, therefore, attests to two things: the singularity of the transformation occurring in that specific institution, and the almost universal prestige of great libraries in general. And politics aside (which is pretty much impossible in France), the public controversy over the BNF renaming indicates, in a paradoxical way, that the public accepts and will even embrace it, now that it is built. By passing through the kiln of cultural challenge, the Bibliothèque Mitterrand has finally been accorded the symbolic stature of the old Bibliothèque Nationale just as it has taken possession of most of the national collections, sharing both the resources and the grandeur of the older institution.

As the Benton report found (*Buildings*), libraries hold important symbolic and civic significance for the public. Library leaders surveyed for the report agreed that "the library is a symbol of trust and a locus of community culture, values, and identity that even nonusers care about" (14). The report also found that the American public agrees wholeheartedly with them. One respondent observed, "I think as we are seeing the population ... stratifying along class lines in a huge way ... the library is one of those symbolic things that is left, that is a cornerstone of 'we all do this for everyone' so that everyone can use it" (28; ellipses in original).

The sentiment for libraries seems to be the same internationally, as this book demonstrates. So whatever the thought behind the renaming of the BNF, it worked a very effective transfer of symbolic power from the old, honorable media and precincts of the Richelieu site to the new and more modern locale, formats, and purposes of the Bibliothèque Mitterrand.

Symbolic Librarianship

I freely and quickly admit that Paris is by far my favorite place in all the world. But that is not the reason for including two chapters on the BNF in this book. Rather, it is because of the antiquity of the institution, and because of the changes it has seen, and because its sheer longevity has contributed immensely to its symbolic power. No other library has achieved the symbolic stature of the organization now re-christened the Bibliothèque Nationale de France, nor carried that symbolism intact into the dawn of the new century and, if *Le Figaro* is correct, for an entire millennium. No single chapter could communicate the grandness or the scope of the mission the BNF has set for itself. So in chapter 13, Jack Kessler gives the background and a view from the outside. In his chapter, Daniel Renoult is certainly no less respectful from his inside perspective, but he is in possession of and communicates the sure sense of place the BNF exudes. Between them, they provide the essential information to understand how the new facility succeeded in securing its place as a prominent monument in a city populated by monuments.

Few locations on the planet can evoke a sense of place as powerful as that elicited by Paris. And within the city, innumerable monuments, vistas, and even cafés, nightclubs, and street corners work their own magic or majesty. So do many of the institutions in Paris — the museums, theaters, schools, and churches — but none more so than the BNF. The fact that this sense of place has been recently transmitted into a new domicile where it will reside perhaps for centuries makes it of such particular interest that Unit 4 is devoted to the BNF. It epitomizes many of the symbolic values attached to libraries.

Symbolic librarianship, as I call it, is the little-recognized portion of library practice that acknowledges the library as a system of symbols and calls for proper management of those symbols as an important part of a library's resources. It is the interpretation and utilization of the symbolic value of a library to strengthen and extend the library's influence as a social institution. It is the ability to interpret, be sensitive to, and build upon public perceptions of a library as a societal asset that is as much symbolic as functional. By "building upon," I mean: 1) extending that symbolism across societal changes, and 2) working with the public sentiments for libraries to preserve and strengthen the library during social change.

Earlier chapters have provided numerous examples of architectural devices designed to capture the symbolic power and stature of libraries, and express their unique role in society: Bruder's "flaming" columns in the Phoenix Grand Reading Room; the focus of Freeman and Shepley Bulfinch Richardson and Abbott on addressing the memorable, the attractive, and the other "immeasurables" that users expect in their libraries; and the imposing, beacon-like tower of the Walsh Library. The efforts at Beijing University and Indiana University–Purdue University Indianapolis to make these new libraries the emblems of their respective institutions are explicit examples of librarians' intentions to broker these recognized qualities to the larger community, thereby bolstering their prominence in those environments. The layouts of the libraries at George Mason University and Kapiolani College are experiments in adapting traditional symbols of libraries to new arrangements and uses to communicate their expanded role in a new information age.

Meanwhile, in Paris

The new libraries in Chicago and Paris are connected by a French 19th-century architect, Henri Labrouste. For not only did Labrouste design the Bibliothèque Ste.-Geneviève, which Thomas Beeby said was his inspiration for the new CPL library design, but Labrouste also designed the magnificent reading room in the Bibliothèque Nationale at Richelieu, which is now surrendering the large part of its collections to the new Bibliothèque Mitterrand, a structure of a very different style. These two cities, Chicago and Paris, plying their libraries, send a single strong message that surpasses their contrasts — a library is a movable feast in its own right, a potent, if very malleable symbol.

There is a circularity between the Chicago and Paris libraries. They are like two lines of the same family tree. The CPL facility is a direct descendant that carries the outward resemblance of Labrouste's work, which has been called rationalist, neo–Greek, or revolutionary classicism. In his use of interior iron work at Ste.-Geneviève and the Richelieu reading room, Labrouste trained new materials to assume classical forms; in the exterior of Ste.-Geneviève, he built a visual rhythm that suggested orderliness and control.

From his very first sketches for the CPL competition, Beeby's design alluded to classical motifs, Greek prototypes, and the "imagery" of the Labrouste facade. The building was to look "historic" (Marzynski, n.p.). Norman Ross said the building "looks like a library." Yes, because it recalls a very specific, famous library, and because that library, and all its reiterations through time, communicate a very rational and regular pattern that many people can relate to the intellectual and cultural purposes served by libraries.

But according to Renoult's chapter, even in his modernism Dominique Perrault, the young French architect who designed the new library in Paris, retains a characteristic French simplicity by presenting a formal and monumental structure, but rejecting architectural overstatement and contortion in favor of an almost minimalist simplicity of glass and metal. Perrault is reported to have said, "It is a simple idea. I took everything but the four corners of a square, and put it into the ground. So you have the *absence* of a building. It is a paradox" (quoted in Adler, 73; emphasis in original). So Perrault is also following Labrouste in spirit perhaps, but less in outward appearance than Beeby does.

Quite different in style are the new facilities of the Denver Public Library (not included in this study) and the San Antonio Public Library. Where the CPL and BNF buildings are regular and orderly, with broad, stately planes that bespeak control, San Antonio is sharp-edged and incisive. Denver is a conglomeration, with bulk, contours, bulges, and a crown. But which is the most accurate depiction for a treasure house of knowledge? Each conveys its message as it pays homage to the forms that knowledge might take symbolically, since knowledge and learning have no real forms of their own. There is still no single acceptable architectural formula for representing accumulations of knowledge and teeming information. The rendering is a matter of taste, a matter of style. But the significance remains the same in all these architectural instances: knowledge, be it perceived as orderly and organized or raw and disjointed, can be fully accommodated in the library.

While Chicago was building its replica of 19th-century Paris and using Labrouste to backfill its culture gaps, the French were building in Paris a very modern-looking edifice. There, Labrouste is still revered, as Renoult makes clear. His reading room for the Richelieu library remains one of the marvels of the French national library, which the French are now refashioning into the complex of modern and traditional edifices that Kessler and Renoult describe in their chapters. But the French are spanning from the past glory into a new kind of library that Kessler calls a blend of a monument to knowledge with an information system. Looking for the future, the French are adding on to the present; they have a new library, but its mission has not changed; they simply realize that the mission must be added to greatly. And they have created a modern palace of knowledge in which to do it. The French are now traveling on some different roads than before, but the direction is the same.

12. The Bibliothèque François Mitterrand of the Bibliothèque Nationale de France: Books, Information, and Monuments

Jack Kessler
kessler@well.sf.ca.us

> In 496 the Allemani, a Germanic confederation like the Franks ... crossed the river and invaded the settlements of the Franks on the left bank. Clovis went to the aid of his confederation and attacked the Allemani at Tolbiaç near Cologne... —(Guizot)

Introduction

Marriages can be blissful or they can be a burden; combinations can be fortunate or they can be chaotic. The Bibliothèque François Mitterrand (BFM), just completed by the Bibliothèque Nationale de France (BNF) at their Tolbiac site in Paris, mixes information systems, library mandates, an ancient institution, and one of the world's largest and newest library buildings, in a combination which has yet — as of early 1997 — to prove itself a marriage at all, much less a happy one. But at least, so far, it has been a very brave attempt. Each of these four aspects of the BFM project — the building, the institution, the library, and the systems — will be considered in turn here.

The overall concern in what follows is architecture: forms in space. But forms do not exist in space without some sort of function. A building shaped like a duck once was used to show several generations of architecture students that "form" could be independent.[1] But similar buildings — these shaped like oranges — now face demolition in California because the function which they once served, the provision of fresh orange juice, has migrated to competing fast-food chains and giant supermarkets.[2] A building cannot live from "form" alone.

So the various "functions" which have been and might be attributed to the BFM "form" are examined here, for the light which they might shed on both the physical shape of the new building and on the systems which it is thought to contain.

This becomes particularly interesting in the case of a library — and particularly this library — at this time when information systems are said to be divorcing themselves, quickly, from any dependency upon individual buildings, special sites, or even any physical location whatsoever. This is supposed to be the age of "distributed information systems," of information which "wants to be free" — of buildings, perhaps, as well as in other senses: of "The Global Village," of "tele-work" and "distance learning" and "telecommuting."

Michel Melot poses the problem with his customary eloquence:

> The era which brings us the circulation of information freed of its media, carried on electronic waves, released from all its attachments, is the same era which is covering the world with giant libraries, solidly anchored in the soil, forever immobile and self-contained within their own walls…. The library today is everywhere, at our fingertips on a keyboard the knowledge of the world is online — why reconstruct the Great Library of Alexandria, the powerful symbol of the closed knowledge of our ancestors, of the belief in thought which was halted by writing and encased by the book?[3]

At such a time, when function is said not only not to follow form but increasingly to have little to do with it at all, it is interesting that the French have invested so much time and effort — and so much pride, and so much money — in one of the world's newest and largest, certainly most expensive and, some say, most magnificent library buildings.

A Magnificent New Building — Some Say Too Magnificent

MEASUREMENTS

Each of the four towers of the giant BFM, which the BNF opened to the public on December 17, 1996,[4] measures 20 stories or 79 meters in height, making them among the tallest structures in Paris. They stand on an immense plaza, raised alongside the Seine River, on a Left Bank site formerly occupied by warehouses and train yards: the site for all of this measures nearly 7.5 hectares, or the size of the Place de la Concorde. In the densely built-up and overcrowded Paris central city, next to the Seine River itself and too few parks, the Bibliothèque

First sight of the new library typically is from the west, from the river. (Courtesy of Bibliothèque Nationale de France François Mitterand, Dominique Perrault, Architect. Photograph by Alain Goustard.)

François Mitterrand is one of the largest open areas in downtown Paris. [I am indebted to Daniel Renoult for his clarification of various measurements. JK.]

Perhaps the most distinguishing architectural feature of the new building, however, is its large, central, sunken garden. The garden is the feature of which the architect, Dominique Perrault, is most proud: "The stroke of genius," writes Jacqueline Leroy, "is to have constructed not a 'French Garden' but a small forest..."[5] modeled on the forest of Fontainebleau. After hard fights to preserve it through the design process changes, the BFM "forest" will contain 120 tall pines, oaks, and other trees, some reaching 12 meters in height. Paris is a city which possesses beautiful vegetation. The central city parks which it does have boast plush lawns — at last, as of this year in fact, available for picnics and simply for being walked upon — and glorious trees. The boulevards, as well, have trees — those spared the depredations of Haussman, and various revolutions — and countless small private gardens lurk behind Paris city walls. A large city, though, never can have enough trees at its center. The tall trees of the garden/forest of the BFM are intended to provide a sylvan oasis in the center of crowded Paris.

Trees also go well with books. The idea of readers being able to "take a good book out to read it beneath a tree," or being able, at least, to see trees through a window as they read, is as attractive to the French as it is to Americans who know Joyce Kilmer's poem.

Among the building's measurable features[6] are 395 kilometers of book-shelving, meeting rooms ranging from small seminar closets to auditoria of various sizes — 350 seats, 200 seats, and six rooms each containing 50 seats — and, most significantly perhaps, 3,600 seats for readers, as against the always over-crowded mere 700 seats at the predecessor BN. The new BFM's "garden/forest" measures 12,000 square meters; the plaza on which the towers rest, 60,000 square meters; and total usable space in the building amounts to nearly three million square meters. The collection which eventually is to be housed in the building — although this may be subject to great change and even greater controversy, as discussed later on here — is supposed to include over 8 million and as many as 10 million printed books. There are to be 2,500 staff, keeping the BFM open 12 hours per day, six days per week, 300 days per year.[7] The public attendance expected for all of this is a breathtaking 12,000 people per day: 7,500 readers, 4,500 tourists. The cost so far has been an enormous 7.2 billion francs; at current rates, U.S. $1.4 billion: this is for the building and its outfitting alone. Annual costs of maintenance and operation going forward appear still to be anyone's guess (per the BNF's Daniel Renoult, as he states elsewhere in this volume, these figures have risen to U.S. $1.5 billion for the construction, with U.S. $1.8 million per year projected for maintenance and operations). On the numbers alone — merely its measurable quantities — the Bibliothèque François Mitterrand sets a number of new records.

THE INTERVIEW IN THE GARDEN: HOW MONUMENTAL BUILDINGS ARE MADE, IN PARIS

Buildings as monumental as the BFM have originated recently from the curious process of the "international jury." Modern projects are the result of design competitions: the Centre Pompidou, the Sydney Opera House, the Bibliothèque François Mitterrand, all saw entries submitted by design teams from all over the world, analyzed endlessly in the popular press, the choice narrowed down by juries of international experts, final decisions made by luminaries who then defended them for some time after, again in the popular press.

This process, in the case of the BFM, began with a Bastille Day 1988 interview in his Elysée Palace garden, given by then–President François Mitterrand, and the following announcement: "I want a library which can take into account all the products of knowledge of all the disciplines, and above all which can communicate this knowledge to all those who are looking for it, those who are studying it, those who have the need to know it…. I have this ambition and I will do it."[8]

There had been plans for an "additional" BN — a "BN bis"— before,[9] and a need for expansion of the old BN premises for many years. Recent "Administrateurs" of the BN, from Julien Cain to Emmanuel Le Roy Ladurie,[10] had searched earnestly for solutions. By 1988, however, there just was no more space: the BN was faced with an overcrowding problem in which simply the space available for storing the books — not to speak of the staff and the workshops and the exhibits and the readers, in this major national cultural institution — would run out very soon.

The jury was composed of practitioners of various professions, drawn from various countries: mostly French, and mostly architects, but with a couple of experienced library directors and even some writers and a practicing artist.[11] The initial submissions numbered 244, and the initial selection was narrowed by the jury to 20, and again to 4. President Mitterrand himself chose the design submitted by a young French architect named Dominique Perrault, who called for "A place for Paris, a library for France ... a new Place de la Concorde, open to pedestrians ... at the heart of this public place a vast garden ... all around this site of calm and serenity reading rooms will develop, in the image of a cloister ... four towers, like lighthouses a hundred meters high, will mark the presence of the and affirm its identity...."[12]

Among the interesting aspects of this "international design competition" process is the perceived necessity of defending a monumental project of this size and importance before "world opinion." Partly for publicity, perhaps, but perhaps also because of a growing feeling of a common global interest in humanity's more significant undertakings, the sponsors of such large projects increasingly seek to discuss and justify them globally, both before and after crucial decisions are made. In the BFM case this even involved an expensive trip to the US made by all of the project leaders and luminaries.[13] One cannot imagine Francis I or Louis XIV or Philip Augustus making such an effort of discussion and self-justification for Chambord or Versailles or the Louvre. That the modern efforts are in part defensive is discussed later here, as one of the significant aspects of the entire BFM undertaking.

CONTROVERSIES

The design and building of the Bibliothèque François Mitterrand have generated great amounts of controversy. But this should come as no surprise, either to the French, or to friends of the French, or to anyone who ever has been involved in a good-sized design and construction project.

Objections to any move of the BN at all, of course, were raised early on, as were objections "in principal" to the erection of any such mammoth and expensive and disruptive project in the heart of Paris. Critics from these broadest perspectives objected first to the necessity of a BN move and new construction at all, and then, convinced of the imminent outgrowing of the site at the site at the Rue Richelieu, to every conceivable aspect of the logistics of the move.

Most famous of these last was the debate over the "coupure" or "caesura." When it was thought, at one point in the design development, that no single site would accommodate the 10 million printed books of the BN, the problem of where to draw the line — a "Solomon's" choice of how to divide up the collection — presented itself. Someone, somehow, had to decide what would "stay" and what would "go." There were many suggestions made, and much sound and fury. Some thought that certain subject classifications might migrate while others remained, the more organized of these suggesting the established classes of the BN's ancient alphabetic "Système Clément" be used in making the division. Others protested against this "alphabetic determinism," insisting that modern cross-cultural and cross-disciplinary trends in research rendered such a division obsolete.

The suggestion was made that a cutoff date be chosen, the books printed after that date to move to the new building, those from before to remain behind. Lacking a better or braver candidate for the role of Solomon, President Mitterrand himself was asked to decide, and he backed the date 1945.

The outcry was immediate, immense, and furious. Most of all, it came from the ranks of the historians, who are exalted figures in France. There were mass meetings, and "open letters" to the international media, interviews with "household name" intellectuals, apoplectic opinion pieces. Objections ranged from the impossibility of doing historical research restrained by an arbitrary date, to dark suggestions of a desire to disguise France's pre–1945 past. Prudent politician that he was, President Mitterrand finally made the even more Solomon-like decision to retreat; a way was found to suggest that indeed all of the books might move after all, and the idea of cutting the collection at the year 1945 disappeared quietly from view.

CRITICS

Criticism of the architecture has been as biting — and as furious — as have been the critiques of the more general issues of the BFM. They have centered upon three of the basic elements of the design scheme: the towers, the garden, and the subterranean readers' quarters.

The initial objection to the towers was that leveled at any tower, an objection to the height. The original plan called for 100 meters, making them rival the tallest structures of central Paris, such as the nearby Faculté de Médecine, Notre Dame, the Eiffel Tower, and the Tour Maine-Montparnasse. (This last-named 209-meter office tower was extruded into the heart of Paris' famous Montparnasse neighborhood — contributing greatly to that neighborhood's destruction — during the 1960s, over belated but then nearly violent protests of opponents, and the memory still rankled when the BFM design was announced in 1988.) In a mood of compromise — implacable opponents called it "co-optation" — the BFM towers' height gradually was "adjusted" down to their still tall 79 meters.

The BFM garden, then — the design's most precious feature, to its designer Perrault — has received many volleys of the sarcasm for which the Parisian press has been so well-known for centuries. The very idea that tall trees would even grow in such a location has been questioned. The trees selected — pines and oaks among others — are to reach 12 meters in height, and gardeners and tree lovers have ridiculed the idea that the shadows, heat, cold, wind, and shallow root space provided at the BFM site would support them or any other tall tree for long.

The subterranean chambers into which the readers originally were to have been placed offered a third focus for criticism. The idea of putting people underground, particularly in a city priding itself on being "The City of Light," seemed counter-intuitive, even if quite a few of these people were to be given a sunken garden to look out upon. The level of sarcasm was heightened greatly, then, when — to resolve one of the building's greatest controversies to date — it was decided that rather than store the precious books in the towers, where the glass windows and hot Parisian sun would have done their worst to yellowed pages and fragile bindings, at least some of the books were to go below into subterranean storage.

The problem with this last suggestion, critics almost gleefully pointed out, was that the storage then would be below the water level of the nearby Seine River. All the assurances of the engineers who have tested the riverbank have not been sufficient to assuage gloomy fears that an even greater enemy of cardboard and paper than light — moisture, that is, and the "champignons" which accompany it in the case of books — might beset any subterranean BFM book collection.

FINISHED PRODUCT

There have been many other criticisms made of the BFM's architecture and design plan. The rare or at least protected hardwoods proposed for use in the louvered shades of the tower windows caused an outcry. Street protests for the "sans abri"— the Paris "homeless"— have taken place at the Tolbiac site. Parisian sarcasm has been directed at the extremes of heat and cold and wind which will sweep across the broad plaza, the tall glass towers, and the great open garden. Soul-searching has been done in the public access program: advocates of public access, advanced research, and student needs squaring off, for example, in debates which have provided classical standoffs in central Paris for nearly nine centuries.

France, being no stranger to such controversy, knows very well how to cope with it. There have been sincere attempts at public consultation, or at least at the provision of information to the public: attempts far more sincere — in spite of the sarcasm, Parisian and other, which this view itself will occasion — than similar public consultation and information efforts made on behalf of other such projects elsewhere. There also have been several grand ignorings of the furies of the critics, at times to the detriment, at times to the benefit, of the overall project.

The outstanding feature of the BFM, however — a feature which both resolves many of its controversies once and for all and distinguishes the BFM from many of its competing projects — is that it has been built. So many such grandiose schemes never leave their drawing-boards. There are plans for mere library capital campaigns, much less enormous library buildings, which exist only as pipedreams in nearly every library in any country. Here, in Paris, is one which has succeeded, beyond the wildest nightmares of some of its critics, beyond the wildest dreams of its proponents and of many librarians and library lovers.

Even more, though, a new building for France's Bibliothèque Nationale is something in addition to a new, very big, library, to a new large building in the center of Paris, to a new piece of monumental civic architecture — something more than the sum of its parts. Advocates of libraries and civic monuments everywhere are wondering what form the cultural monuments of the new Information Age are going to take, at a time when information appears to be wresting its independence from the physical structures which until now have contained it. The BFM, whatever might be the normal and traditional criticisms which might be leveled at it as a building, stands at least as a completed example of what the new Information Age's own "information" structures may resemble. As a normal — if large and expensive — building, then, but also as a cultural phenomenon, the BFM deserves a close look. More than just a building, it is a cultural phenomenon which has a long and fascinating history.

An Ancient Institution — Some Say Too Ancient

> The difference between an Englishman and an American is that to an Englishman 100 miles is a long way, while to an American 100 years is a long time.

ANTIQUITY — THE INSTITUTION

One of the least remarked-upon aspects of the new BFM building at Tolbiac is the great antiquity of the cultural institution which it is intended to house.

The BN was founded in the 18th century, inheriting collections — and much pride, and many traditions — from its predecessor Bibliothèque du Roi, which claimed lineage back to the 14th century and before. From the earliest times of France and of the Frankish Empire, books were a treasured possession. One of the earliest recorded transactions in the country's history describes the donation of a book by Charlemagne to the Monastery of the Île Barbe, near Lyon, a transaction which took place in the 9th century.

The greatest period of growth in the BN's collections occurred, as it did for most European and North American libraries, during the 19th century. But the BN collections also saw significant additions made during the 18th, 17th, and 16th centuries, times when other European libraries which rival the BN today still were in their infancies, and North American nations — much less North American libraries — had not yet even begun their existence.

Within the BN, as well, the great system of classification still used to organize its collections derives from one formulated during the 17th century, and thence from the Latin alphabet system which once had united all of the learned of medieval Europe. A classification system — the way a culture organizes its knowledge — says a great deal about the use of that knowledge by that culture, as both advocates and critics of classifiers, from 4th-century BC Aristotle to the BN's 17th-century Clément to U.S. librarianship's 19th-century Melvil Dewey, can attest: that the BN would be using, still in the 20th century, a system for organizing knowledge first constructed in the 17th century and derived from the Middle Ages, distinguishes it from other libraries, including many in France, where the novelty and modernity of more recent approaches is so prized.

ANTIQUITY—THE BUILDINGS

The buildings which the printed books of the BN only just now are leaving are ancient as well. The site is one acquired in the 17th century from Louis XIV's minister Colbert, after several decades during which the BN's collection wandered around through several sites in central Paris, and previous centuries spent wandering around — following the King — from the Louvre to various chateaux in the valley of the Loire. The great expansion in the collections during the late 18th-century Revolution — largely confiscations of church nobility and émigrés' libraries — made a corresponding 19th-century expansion of BN premises necessary. The 19th century saw the construction of most of the great buildings of the BN site which still are in use today: restoration of the existing Hôtel Tubeuf and Galérie Mazarine, new structures along the Rue de Richelieu and the Rue des Petits-Champs, the famous "Salle Labrouste" reading room for the Printed Books collection. Twentieth-century building additions have been made both on the site and away from it: the subterranean catalog and bibliography room, the Periodicals reading room, locations in the Rue Louvois and at Versailles, and the conversion of the Galérie Colbert. Since 1960, however, there has been little further space available in the immediate Rue Richelieu area — any walk through the quarter's narrow streets and constant crowds will confirm this — and most of the BN buildings there date from the last century and before.

ANTIQUITY—SIGNIFICANCE

The simple fact of antiquity — of physical buildings like those of the BN or of a cultural institution like the BN itself — suggests but does not fully reveal the significance of that antiquity. The most obvious manifestations, such as pride and traditions, some of the latter curious and a few of them even bizarre, are common to the BN as they are to other ancient institutions. Just as Oxford students still recite a Latin prayer before dinner and throw hard rolls to land up in back of the hanging portrait of a college founder, and as members of the British Parliament hang their coats on hooks still festooned with cloth loops for the hanging of swords, so BN librarians generally still respond better to a written note than to an email message or — heaven forbid — a telephone call, and best if the note is written with a fountain pen.

More serious pride and traditions also permeate the BN, however, serious in their effect on the institution's — and its old buildings' — adaptability to change. Not only is the BN physically and institutionally ancient, it stands as a monument and in fact a cultural repository for the very antiquity of its entire surrounding culture. Even more than the cathedrals, which Victor Hugo called the "books" of Medieval France, and certainly more than a modern corporation or government ministry, or a school which might happen to be housed in an ancient building, the preservation of antiquity is a part of the BN's own institutional mission, and is to a great extent the purpose for that institution itself.

It becomes more difficult, then, in the case of such an institution, to alter ancient and historically preserved buildings, to change time-honored practices, to innovate: more difficult than, for example, in a government industry or hi-tech corporation in fact devoted to change and innovation, to "keeping up with the times." This has been the case somewhat at the BN. Enthusiastic though many of the staff and outside BN supporters have been for the innovation promised by the BNF/BFM project and the new buildings, the greatest concerns have been conservative: the continuation of traditional practices, uninterrupted reader access during any move, above all the preservation of the collection. How different from a government department or a hi-tech firm, where the mere establishment of an archive during normal times often is difficult, and always is a least rather than a most important priority.

Longevity, finally, is a consideration similar to antiquity but bearing one important difference. The BN is not only ancient but has been in nearly continuous operation for all of its long history. Libraries, like museums and other cultural institutions, may claim ancient antecedents but be of modern origin themselves.

One example might be the Olympic Games, which identify to some extent with cultural practices over 2,000 years old but in fact are largely an institution dating back only 100 years. The BN, though, not only claims origins in the European Middle Ages but has operated nearly continuously since then. It holds an institutional record for longevity equaled perhaps only by the British monarchy and a few of the older religions. Such record longevity makes for an institutional momentum far greater than might be found in organizations boasting a shorter record of practice. Staff or any other advocates wishing to propose or oppose a change, and who have over 800 years of continuous practice to use to justify their positions — in the BN's case usually less but occasionally even more — become difficult to argue with.

Antiquity—Change

Among the changes which have been imposed upon the ancient BN institutions by the current BFM moving and reorganizations, two are both most revolutionary and most fundamentally related to the design of the physical building.

The classification system for the books — the overall approach to the organization of knowledge inherited, in the BN's case, from 17th-century systematizations of medieval practices — has been restructured to reduce 23 categories to 4: 23 medieval Latin letters, each standing for an area of knowledge, became, in early BFM planning terms, subdivisions of four basic units: 1) "philosophy, history, human sciences," 2) "law and economics," 3) "science and technology," 4) "art and literature."

Why four? Because there are four towers in the architect's design and — originally, anyway — the books were to be stored entirely inside the towers. "Architectural determinism" had replaced the "alphabetic determinism" of an earlier age. To those who might think that it might not matter, the French themselves, at least, recently have considered the "structure" of knowledge to be nearly as important as — and in some cases determinative of — the content of knowledge itself: the decision to reclassify all knowledge because of an architect's design caused a commotion in French educational and intellectual circles.

A second significant change, related to both the architectural design and building program and to the antiquity and longevity of previous BN practices, is that involving the offsite storage of portions of the collection. Early on in the project the BNF acquired a site at Marne la Vallée — the giant real estate development in the suburbs east of Paris, the most prominent feature of which is the "EuroDisney" theme park — originally to be 5,000 square meters in size: now 16,000 square meters are in use, and the usage is expandable to the more than 60,000 square meters of the full site. Five thousand square meters is a good-sized office and workshop, but small by industrial, and certainly BNF, standards; 60,000 square meters is a large piece of real estate by anyone's standards, and one always can build "up," as well.

At this point — now that the Tolbiac building has been completed, the decision to move the entire printed collection made in principle, and the physical move actually under way — the outstanding question remaining about the BFM is how many, and which, of the BN books actually will go to Tolbiac and how many in fact will end up being shunted off to Marne la Vallée? The original BFM planning did not call for anything but a preservation workshop at the suburban site: this has evolved to the most recent formulation — this from the BNF W3 site[14] — calling for, "Stocking a 'collection de sécurité': the creation of a 'collection de sécurité' involves the storage of one exemplar of all printed, audiovisual, and digital documents received by the dépôt légal [French copyright service]. This exemplar will not be available for consultation by anyone." The BN dépôt légal already receives about 40,000 print titles, 24,000 hours of audio, 15,000 hours of video, and 2,500 multimedia documents each year: at this rate, Marne la Vallée will be building a substantial collection soon, just from "dépôt légal 'exemplars'" alone.

It would make really very little financial sense, in fact, not to send most of the BN printed collection to the offsite storage site rather than to Tolbiac. Large amounts of the collection — over three million volumes — already are damaged or endangered, by acid paper and other traditional book preservation problems, and a great amount of that which remains is rarely used; it is very arguably the "dead stock" which clogs any merchandise inventory; and central Paris real estate — certainly the BFM site — is expensive, while suburban Marne la Vallée is cheap.

The precedent for using offsite storage space at Marne la Vallée to warehouse significant portions of the BFM collection is great. Such facilities, where books may "properly" be stored in dehumidified and temperature-controlled conditions, and arranged by size and weight like any efficient merchandise inventory rather than by some arcane "classification" system, exist in many places elsewhere. Large university libraries throughout the United States either already have such "surplus" facilities or are planning them.[15] Similar "surplus" or "offsite" facilities, organized around modern "warehouse/ distribution center" rather than "library" lines, exist for many large institutions in Europe.[16] Book storage by libraries is perhaps the last inventory-intensive activity to remain in the central city: most merchandise inventory or records storage businesses migrated to the suburbs or even further out long ago. The idea of reorganizing the BNF or any other large library along such "efficiency" and "modern distribution center" lines — let alone of exiling the books to locations far from the traditional city center — presents one of the most revolutionary changes to libraries and librarianship involved in the BFM project.

ANTIQUITY—RESISTANCE TO CHANGE

There has been resistance to change at the BFM, however. The resistance comes from both outside and inside of the older BN institution. It comes largely from those very familiar with, and very concerned about preserving, the continuity of the institution's long-standing practices and ancient traditions.

The historians who successfully opposed the early proposals — some of them even presidential — for a "coupure" or "caesura," cutting the BN collections at 1945 or at some other date, argued from the point of view of practical research needs: few topics requiring research in materials close to a given year, such as "1945," could be found which might not — which would not — require materials from both before and after the cutoff date, they said.

More generally there is danger, in fact, in any solution, "architecturally-determined" or other, they reasoned, which might impose some arbitrary limit like a chronological cutoff date upon the course of historical research. The availability of sources always has, after all, conditioned much of historical research and interpretation: has been one of the historical discipline's outstanding problems, in fact, and the deliberate introduction of such a barrier — the inevitable suggestion to researchers that materials not readily available might be omitted — would be a retrograde and highly dangerous step.

A more recent change and challenge to traditional BN procedures now is arising in general French politics, where pressures from a recently elected extremist-right party in four southern towns have resulted in the removal of left-wing periodicals from library shelves there. The BN's long history of comprehensive collecting — certainly of anything French — is being offered now to reassure those who fear that the censorship contagion begun in those four southern towns might expand and spread. But some worry over other long-standing BN traditions — the "Enfer," for example, which for many years famously hid materials from view which were deemed pornographic and otherwise improper — which suggest that the institutional mechanisms for censorship might exist within the BN itself: occasioned overtly by politically motivated censorship, or perhaps masquerading covertly behind the mandates of an architectural design program: "no space left — it has to go out to Marne la Vallée...."

Indeed there is general worry throughout the world community over such looming choices which will have to be made — at the BFM but also elsewhere — as the transition in media from print to digital proceeds. Says Umberto Eco, "The issue which gives me the greatest anxiety of my life: the conservation of books.... I am terrorized by the idea that all the books which have appeared on cellulose paper since the 19th century are destined to disappear because they are so fragile.... When I pick up a Gallimard from the 1950s, I have the impression of having in my hands a lamb being burned as a sacrifice.... We are confronted by a fundamental choice of civilization. The Bibliothèque de France is studying all the methods of conservation. It will cost a fortune.... But who, what authority will decide which books to retain?" Eco warns darkly against such choices being guided by current political opinion and cultural fashion — for, he reminds us, "Plato and Dante have known their periods of disgrace, although they have been able to transcend the centuries...."[17]

A Library — One in the Throes of All of the Most Difficult Problems Faced by All Modern Libraries

LIBRARIES, GENERALLY

The Bibliothèque François Mitterrand is more, though, than just a possibly magnificent new building and a set of very ancient and still living traditions and concerns. It is a library — or its declared intention is to house a "library," or at least to provide "library" service — and, as such, it exhibits all of the problems and possibilities which beset most libraries anywhere today.

Problems of the mix of services to offer, for example, confront the BFM as they do any modern library in this time when the definition of the "user" is shifting radically. Traditionally the BN was a research institution of "last resort": it was expected that all other avenues were to have been pursued before the precious resources of the BN were called upon. There is in Paris as elsewhere, however, a great need for library service for the general public, a need very much at odds with the BN traditionalist ideal of selected scholars obtaining limited access only to selected books. Paris also has a more unique need for library space, or at least resources, for its enormous student population. The BFM has struggled with all three of these — with all three user publics and with every possible combination of them, erudite researcher, general public, and student — and with how to accommodate them, and whether to, and in what proportions. But then, so have libraries elsewhere.

Funding also is a problem, at the BFM and the BNF generally, again as it is at most modern libraries. Like the British Library and the U.S. Library of Congress, the BNF has discovered that direct central government largesse — so envied by smaller state, regional, local and private institutions — is a two-edged sword: as the politics at the national capital change — and they often do with an alarming regularity far more frequent and radical than that of political change at local levels — so does the state of central government library funding. Political climates favoring "private enterprise" and "privatization," and making up for perceived overspending by previous opposition regimes, can wreak havoc with central-government-funded library budgets.

Cultural and social trends also generally affect the BNF and its BFM, as they do most libraries. Censorship — the need for it against pornography and violence, the threat of it in politics — is an old and constantly shifting balancing process for libraries. "Political correctness" is a phenomenon which touches any cultural institution: BNF librarians debate the role and proportion of "Maghreb" literatures in their collections just as U.S. librarians debate the roles and proportions of "Native American" and "African American" literatures in theirs.

PRESERVATION

There are, however, several issues still common to all libraries which assume a special significance at the BNF, at least in part directly because of the new BFM building.

Preservation is one of these. The BNF faces a unique preservation problem to begin with: over three million books in need of fairly immediate attention.[18] These are primarily acid paper problems, but also involve decaying bindings, molds and occasional infestations, the whole host of usual book preservation maladies; only in the BNF case the sheer size of the problem is unique, "three-plus million books" being greater than the entire contents of most libraries elsewhere in the world.

The new BFM building also has added several new dimensions to the BNF's preservation problems. First is the move itself: the packaging, transport, unpackaging, and general handling of the material — much of which rarely if ever has been handled since it was first put in place on the shelf — pose perhaps the greatest threats to the material's preservation.

Then there is the problem of the reclassification and general reorganization of materials at their new site, wherever that new site may be. Inevitably this reorganization will increase handling — reclassification and reorganization reduce the chance that entire groupings of materials might be moved intact — thus increasing the possibility of damage in handling.

The architecture of the new BFM, also, presents risks to the preservation of materials. The idea of storing materials damaged most frequently by heat and light and moisture, either in glass-enclosed towers in a hot and humid city, whatever the temperature and humidity control guarantees offered by the designers and engineers (already there have been severe sprinkler system malfunctions which have flooded the new building — without doing too much damage, yet), or in subterranean vaults on a river flood plain, separated from the river water itself only by a levee and the assurances of a different set of engineers, conjures up age-old nightmares to all librarians, particularly acute here as these have been the precise plans for the BFM. Add to this the various automated book retrieval systems, and their possibilities for error and for damaging fragile books — recent disasters of similar luggage-handling systems at Dulles, Fort Worth and Denver airports are well-known in the field, and are on the minds of many architects — and it is easy to understand why preservationists are particularly worried about the BFM.

The entire problem of offsite storage, then — and the underlying selection problem which so worries Umberto Eco— also poses great threats, although great possibilities as well, in the minds of the preservation community concerned about the BFM. If there will be two sites in fact — the one at Tolbiac and the other at Marne la Vallée — perhaps inevitably people will worry as to which will provide the better protection. Tolbiac will have all the risks of heat and water and glass-enclosed towers and handling by users, by now well-known to those who have followed the project. But a tens of thousands of square meters modern warehouse and distribution facility at Marne la Vallée might pose the threat of "single" disasters which any large-scale "single" solution always offers: a massive failure in some highly automated system, such as those for automated shelving or heating or humidity, for example, or fires, or — notoriously — accidents with automated fire protection systems.

Perhaps the greatest assurance for preservationists might be derived, however, simply from the fact that now the BN print collection at least is destined to be split between two locations: even if one does not trust systems, modern or ancient, or the assurances of experts, at least the old actuarial adage about "spreading the risk/not putting all the eggs in one basket" will ensure that whatever disasters befall the one BNF site, the other will escape them.

ACCESS

Access, then, is the traditional complement to library concerns about preservation. As with preservation, the BNF faces most of the usual access problems and possibilities faced by other modern libraries. Primary among these concerns at the new BFM is the library effort to cope with the challenges of the era of digital information.

The French president said, in calling for the building of what was to become the BFM, "One must be able to connect this national library with the great universities of Europe, and thus we will become an instrument of research and of work which will be incomparable."[19] Access thus has been built from the beginning into the BFM charter.

The difficulties in carrying out the presidential mandate, however, have stemmed from an unexpected source. There have been the usual technical problems. The "PLAO/Poste de Lecture Assisté par Ordinateur" concept, for example, into which much BFM money has been poured, has proven to be unwieldy in the face of rapid changes in the digital information industries: a "one-size-fits-all" work station like the "PLAO," designed for the stand-alone personal computer environment of the early 1990s, is ill-suited for the Network Computer/Internet, "multiple platform" and "Java/Activex" environment which may — these things change quickly — characterize digital information access already in the late 1990s. And neither model, neither "work station" nor "Network Computer/Internet," may have much to do with user access needs and practices by the fast-approaching early 2000s. The integration of BNF cataloging — both within the BNF itself and also among the various "pôles associés," the regional libraries which have shared in this activity — also has been successful but extremely difficult to implement.

The BNF, like all libraries, faces the problem — the challenge but also the difficulty — of bridging the transition in media between the older print tradition and the newer digital information age. The problem is exacerbated now in the BNF case by the division into several locations: for the BFM at Tolbiac, printed information and a presidential mandate to implement the latest digital techniques, and back at the Rue Richelieu all the considerable non-print treasures of the old BN — prints, coins and medallions, manuscripts, maps and plans — and the concerns for imaging and image storage and description, which ironically are even more central to the digital access revolution now than are the primary interests of the BFM in printed text.

STAFF

The new building is also affecting the library staff at the new BFM, in fundamental ways. There will be a large staff. Of the projected 2,500 positions, it has been suggested that 700 will be brought over from the old BN.[20] What has not been made clear, though, is who these new staff are to be: whether they will be professional librarians, or primarily "support" personnel. One expects the latter, given the budget problems of the BFM and general trends and problems of the library profession at the moment, and this will create difficulties over the long run. Is the BFM to become yet another institution overflowing with computers and information systems and information, churning out "information overload" to users who can handle only a small portion of it? To quote Umberto Eco, an avid library user, once again, "A bibliography of 20 titles is useful.... But what do we do with one of 10,000 titles obtained by pushing a computer button? Into the wastebasket!... The problem is to filter this information overload...."[21] The BFM is going to need trained information professionals to help users with such "filtering," not just "support staff."

Staff training is a problem posed directly by the innovations being brought in by the new building. The general mandate for the BFM favoring automation and computerization — what the French call, generally, "informatisation"— has created a demand for training, and retraining, in these areas which the profession and its schools are straining to provide. Shifting BFM mandates regarding the public to be served, as well, cause strains and changes for the staff: a user public composed primarily of academic researchers requires a far different professional staffing approach from that needed for one composed of the general public, or one composed of university students. Any radical shift in the allocation of the collection between Tolbiac and the Marne la Vallée offsite storage, as is likely to develop, likewise will affect professional staff demands and training: the warehousing of books is a very different activity from the provision of reference service.

Downsizing, furthermore, does not involve solely reductions in staff size. The construction of the BFM building has cost a great deal of money, and its operation will cost more, and the strength of the general French economy and the financial health of the French government lately have not been good. This is a recipe for what, in the U.S. context, would be called "downsizing": overall reduction in financial expenditure, whether or not this involves cuts in staff size and compensation, or reductions in any other institutional asset. In a library situation there are many assets and expenses which thus might be reduced — the book budget, for example, or subscriptions, opening hours, service levels — but there also is total expenditure on personnel which can be cut, and usually it is. More people might even be hired, but they may be less qualified than those whom they replace, having been hired at lower rates.

Ultimately, however, the greatest problem for staff at the new BFM will be presented not so much by any given situation, such as downsizing or the need for new training, as by uncertainty. The severe changes which already have occurred are only the beginning. Change in the computer and general "hi-tech" industry currently runs in generations lasting only six months — every six months there is a need to release a new "version," a new "product," a new "solution," to stay ahead of the competition — and that six-month "window," which used to be one year, quickly is reducing itself to four months. Insofar as this sort of thinking continues to dominate the digital information industries, libraries and librarians are going to have to learn to work with it. Techniques have to be developed to accustom staff and institutions to invent entirely new solutions to information service tasks and problems every six months, to accommodate the digital innovations which literally are pouring out upon them from the computer and hi-tech industries, and to enable them to see professional development as a renewable cycle rather than as a static achievement.[22] Such techniques are not yet in place, and libraries and librarians themselves, along with Eco and the rest of the users, literally are drowning in too much information.

An Information System — One on the Cusp of the Very Latest Developments in Online Digital Information

INFORMATION SYSTEMS

The most advertised aspect of modern librarianship, however — and of modern libraries, including this Bibliothèque François Mitterrand — is the large and increasing role of libraries in the actual development of online digital information itself: in the Internet, the World Wide Web, and the increasing digitization of everything — text, images, sound, "multimedia" combinations of these and other things — for the provision of information to users over long-distance telecommunications channels.

This is not the warehousing of books. It is not the provision of traditional "reference service." It is something new, and it is revolutionizing the "function" performed by libraries everywhere. The old French president was to some extent aware of this. In his original mandate for the construction of the building which eventually was to bear his name, he declared, "This great library will cover all the fields of knowledge, will be at the disposition of all, will use the most modern technologies of the transmission of knowledge, and will be able to be consulted at a distance, and to enter into relations with the other European libraries."[23]

The planners of the BFM took this mandate to heart, and invested heavily in computers, library automation, digitization schemes, and information systems. Computers, online access, and a sophisticated presence on the Internet and the World Wide Web are among the BFM's proudest achievements. As they were planning for the construction of architect Perrault's new building, the BNF planners were investing in anything which might smack of "the new technologies." As they were breaking ground at the building site at Tolbiac, ateliers were being formed, in various locations, to extend or inaugurate online information systems innovations in cataloging, preservation, access, and other aspects of traditional library information service.

LOCATION AND INFORMATION

But there is a problem. Information, in its most general sense, is independent of physical location: information is rootless. It does not matter any longer, to anyone — to the user, to the provider, to the publisher or the distributor or even to the person who stores it — where, physically, the information resides.

Functionally, information is a part of a process or a system — the French refer to a "chain of publication," proceeding from author to reader by way of editors, publishers, printers, distributors, and all the others who may be involved — in which the ends are satisfied simply by getting the information to the user: so long as this is accomplished, it does not really matter *where* the information, or, for that matter, the user, "is."

The preoccupation with physical location which many involved with libraries exhibit is one not with the information but with its containers: with reels of tape and microforms and paper catalog cards and printed news periodicals — and with books. These all require a "place" to "put" them.

Information, however, does not require a location, or it no longer does — or at least it requires a specific location less and less. The modern computer modem user's process of looking up a text reference in an online Internet index, finding and reading it, and even downloading and printing it in the privacy of his or her own home, has very little to do with the physical location of the computer disk which may store the digital representation of that text: the disk could be in a giant building, labeled a "library," in the expensive heart of Paris, but it might also be in a less expensive warehouse in suburban Marne la Vallée — or in an information center in Italy, or one in Iceland, or someplace in Kansas, or in Bali or Tahiti. The user, at any rate — the customer — does not care.

There is some precedent for this rootlessness of information, and interestingly it comes from Paris. During the Middle Ages scholars "wandered": itinerant students and lecturing professors both traveled all over Europe, from learning center to learning center. The medieval schools which formed the foundations of many of Europe's modern universities originally were collections of students which such "wandering scholars" visited: at times invited to stay on, "in residence," at times invited to leave. The period of the "wandering scholars" was one of the most fruitful intellectually in the entire course of European history. Perhaps one of the greatest and most interesting ironies of the BFM situation being described here is that the city which was among the first to cause the "wandering scholars" to settle down is now again in the forefront, intellectually, but this time in encouraging information to set itself free to "wander" again. The trend and its battles are not over yet, but it is comforting perhaps to consider that it is not a set of entirely new issues.

DIGITAL VERSUS NON-: AT THE BNF

Online digital information development at the BFM is taking several forms, which roughly can be grouped into three categories: access, preservation, and technique.

The international library community has been using online digital information for providing access to printed collections for many years. Bibliographic description, and its cataloging, including extensive indexing and cross-referencing, have been available for most large libraries since the 1980s. The BNF's own "OPALE" online catalog service for printed books and periodicals, and its companion "OPALINE" for non-print materials, now are reached easily online on the Internet.[24]

Libraries have been slower, however, to adopt the next logical step and provide reference service access online. This may have been wise, in retrospect. There has been such an explosion in the use of online digital information systems recently — from thousands of users to tens of millions, within very few years — that half-hearted attempts to provide, for example, reference service via email, would have swamped meager library staffs, as similar efforts have swamped "help desks" elsewhere. The BN has had email as long as others have had it, but not for access to reference service: one still is best advised to send a handwritten note, in good French.

The World Wide Web (W3), however, is revolutionizing library information access as it is information use elsewhere and in other contexts. The W3 provision of an easy, accessible and attractive graphical user interface enables librarians to provide access to reference service, and even to the information sought itself, in ways impossible in previous "ASCII américain — only" textual interfaces. The excellent and imaginative BNF W3 site — Internet address http://www.bnf.fr, and the W3 site includes a fascinating pictorial "tour" of the new Tolbiac BFM building — now provides much of the general access information which users previously had to travel to Paris to obtain.

Preservation, also, is a major area of online digital information use being developed by libraries, among them the BNF. With over three million "endangered" volumes of printed text — problems ranging from molds to bookworms to decaying leather and users' depredations to, above all, the destruction caused by 19th- and 20th-century acid paper — the BNF faces a massive preservation problem. The digitization of texts and images, and sound and multimedia formats, and their distribution to users in the digital formats rather than on their original and more fragile paper or celluloid media, is an important function everywhere now. At the BNF, as usual, the aspirations and statistics are impressive to the point of being overwhelming: by 1998 it is hoped that 100,000 works representing 30 million pages will have been digitized.

The BNF work on the World Wide Web concerns access to some extent — an adequate online digital version certainly has the possibility of reaching far more people, via the Internet, than did the earlier printed paper text — but preservation of the earlier more fragile version is an equally important goal. The balancing of "preservation" with "access" has led to some interesting dilemmas. For example photographers, asked by the BNF staff for permission to digitize their photographs for the collection, seem divided into two camps: those who will not give permission — still by far the majority — and those who give it only on the condition that the digital version be shown on W3.

Full "digital libraries," though, also are being assembled by the BNF, and these efforts eventually will merge with the more general projects for digital preservation and access. Already, online on the BNF W3 site, any user anywhere can view magnificent images and scholarly text for "Tous les savoirs du monde," the December 20, 1996–April 6, 1997, BNF exhibit on encyclopedias and movements to assemble encyclopedic knowledge of France: Diderot's effort and much more, "Le roi Charles V et son temps (1338–1380)," 1,000 illuminated manuscripts including some of the finest of the "cabinet des manuscrits" collection, and "Naissance de la culture franse," an exhibit shown by the BNF at the Library of Congress of some of the greatest historical treasures — printed books, manuscripts, even an image of the "throne of Dagobert." The BNF as online digital library is emerging.

DIGITAL VERSUS NON-: LIBRARIES IN GENERAL

These are trends which are emerging in other libraries besides the BNF. All over the world, in nearly every country which has any major library infrastructure, including libraries in Latin America, Africa, and Asia, and nations such as Thailand, China, Estonia, Ecuador, "digital libraries" such as that being assembled by the BNF are appearing.[25] The problems which beset all of these efforts are both local and held in common: local difficulties with budgeting and resistance to innovation, common problems of development of the techniques and the evolution of acceptable standardization. All these problems are being swept aside, though, in the current tidal wave of digital information usage growth worldwide: Internet total host counts which have soared from nine million in January 1996 to 12 million that July, to 16 million by January 1997 and 19 million by July 1997.[26] The more long-term problems may come back to haunt, however: as the Internet juggernaut rolls, it is not clear whether issues like the amenability of online digital information to international users, users who are not comfortable with the Internet's still overwhelmingly native American English, and general public users, people whose greatest interests in life are not the reading of computer screens and the pushing of computer keys, will be satisfactorily resolved. Both of these issues, and many of the others with which the Internet grapples now, are being addressed directly in the development of digital libraries at the BNF.

CONTRADICTION

Creativity very often is the fruit of contradiction. France has a long history of using controversy in this manner. The French revolution added greatly to the collections of the BN. The controversies which attended its creation probably have added greatly to the BFM: whether they improved or damaged it remains to be seen; the important thing is that there has been "value added," controversy changed something.

Once again, then, there is controversy looming at the BFM. As the information system develops — as it seems it must, inexorably, under the immense pressures of current digital information and "informatisation" development — and as the book collection gets set to move into the expensive new building, or elsewhere, there will be more clashes. Someone, somewhere — in a journal, during a political campaign — will begin to suggest, strongly, that the building is not needed for the books. Worse, the suggestion might not be made overtly, but things simply might begin to happen, and we all might wake up belatedly to Umberto Eco's nightmare of someone or something having made the painful "selection" decisions rued by all of us but which must be made: too many of the books will be found to have been sent "out to Marne la Vallée," or, as already is happening in some other "new" library projects, significant numbers of the old books will be found simply to have disappeared. It would be better if these decisions were to be made openly.

One hopes that there will be many discussions, some decisions, much debate, before all of this is "fait accompli." In the meantime, however, in France at least they now have a large, new building and some new ideas to contribute to what is essentially an old if now increasingly — globally — widespread set of library and information issues.

Conclusion — Form and Function, Monuments and Information Systems

FORM AND FUNCTION

The debate about form versus function is the oldest in architecture. It is one of those dynamic discussions, surging back and forth between two opposite and irreconcilable poles, which pit purists against compromisers, artists against engineers, political organizers against aesthetes. Like most such debates it is a matter of the cup which may be seen as being either "half empty" or "half full," depending on what sociologists euphemistically call the "observational standpoint" of the debater: buildings have to have both form and function, and the two must balance, and most serious participants in such discussions realize this.

The question, in considering any new and interesting "form in space" such as the Bibliothèque François Mitterrand, then, is not so much whether form follows function or the reverse, but whether a new balance may have been struck — in this old debate — as a result of something unique about this particular building. One has, I think.

MONUMENTS AND INFORMATION SYSTEMS

The BFM is both a monument and an information system, more starkly and more significantly than any other building so far built. Other structures have been erected to be primarily or merely monuments. From Egypt's Pyramids to Corbusier's Ronchamp to Maya Lin's Vietnam Memorial, one can think of many edifices with functions which primarily are monumental. Few, however — certainly few of recent origin — have been intended so completely to embody the full history, culture and aspirations of an entire people as has the Bibliothèque François Mitterrand of the Bibliothèque Nationale de France. And few have been so large. In France itself there have been Versailles and the Eiffel Tower, and more recently the Centre Pompidou, I.M. Pei's wonderful Louvre courtyard, and the Grande Arche de la Défense. The BFM ranks easily with these now as being among the large architectural monuments best said to represent the entirety of France.

The BFM, however, makes additional pretensions. In addition to the monumental form of its "bricks and mortar," it brings to France an architectural "function" which, combined with that monumental "form," makes it unique and very interesting for all current building. For information systems do not need locations. They can be — they are — anywhere and everywhere. A computer modem user in the Alpine resort town of Annecy "dialing in" via her modem to an online catalog, looking up a text, "clicking" to a database which contains that text, and reading and downloading and even printing — all in her own home in Annecy — that text and its images (and its sounds, and one day perhaps even its smells and its tactile "textures" and "sensations" ["Virtual Reality Markup Language/VRML" is under development already]) — does not need to know and may not care "where" any of this is "located." It may all be in a big building in Paris, or in one in Marne la Vallée, or it may be scattered among linked resources themselves located in several small towns in France, or it may be stored in mainframe computers in Cambridge, England or in Cambridge, Massachusetts, or for that matter in Alice Springs, Australia. All of this, located wherever, still may be online information service brought to her by the BFM in Paris, but to her its location does not matter. The BFM is a giant building, of giant monumental "form" apparently dedicated increasingly — like so many other libraries, and increasingly also distance-learning-oriented universities, and multinational corporate campuses — to an information system "function" for which physical location simply no longer matters.

SOME LOSSES

Something is gained and something is lost in all this. The social and economic gains appear to many to be obvious. The advantages of decentralized location made possible by telecommunications have spawned entire new industries in "industrial location," "distance learning," "tele-work" and "tele-commuting." Ever since J.P. Gravier's landmark work from the 1940s, *Paris et le Désert Français*,[27] the decentralization of the Paris behemoth has been the constant dream of French city and regional and economic planning. To some, everything — prices, family activities, environmental surroundings and village atmospheres, health, education, and general quality of life — seems better in the suburbs, or in the countryside or villages or towns or smaller cities, anywhere that is but in the big central city. Telecommunications appears to offer all this promise, the promise that the BFM user can stay at home in Annecy, a small and pleasant resort city on the shores of a beautiful lake high in the Alps, and that she need not travel to the noise and dirt and congestion and high prices of central Paris, to use the services to which the giant new BFM building supposedly is dedicated.

Why build the building, then? Why spend the time, effort, and enormous amounts of money to construct a "form" — the new library building at Tolbiac — which increasingly is becoming separated, by telecommunications and "digitalisation," from its "function" of providing information to that user way out in Annecy? The answer lies in some of the losses which are beginning to crop up amid the undoubted gains which have been realized from telecommunications and digitization.

Socially and economically, for example, it is not clear that the decentralization dreams, of the Paris planners among others, yield results entirely in their favor. These are old dreams. Before networked information they relied on other instrumentalities — the automobile and its freeways, and before them television, and before that radio and the telephone and the railroad, the steamship, the clipper ship — to provide their panaceas for all social and economic ills. Always the argument was that the technological innovation would stimulate decentralization — from an overcrowded Europe to a New World, from overcrowded East Coast regions to new "frontiers," from overcrowded cities to smaller towns and cities and suburbs.

All along, however, nightmares have accompanied the dreams; somehow the very social and economic ills being escaped traveled along with the new technologies. The New World, for many, offered hardships to equal or surpass those left behind in the Old. New regions never were entirely uninhabited, and their existing residents resented and resisted the incursions of newcomers from the crowded areas. Even the dream of suburbs and small towns — the motivation for famous planning movements from "Garden Cities" to "New Towns" to "City Beautiful" to "La Ville Radieuse" — was not without its disadvantages: decentralized people found themselves to be too removed, too distant, "alienated" — far from the "community" which they once had enjoyed, or at least imagined that they had enjoyed — decentralized, literally, too far from the "center."[28]

What has been needed all along — what perhaps has been present, but rarely recognized enough to prevent some severe suffering has been a balance between the forces of decentralization and the center, a dynamic "sense of place." The BFM building, and the apparent contradiction between its monumental "form" and the growing networked information "function" which no longer needs it, is an instance of all of these decentralization pressures in microcosm, and an object lesson to all the many social, cultural and political institutions now facing similar situations. The BFM perhaps no longer is needed for its traditional information "function." Its monumental "form" remains, however, and ironically evokes — and just may answer — the losses and problems associated with decentralization.

SOME GAINS: A SENSE OF PLACE

What might be gained — in the new lands, in the new frontiers, in the suburbs, amid the increasing trends toward "tele-research," "tele-commuting," "tele-work" — is a "sense of place."[29] There is a tremendous freedom associated with the increasing ability to call up, read, and download any text, anywhere, from the privacy of one's own home. But any unbounded freedom brings insecurity. There is that insecurity today, among suburban dwellers — and particularly their children — who long for the excitement and stimulation of the city center; among "region" dwellers increasingly uncertain whether they inhabit their "region" or their "nation"; among people imprisoned by poverty in both small towns and large cities who wonder increasingly what their own lives have to do with the lives depicted on their televisions. There is that insecurity as well among digital information users, hammered with the message that they have to "get that thing" but flooded with its "information overload": Umberto Eco [*supra*], dumping his "10,000 citations" into the trash can and crying for some sort of "filter."

One interesting exercise which anyone might perform on a group or even on oneself, is to ask, "What was your earliest happy memory?" — in this case, "What was your earliest happy memory of a library?" I have tried this myself on graduate-level classes which I have taught, and the answers I have received from students have been extraordinary: "the *smell*" — these are adult people remembering the sensations perceived when they were little folks, four and five years old — the *smell* of a library, of the old books and rugs and wooden furniture and general warm and comfortable mustiness, was their earliest happy "library" recollection. There were memories of light and of color, as well — of soft reading lamps, and gentle light filtering in from large windows, of the warm colors of rows of book bindings — also of the touch, of cloth and of leather, of polished wood.

All of this, any architect will tell you, has to do neither with "information" nor with the "containers" in which it comes but with "place," with a certain place called a "library," a place which perhaps enhances the experience of using that "information" and its "containers." What has been lost, in the final analysis, in all the focus placed recently on the development of digital information and its battles with the "book" medium which preceded it, has been a "sense of place": a sense of what libraries have meant in the past to a small child, the contribution which the "place" made in the past to the enjoyment and even the effective use of information — a combination, in fact, of both "form" and "function," in that the "place" called a "library" offered both.

TOLBIACS NEW AND OLD

Clovis, the tribal chief who defeated a rival at the original Tolbiac, near Cologne in AD 496, went on to become a Christian in a famous baptism, some say in gratitude for his Tolbiac victory, some say as part of a devious and complex plot in the politics of his day. Some say, too, that Clovis was a German, others insist violently that he was French, in this era so long before either "Germany" or "France" existed. All seem to agree that his military action that day at Tolbiac was, like all military actions throughout history, defensive; all, that is, except perhaps the Allemani.

The new library building just opened at the place called Tolbiac in Paris shares certain things in common with the old Frankish chieftain's AD 496 victory. Like the earlier event, the new library has involved controversies. Like the earlier, the controversies have been cultural. France never is quite sure where the dividing line between French culture and the rest of the world lies, and continually is preoccupied with its self-definition. Like Clovis' battle, the BFM construction is in a sense defensive. French culture is forever under siege, according to the French: the language of the English, the cinema of the Americans, the cars and computers of the Japanese, the soldiers and more recently the economic might of the Germans — all are deemed by the French to threaten the "Hexagone" and "la Francophonie." The new building at the Paris Tolbiac might be seen as a "temple of culture," but it might also be seen as a battlement: a defensive — and sometimes offensive — bastion against the forces loose in the outside world which might pose a threat to French culture, and to France.

Crenellated towers? Hoardings? Oubliettes, moats and "murderholes" for pouring hot tar and pitch and boiling water down upon the intruders? Dominique Perrault's building does not contain these, explicitly. But perhaps they are there a bit: hidden, understated with the subtlety so prized by the French in their language and cuisine and general culture. The building now is open, and it is inviting: there is a garden, after all, and a majestic stairway, and a great open plaza, and broad public spaces and great reading rooms and far more seats for users than its predecessor had. But there are things which are hidden and defensive nevertheless: as for any display, it is not immediately apparent why the display is being made. One shows the best of what one has perhaps to share it, but perhaps also to protest that it exists: to protest against critics, against insecurities, defensively or offensively.

The Germans used to call this tendency "Kulturkampf"—Culture War. In French, with more gentility, or perhaps subtlety, they say "engagé": "engaged"—things can be removed—above, below, or just distant from strife, or they can "take arms against a sea of troubles." The new Bibliothèque François Mitterrand building at Tolbiac might best be described as this: as an edifice which is, above all, "engagé."

Postscript

Michel Melot's answer to his own question, posed earlier here, as to the reason for the continued existence—in fact the flourishing—of grand library buildings in an age of online digital information, is that the building functions as a "symbol" and a "territory": an emblem of the knowledge—and the thirst and quest for, and use of it—traditionally associated with libraries, and a special place in which to indulge all of this.[30]

As I sit writing this article, on a weekday afternoon in the little one- (large) room local public library close to my home in San Francisco—able to reach Melot in Paris or my editor in Hawaii in an instant via email, but having come to my library to write—I watch schoolchildren and mothers browsing, doing homework, and reading both computer screens and books. These all are activities which today might be undertaken elsewhere—it now is the user's choice, thanks at least in part to online digital information—but perhaps not so easily and not so well: schools are crowded, noisy places; offices (and kitchens) have many distractions and interruptions; even a grassy field beneath a pear tree is not always the ideal place to do research, no matter what the reach of one's radio-modem. The library building may offer nothing more than a congenial place to go to read—in books *or* on computers—and to think, but that may be enough.

References

1. Venturi, Robert, Denise Scott Brown, and Steven Izenour, *Learning from Las Vegas* (Cambridge, Mass.: MIT Press [1972]; Mead, Christopher, ed. *The Architecture of Robert Venturi: Essays by Vincent Scully [et al.]* (Albuquerque: University of New Mexico Press, c1989).
2. "Doggone Dilemma," *San Jose Mercury News*, March 19, 1997.
3. Melot, Michel, ed. *Nouvelles Alexandries* (Paris: Éditions du Cercle de la Librairie, 1997), p. 7 [excerpt translated from the French by JK].
4. Kessler, Jack, "FYI France EXTRA: Opening of the Bib.Nat.deFrance/F.Mitterrand!" archived in http://www.fyifrance.com/restricted/Fyarch/fy961218.htm; Edelmann, Frédéric,

and Emmanuel de Roux, "La bibliothèque François Mitterrand," http://www.lemonde.fr/dossiers/BFM/index.html.

5. Leroy, Jacqueline, "Paris: Bibliothèque Nationale de France," in Melot, Michel, ed. *Nouvelles Alexandries* (Paris: Éditions du Cercle de la Librairie, 1997), p. 273 [excerpt translated from the French by JK].

6. The BFM program has changed, considerably and constantly, since it first was announced, and it still is changing: the number of books which in fact will make it to the new site is not the only figure subject to change — walls still are being re-thought, internal usage patterns re-configured. Numbers given here are taken from the latest (April 1997) sources available — primarily "Bibliothèque nationale de France — Tolbiac — 1996–1998 l'ouverture" (Paris: Bibliothèque nationale de France, [1996]) and *The Bibliothèque nationale de France into the twenty-first century* (Paris: Bibliothèque nationale de France, [1995?]), both brochures produced by the BNF itself, and the BNF website at http://www.bnf.fr which currently shows an updating date of April 10, 1997. Caveat lector, however: this is a project undergoing constant, as the French say, "mutation."

7. These last numbers are from Jacqueline Leroy — Note 5, above, page 282. Staffing at the BFM is a rarely addressed subject in the BNF literature. Mme. Leroy takes a much needed look at this in her article. She has been a librarian herself: perhaps only a librarian really can appreciate what it is going to take to run an enterprise like the BFM on a daily basis.

8. Declaration of the President of the Republic, July 14, 1988. [Translated from the French by JK. To those unaccustomed to the language of French Presidential declarations, that which appears here was not intended to be as grandiose as it sounds in translation. It perhaps is intended to sound more "final" than "grand." English speakers might think of the "Royal 'we,'" in Crown proclamations, and American speakers might remember that other French presidents of recent memory have made declarations far more "grand"-sounding than this one.]

9. Gattegno, Jean, *La Bibliothèque de France à mi-parcours: de la TGB à la BN bis?* (Paris: Éditions du Cercle de la Librairie, c1992). ISBN 2765405123.

10. Le Roy Ladurie, Emmanuel. *Coping with change: the experience of the Bibliotheque nationale (France).* [Paris: International Federation of Library Associations, 1989]. Series title: Proceedings (IFLA General Conference and Council Meeting 1989: Paris, France); 4.

11. The competition jury for the Bibliothèque François Mitterrand consisted of:

Name	Nation	Occupation
Annaud, Jean-Jacques	France	Filmmaker
Belmont, Joseph	France	Architect
Bouchez, Gilles	France	Architect
Chaslin, François	France	Architect
Fuksas, Massimiliano	Italy	Architect
Galfetti, Aurelio	Switzerland	Architect
Gregorian, Vartan	USA	President of Brown University (also former director of the New York Public Library, and largely responsible for having rescued that institution from severe difficulties)
Guimard, Paul	France	Writer
Jamet, Dominique	France	Writer
Larsen, Henning	Denmark	Architect
Orsenna, Erik	France	Writer
Pei, I. M.	USA	Architect (the Pyramid-foyer of the Louvre is Pei's)
Pelikan, Jiri	Italy	Publicist
Rogers, Richard	UK	Architect
Simounet, Roland	France	Architect
Soulages, Pierre	France	Artist
Verba, Sidney	USA	Professor and Director of the Harvard University Library

12. Leroy, Jacqueline, "Paris: Bibliothèque Nationale de France," in Melot, Michel, ed. *Nouvelles Alexandries* (Paris: Éditions du Cercle de la Librairie, 1997), p. 267 [excerpt translated from the French by JK].

13. Kessler, Jack, "The Bibliothèque de France at Berkeley," gopher://library.berkeley.edu: 72/11/ejrnls/FYIFrance, or, http://www.fyifrance.com/restricted/Fyarch/fy920414.htm; also, Bloch, Howard, ed., *Future libraries* (Berkeley: University of California Press, 1995) ISBN 0520088107, 0520088115.

14. http://www.bnf.fr/web-bnf/infopro/conserv/sites.htm#marne.

15. Several resources on offsite library storage: Boss, Richard W. *Information technologies and space planning for libraries and information centers* (Boston, Mass.: G.K. Hall, c1987), ISBN 0816118701, 0816118590. Steel, Virginia, *Remote storage, facilities, materials selection, and user services* (Washington, D.C.: Association of Research Libraries, Office of Management Services, Systems and Procedures Exchange Center, 1990). Department of Facilities Management, University of California, Berkeley, *Initial study, environmental assessment, Northern Regional Library Compact Shelving Facility, Richmond Field Station* ([Berkeley]: University of California, Systemwide Administration, [1980]).

16. Several resources on a remarkable facility in Britain which not only stores library information "offsite" but in several respects replaces library service "onsite" altogether: Houghton, B. (Bernard), *Out of the dinosaurs; the evolution of the National Lending Library for Science and Technology* ([Hamden, Conn.]: Linnet Books, [1972]). Series title: The Management of change: studies in the evolution of library systems 1. ISBN 0851571425. *National Lending Library for Science & Technology* (Boston Spa) (Yorks.: National Lending Library for Science & Technology, 1967). Watson, Peter G. *Great Britain's National Lending Library* (Los Angeles, University of California, School of Library Service, 1970).

17. *FYI France* ejournal, ISSN 1071-5916, issue of February 15, 1993, archived online at http://www.fyifrance.com/restricted/Fyarch/fy930215.htm: a translation of an article which appeared originally, in French, in *Le Nouvel Observateur*, n.1406, 17–23 Octobre 1991, an issue entitled, "No, Imaging Has Not Killed the Civilization of the Written Word: The Revenge of the Books."

18. Oddos, Jean-Paul, "Politique de préservation et de restauration à la Bibliothèque de France," in *Bulletin des Bibliothèques de France* t.36 n.4, 1991, p.317 ISSN 0006-2006.

19. Declaration of the President of the Republic, July 14, 1988.

20. Leroy, Jacqueline, "Paris: Bibliothèque Nationale de France," in Melot, Michel, ed. *Nouvelles Alexandries* (Paris: Éditions du Cercle de la Librairie, 1997), p. 282.

21. See note 16.

22. Kessler, Jack, "Limiter l'accès à Internet dans les bibliothèques: le modèle américain?" in *Bulletin des Bibliothèques de France* t.44, n.5 1999, pp.66–77. ISSN 0006-2006. Online at http://www.enssib.fr/Enssib/bbf/feuilleter.htm; and http://www.fyifrance.com/fy1275a.htm (in English).

23. Letter of Mission from the President of the Republic to the Prime Minister, August 1988, quoted in Cahart, Patrice, and Michel Melot. *Propositions pour une grande bibliothèque* (Paris: Documentation française, c1989). Series title: Collection des rapports officiels. ISBN 2110022264.

24. Connections to both "OPALE" and "OPALINE" may be made from the BNF W3 site, Internet address http://www.bnf.fr, or via telnet for "OPALE"—print resources—telnet://opale02.bnf.fr, login opale—as of January 1, 1997:

> 2,100,000 records, composed of:
> — all French and foreign books since 1970,
> — all French periodicals since 1974, — all foreign periodicals since 1965,
> — microforms records mounted by the Centre de Sable.
> OPALE grows by about 6,000 records per month.

for "OPALINE"—non-print resources—telnet://opaline02.bnf.fr, login opaline—as of April 15, 1997: record counts:

> 71,584   cartes et plans
> 52,019   estampes et photographie

266,740	audiovisuel
32,564	musique
3,664	monnaies, medailles et antiques
20,374	arts du spectacle

25. Kessler, Jack, *Internet Digital Libraries: The International Perspective* (Norwood, Mass.: Artech House, 1996). ISBN 0-89006-875-5; also the brave attempt by the International Federation of Library Associations, IFLA, to keep up with digital libraries growth online, as it develops, at Internet address http://www.nlc-bnc.ca/ifla/II/index.htm.

26. Network Wizards, http://www.nw.com/zone/WWW/report.html.

27. Gravier, Jean François, *Paris et le désert français; décentralisation, équipement, population* ([Paris]: Le Portulan, [1947]); see also Gravier, Jean François, *Paris et le désert français* (Paris, Flammarion [1958]).

28. City and regional planning is not the subject of this essay, but is offered only as an example of the possible long-range implications of the BNF's remarkable new "monument/information system" BFM building. The reader is referred generally to the classic works of Lewis Mumford, and to Mumford's many supporters and attackers — of great ability and aggressiveness on both sides — who together constructed much of the modern city and regional planning ethos, in Europe as well as in America. Mumford also was a great historian, and lays generous tribute and occasional blame on his European precursors in his work.

29. The discussion here of "sense of place" owes a great deal to Francis Violich, of the University of California at Berkeley: specifically to a recent extensive conversation about his own new ideas of "sense of place." The views on "sense of place" expressed here are not his but my own, however: for his please see his new book, *The Bridge to Dalmatia: A Search for the Meaning of Place* (Baltimore: Johns Hopkins, 1998). ISBN 0801855543.

30. Melot, Michel, ed. *Nouvelles Alexandries* (Paris: Éditions du Cercle de la Librairie, 1997), pp. 36–42.

A Selective and Partially Annotated Bibliography and Resource List

Because the Bibliothèque François Mitterrand (BFM) has been a project, completed over time — and because the antiquity of the old Bibliothèque Nationale (BN) has been emphasized in the text above as being among the most important and unique characteristics of the new Bibliothèque Nationale de France (BNF) — the resources suggested here are presented in chronological order, most recent first, rather than in any subject-oriented or alphabetical list. The serious history student is encouraged to explore the items on this list beginning at its end; those wishing merely to update information which they already have about the BNF and its BFM might want to begin at the list's beginning. Either way, there is far more omitted from this list than ever could be imagined, much less included here.

CURRENT AND FORTHCOMING RESOURCES

http://www.bnf.fr

This is the BNF's own World Wide Web (W3) site, which — to those who have access to W3 — undoubtedly offers the best resource available nowadays for current information, distance access to the cataloging and the collections, and glimpses of the great amount of work already under way in Paris to assemble the "digital libraries" of the future. The site also contains an excellent "point-and-click" tour of the new Bibliothèque François Mitterrand building at Tolbiac: "you feel as though you are there," almost.

biblio-fr@cru.fr

BIBLIO-FR is the French librarians' online electronic conference, and the best place to read and even engage in current ongoing debates about the BNF, the BFM, and other aspects of French librarianship. It is superbly moderated by Hervé Le Crosnier, and is a model of reasonableness and equanimity in an e-conference world populated largely by the opposites of both. These are librarians, so of course BIBLIO-FR is the ideal place to pose whatever burning questions you might have: everyone is happy to help, nearly always. On parle français, however: discussion is entirely in French. To join BIBLIO-FR, send an email message to listserv@cru.fr saying (only) SUBSCRIBE BIBLIO-FR <Yourfirstname> <Yourlastname>. The BIBLIO-FR archive — its most recent 500 messages, at any rate, can be consulted very conveniently, with very convenient search engine access, at http://www.cru.fr/listes/biblio-fr@cru.fr/ ("Recherche dans l'Archive).

Violich, Francis, *The Bridge to Dalmatia: A Search for the Meaning of Place* (Baltimore: Johns Hopkins, 1998). ISBN 0801855543.

This is a book which I have not read myself — it was not yet published as this essay was written — but I can highly recommend its author. Fran Violich is one of the distinguished senior members of the international city and regional planning community. His long career has given him experience with Latin America and Latin American planners, and the United States and U.S. planners, and he even has been up against quite a few of the more famous French in his field. His ideas about "Place," which he promises are developed in this book, are a significant part of the thesis which I present myself in the text.

1996

"Bibliothèque nationale de France — Tolbiac — 1996–1998 l'ouverture" (Paris: Bibliothèque nationale de France, [1996]). Pamphlet.

The latest printed publication actually produced by the BNF itself, replete with facts and figures. Beware of the latter, as they are severely subject to change, judging by my own previous experience with BNF facts and figures: construction politics — and economics — and library planning are matters of realpolitik. Nevertheless this is the "latest official word."

Melot, Michel, ed. *Nouvelles Alexandries: les grands chantiers de bibliothèques dans le monde* (Paris: 1996). ISBN 2765406197, ISSN 0184-0886.

Excellent architectural descriptions, in French, of 15 of the leading "grand library" construction projects taking place throughout the world — Alexandria, Copenhagen, London, New York, Beijing, San Francisco, etc. — including a very good piece on the Bibliothèque François Mitterrand by Jacqueline Leroy. The volume is particularly distinguished by an erudite article by Michel Melot, former conservateur of the BN's cabinet des estampes, first director of the Centre Pompidou's Publique d'Information, and former president of the Conseil Supérieur des Bibliothèques, asking several of the difficult questions, some of them unasked by those involved in projects, concerning the building of large buildings in an age of online digital information.

Kessler, Jack, *Internet Digital Libraries: The International Perspective* (Norwood, Mass.: Artech House, 1996). ISBN 0-89006-875-5.

If you would like to go further than France, there are "information system" libraries — like the characterization which I make in the text of the BFM — under construction in most parts of the world now. This book describes impressive projects under way in places like Budapest and Indonesia and Northern Thailand. Certain problems and questions common to all are discussed: I never dreamed when I wrote the book last year, though, that I might one day be suggesting a common interest in building library "monuments," as I have here — but things change.

1995

The Bibliothèque nationale de France into the twenty-first century (Paris: Bibliothèque nationale de France, [1995?]).

One of a number of glossy and actually very finely designed and presented promotional brochures on the BNF and the BFM project. As mentioned above, the facts and figures must be viewed skeptically: most now are of historical value only, as so much has changed so rapidly in the BFM's development. Nevertheless the glossy/promotional approach is impressive, and gives anyone interested a good beginning idea of the general dimensions of the BFM project.

Perrault, Dominique, Michel Jacques, and Gaelle Lauriot, *Bibliothèque nationale de France, 1989–1995* (Paris: Artemis, Arc en Rêve, centre d'architecture, 1995). ISBN 3764355905.

Recommended to anyone primarily interested in the architectural aspects of the BFM.

Kessler, Jack, "L'Information branches barricades: La France et les États Unis face au grand public," in *Bulletin des Bibliothes de France* (Lyon: ENSSIB/École Nationale des Sciences de l'Information et des Bibliothes, 1995) t.40, n.2, pp.54–63. Abstract in French, English and German, and full text in French, may be found online at http://www.univ-lyon1.fr//bases_de_donnees/ARTICLESBBF/kessler.html.

The problem of information access by the "general public": a central problem of the BFM's development debates, and the looming central issue — along with "international" users' access — of the Internet. The "information systems" which have been and will be said not to need homes such as the BFM.

Kessler, Jack, "The French Minitel: Is There Digital Life Outside of the 'US ASCII' Internet? — A Challenge, or Convergence?" in *D-LIB Magazine, the Magazine of the Digital Library Forum*, CNRI/Corporation for National Research Initiatives, ISSN 1082-9873, December 1995, http://www.dlib.org/dlib/december95/12kessler.html.

Analysis of a unique and early French approach to the problem of "general public" information access — the Minitel — an approach which the Internet in fact is beginning to take. Also, the entire question of who — which nation, which culture — will dominate "information" as it frees itself from location.

1994

"Sidebar 1: prototyping the library of the future; the Bibliothèque Nationale de France and GEAÇ" *Library Hi Tech* (ISSN 0737-8831) v.12, n.3, pp.10–11, 1994.

An interesting consideration of the highly successful inroads made by French-speaking GEAÇ Corp. in the BNF situation, by contrast to its several non–French speaking competitors, which did not get so far.

"Digitisation of the new Bibliothèque Nationale de France," *The Electronic Library* (ISSN 0264-0473) v.12, pp.301–3, October 1994.

The looming problem, so feared by Umberto Eco as cited in the text, of what to do about preserving information as the books disappear; also what "digitisation" really means — facts and figures — in a library context.

Kessler, Jack, "French Libraries Online — Electronic Hachette?" in *The Electronic Library*, v.12, n.2, April 1994, pp.79–87.

Online publication — by publishing firms themselves — and what this might mean for libraries, publishers, and readers, particularly in the French libraries' case: libraries as information systems.

Kessler, Jack, "The French Case: Networked Libraries, the Internet, and the Minitel," in *Libraries, Networks and Europe: A European Networking Study*, Library and Information Research Report 101 (London: The British Library, Research and Development Department, 1994).

Massuard, Alain, "L'Analyse des processus de travail à la Bibliothèque Nationale de France; une approche nouvelle des ressources humaines," *Bulletin d'Informations de l'Association des Bibliothécaires Français* (ISSN 0004-5365) n.162, pp.21–24, 1994.

Kessler, Jack, "The Bibliothèque Nationale de France project: access or expediency?" in *Journal of Librarianship and Information Science*, v.26, n.3, September 1994; reprinted in Maurice Line and Joyce Line (eds.), *National Libraries 3: a selection of articles on national libraries, 1986–1994* (London: ASLIB, 1995). ISBN 0851423426.
  Overview of the BNF/BFM project, posing the question of what happens when the money runs out — as it already had then — and suggesting, before Marne la Vallée was taken all that seriously, that the budget for "informatisation" might be sacrificed and that all that might happen would be the transfer of the books to Tolbiac.

Carranza, Marianne, "L'Accompagnement du système d'information de la Bibliothèque Nationale de France; la dimension humaine du changement informatique," *Bulletin d'Informations de l'Association des Bibliothécaires Français* n.162, pp.17–20, 1994. (ISSN 0004-5365)

1993

"Architecture: le style Mitterrand," in *Le Nouvel Observateur*, March 25–31, 1993, p.88.
  The Paris journalists were not kind to the former President about the BFM.

De Roux, Emmanuel, "Vaste querelle pour grande bibliothèque," in *Le Monde*, January 7, 1993, p.30.
  One journalist who has been — consistently — thorough, accurate, and relentless has been *Le Mondé*s Emmanuel De Roux.

Kessler, Jack, "Networked Information in France, 1993: The Internet's Future?" in *Internet Research*, v.4, n.1, Spring 1994, pp.18–30.

1992

Le Roy Ladurie, Emmanuel, "A Day in the Life of an Administrator of the Bibliothèque Nationale," notes from a speech delivered to a colloquium "La Très Grande Bibliothèque and the Future of the Library," UC Berkeley, April 12, 1992.
  This exists in ms. only but is a charming and highly recommended introduction both to the personality of Le Roy Ladurie, who is a preeminent French historian in addition to having been the administrator and thus chief shepherd of the BNF during the critical BFM development process. I would be happy to share the text which I have with anyone interested, although I would have to ask its author's permission: please contact me via email at kessler@well.sf.ca.us if you would like a photocopy.

"1992 — Bibliothèque de France — Les résolutions d'octobre — Les espaces de lecture et de recherche" (Paris: Bibliothèque de France, 1992).
    Glossy brochure showing several of the major changes made to the BFM as the initial development stages proceeded.

"La Bibliothèque de France: une bibliothèque pour le XXIe siècle" (Paris: Bibliothèque de France, 1992).
    A full-press package, containing an impressive array of materials displaying the original aspirations of the project's architect and proponents, hopefully still available from the BNF.

"1992, year of the foundation — Bibliothèque de France — A library for the XXIst century" (Paris: Bibliothèque de France, 1992).
    One of the original pro–BFM glossy brochures.

"Document — Bibliothèque de France: la folle histoire," in *L'Express*, December 31, 1992.
    One of the original anti–BFM Paris journalistic broadsides.

Grunberg, Gérald, "Organization of the Bibliothèque of France," notes from a speech delivered to a colloquium "La Très Grande Bibliothèque and the Future of the Library," UC Berkeley, April 12, 1992.
    Thoughtful observations on the management of such a large and revolutionary library undertaking, by one who was involved early in the process.

Gattegno, Jean, *La Bibliothèque de France à mi-parcours: de la TGB à la BN bis?* (Paris: Éditions du Cercle de la Librairie, c1992). ISBN 2765405123.
    Thoughtful observations on both the management and the difficulties of management of any BFM-like project.

"Bibliothèque de France — Mode d'emploi," "— L'Image et le son," "— Les Collections, le réseau," "— Les Nouvelles Technologies," "— Le Circuit des documents" (Paris: Bibliothèque de France, 1992).
    A very helpful and well-illustrated series of brochures on the BFM.

"La Lettre d'information" (Paris: Bibliothèque de France, Sept/Oct 1992). ISSN 1169-176X.
    Included here primarily for its value to anyone looking into the history of the development of the BNF and its BFM. I do not know when this BdF (the previous incarnation and name of the BNF) "La Lettre d'information" either began or ceased publication, but the several issues of it which I myself have were well-done and filled with information. This particular one contains a very interesting interview with then-director of the informatisation process, Alain Giffard.

1991

Biggs, Melissa, "The Very Big Library: Mitterrand Is Building by the Book," in *France Today* v.6, n.1, January 1991 ISSN *088-8663, since changed to ISSN 0895-3651.
    A good example of a well-done presentation of the project by a foreigner, to a foreign audience: there has been much foreign interest in this French national library project, as discussed in the text.

Oddos, Jean-Paul, "Politique de préservation et de restauration à la Bibliothèque de France," in *Bulletin des Bibliothèques de France* t.36, n.4, 1991, p.317. ISSN 0006-2006.
    An early take on the severely difficult — and rapidly increasing — preservation problem, which is building to a critical mass inside the BNF collections, as it is now in most paper materials libraries.

1990

Blasselle, Bruno, and Jacqueline Melet-Sanson, *La Bibliothèque nationale: mémoire de l'avenir* ([Paris]: Gallimard, c1990). Series title: Découvertes Gallimard. Histoire. ISBN 2070531112.

A fine, small book giving an excellent and concise BN history, projecting this smoothly into the future BNF which its authors hope will be realized. Jacqueline Melet-Sanson, a BN librarian, has been one of the principal leaders in the BFM project.

1989 AND EARLIER

Le Roy Ladurie, Emmanuel. *Coping with change: the experience of the Bibliothèque nationale (France).* [Paris: International Federation of Library Associations, 1989]. Series title: Proceedings (IFLA General Conference and Council Meeting 1989: Paris, France); 4.

An early version by Le Roy Ladurie of his adventures as BN administrator, perhaps to be read together with his 1992 presentation described above.

Cahart, Patrice, and Michel Melot. *Propositions pour une grande bibliothèque* (Paris: Documentation française, c1989). Series title: Collection des rapports officiels. ISBN 2110022264.

An important document: the original report ordered by President Mitterrand which analyzed the need for a new BN and laid the groundwork for what was to become both the BNF and the BFM.

Blasselle, Bruno, *La Bibliothèque nationale* (Paris: Presses universitaires de France, [1989]). Series title: Que sais-je?; 2496. ISBN 2130427227.

Readers totally unfamiliar with the French Bibliothèque Nationale would do well to begin here: a very well-written, small and manageable account of the history and general operation of the BN.

Balaye, Simone, *La Bibliothèque nationale, des origines à 1800* (Geneve: Droz, 1988) Series title: Histoire des idées et critique littéraire; v.262.

A larger and much more complete version of the simpler background view offered by Blasselle in the entry above. Balaye's book has become a classic in the history of cultural institutions.

Guide pratique de la Bibliothèque nationale (Paris: Bibliothèque nationale, c1987). ISBN 2717717528.

Previously for the BN user, and now perhaps for nostalgia and the historian: how librarianship was done just before the floodgates of "information systems" fully burst upon libraries.

13. *The Bibliothèque Nationale de France: A National Library for the 21st Century*

Daniel Renoult

Deputy Managing Director for Services and Networks
Bibliothèque Nationale de France

Translated by Jack Kessler, kessler@well.sf.ca.us

The *Bibliothèque Nationale de France* (BNF) was born in 1994, from the fusion of the former Bibliothèque Nationale and the Bibliothèque de France. It is a public entity, under the aegis of the Ministry of Culture. With over 37 million documents in its collections, the BNF is, by the size of its holdings alone, one of the five largest libraries in the world. It is accessible to the public at two main sites, both in Paris: one in the historic buildings (the *Richelieu* site), which contain the manuscripts, prints, maps and plans, music, money and medallions, and theater arts and cinema collections; the other in the new building at Tolbiac (the *François Mitterrand* site), to which the printed and audiovisual documents are being transferred.

Also attached to the Bibliothèque Nationale de France are the libraries of the Arsenal and the Opéra, as well as the theater arts library of Avignon. In addition to the restoration workshops at the Richelieu site, the BNF maintains three other sites devoted to the restoration, conservation and reproduction of documents, at Sablé, Provins, and Marne la Vallée. This last site has been in operation since 1996.

But the terms *Bibliothèque de France* and then *Bibliothèque Nationale de France* also designate an entry on the list of "Grand Projects" of the President of France, of equal standing with those of the "Grand Louvre" or the "Arche de la Défense." It was an architectural project which produced the *Bibliothèque François Mitterrand*. This essay describes this new building, its systems, its organization, and its architecture, which will be counted among the major architectural achievements of the 20th century.

One must not forget, however, that this construction project created only the visible part of a scientific project which, to conclude, we will describe in part. In all, the achievement of all of this will have consumed a full decade, from 1988 to 1998, and a budget of around 7.8 billion francs (about U.S. $1.5 billion).

The Paradox of Novelty

The launching of the Bibliothèque Nationale de France began with the announcement of a radical innovation. On July 14, 1988, during the traditional televised interview given by the President of the Republic on that national holiday, François Mitterrand made public his decision to create "a very big library, of an entirely new type." The term for "very big library," "Très Grande Bibliothèque"—or even more familiarly, "TGB"—would be, thenceforth for several years, the term commonly used to designate the project.

From August 1988 on, the basic idea of the new library was to be that pronounced in a letter addressed by the President of the Republic to the Prime Minister. This very big library was to: "cover all fields of knowledge, be available to all, use the most modern technologies available for the transmission of data, be accessible for distance consultation, and enter into relationships with other European libraries."[1]

All of these objectives together formed the character of the new library. With these objectives in mind, a study panel was formed consisting of two experts, Patrice Cahart, President of the Council of the Bibliothèque Nationale, and Michel Melot, Director of the Bibliothèque Publique d'Information (Centre Georges Pompidou) and former Director of the Département des Estampes at the Bibliothèque Nationale.

In four months they completed the study which would serve as the point of reference for the specifications proposed to the candidates in the 1989 architectural competition. Their report created an initial technical version of the President's basic idea, defined a general policy for all documents, and emphasized in passing the work which would have to be done to build a network including other libraries.

But in response to its political mandate the Cahart/Melot Report also stated a fundamental requirement: "the big library must become the new national library of France." Thus, to the notion of a major architectural project (a very big library), to the idea of encyclopedic and universal knowledge, to that of democratic access and shared knowledge, to the place accorded to new technologies and networked information, was joined the imperative of establishing continuity between the new project and the ancient Bibliothèque Royale.

At first glance, this relationship between the concept of a library "of an entirely new type" and the reality of an historical institution seems to be a contradiction.

The association of tradition and innovation, conservation and communication, represents however the paradox of any national library project today.

The task does appear to be complex. In the case of Paris, the new library must undertake the prolongation of an institution with origins stretching back at least to the 15th century. Its identity remains profoundly affected by an organizational scheme adopted in the 17th century: that is, the classification system for the collections, for the organization of departments and reading rooms according to types of documents (printed books, periodicals, prints, manuscripts, music, et cetera), to even the location in the city, near the old Palais Royal.

In addition, one must reconcile the new missions with the obligations of a national library, obligations amended continually by legislation: copyright deposit (established in 1537), the publication of the national bibliography (1811), the conservation of the national patrimony.

To the complexity of these various mandates, political constraints are added. Thus the President of the Republic imposed a completion schedule which was very short for a project of such magnitude: the new buildings were to be finished at the latest by the end of his presidency, in March 1995.

So the initial dream, progressively, had to confront the requirements of reality.[2]

One other element of complexity was the assignment of managerial responsibility for the project: from 1990 to 1993 this was the job of a public entity specially created for this situation,[3] the *Bibliothèque de France*, so that the Bibliothèque Nationale was simply associated with the project. From this point of view, the fusion of two institutions, foreseen by an official report in 1993[4] and achieved in 1994,[5] permitted — two years before the opening to the general public of the site at Tolbiac — an indispensable synthesis which gave better coherence to the project management.

In sum, the basic idea of the project and of its various innovations may be presented as follows: taking into account the three initial fundamental concepts (encyclopedic knowledge, democratic access, openness to new technologies), what extent and what contents must be given to the modernization and the development of the Bibliothèque Nationale?

To understand the project and its constraints and innovations, the elements of its context are of great value as well.

This context is first of all that of a complete saturation of the historic buildings of the Bibliothèque Nationale. These, installed since 1666 in Paris in the Palais Royal neighborhood, have been extended, bit by bit, to fill a quadrilateral bounded by the Rue Vivienne, the Rue Colbert, the Rue Richelieu, and the Rue des Petits Champs. Most of the 17th-century buildings which were not designed for this use had to be reconstructed, from 1859 to 1873, by the architect Henri Labrouste. With its grand glass vaulting and its elegant wrought-iron columns, the printed books reading room counts today, along with that of the Bibliothèque Sainte Geneviève, among the great architectural achievements of the 19th century.

Nevertheless, and in spite of regular additional extensions, such as the construction of the Annex buildings at Versailles (1934), or the installation of the

Département de la Musique in a new building (1964), or the relocation of bibliographic services to a renovated building across the Rue Vivienne (1985), the site of the Bibliothèque Nationale no longer was able both to house the collections and to serve its users. The exponential increase in publishing, the enlargement of copyright deposit to include audiovisual materials and then digital materials, exacerbated the other problems of conservation and the need for new storage space.

One other element of the context is well understood: the increase in the potential public for research libraries. As in a number of other European nations, France has seen an extraordinary increase in its university population, in two successive waves: the one during the 1960s, the other since the end of the 1980s. The number of students has increased from 155,800 in 1955 to two million in 1994. For historical reasons the Paris region, which today contains nearly 20 universities, holds nearly 38 percent of this student population. At the same time, research has increased considerably, and there are numerous laboratories and institutes in the Île de France.

This concentration of researchers, teachers and students has made it more and more difficult to find a sufficient number of places in the university libraries of Paris, the capacities of which have not increased much for 40 years, or at the Bibliothèque Nationale, where the number of places (around 760, including all of the reading rooms and counting the Annex at Versailles) has grown only a small amount. To obtain a reader's card or a pass at the Bibliothèque Nationale has become more and more difficult over the years.

All of these considerations call for the construction of a building of vast dimensions. But this is not simply a problem of size and space. The evolution of the techniques and media of information, and the development of the digitization of texts and images, make it necessary to reflect on the overall long-term strategy as well — on the means and the methods of the French Bibliothèque Nationale. As will be seen, in spite of many constraints, notably those of the calendar, an important place has been made for innovation and creativity, both in the architecture and in the technical side of the project.

The Architecture

The international architectural competition, which was launched in 1989, was "a contest of ideas." The program brief for the "Bibliothèque de France" given to the candidates by the public entity renewed the basic concepts of the project, as it traced several organizing elements and furnished the main technical specifications typical of library building programs.

In the documentation four primary structural points were defined: a news library, a library for film and sound, an open-access research library, and a closed-access research library. In addition to large spaces for the reading rooms, the program called for a conference center, commercial areas, and a children's library.

Defined only in general terms for the architects, the projected surface areas of the building were estimated to be between 140,000 and 167,000 square meters of usable space, of which 42,000 would be used for book stacks.

In its architecture, a major consideration of the project has been its contribution to the urbanism of its surrounding area. The construction of the library is the first act in the complete renovation of a sector of the capital which in 1988 contained only rail yards, warehouses, and dilapidated buildings, and which had become an industrial wasteland. The building site for the library (seven hectares) is located in the Tolbiac neighborhood (13th arrondissement), and the economic and cultural development of this urban renewal zone is the key to a re-balancing of Paris as a whole towards its east.

After an international call for candidates, twenty architects were selected by a jury presided over by I. M. Pei and Joseph Belmont, and four then were selected for a final round: Chaix & Morel, Jan Kaplicky, Dominique Perrault, and James Sterling. Without doubt because of its strength and its simplicity, the project of Dominique Perrault finally carried the day. As Peter Buchanan[6] and Richard Rogers[7] emphasize, Perrault's style is within the French tradition, being at once formal and monumental, and President Mitterrand doubtless chose the architecture which appeared to him to harmonize best with the grandeur and the tradition of Paris.

This architectural style asserts itself from the first as a project of urbanism, "a place, not just a building." This place is a new plaza for Paris along the banks of the Seine. "The greatest gift which it is possible to give to Paris today," wrote Dominique Perrault in his competition entry, "would be an offer of space, of emptiness: in a word, an open place, free, moving." The library is the first building of this new neighborhood, and its immense plaza will create a link uniting the different zones of the city.

Rejecting what it calls "the over-emphasis and the contortions of architecture," Perrault's plan presents a grand simplicity, recalling minimalist art in its use of repetitive structures. The plaza is the summit of a rectangular base, at the four corners of which stand four angular towers, "like four open books facing each other." The base is excavated to accommodate a garden at its center: a symbolic place, another gift of space in an overcrowded urban place. Inside the base, the project splits itself into increasingly specialized levels, proceeding from the plaza down to the research library.

Horizontally, the base is arranged in concentric spaces which deliberately are designed for change. "One could," wrote Dominique Perrault in the competition, "significantly increase the number of square meters proposed by adding peripheral spaces to the service plan, or reduce it by decreasing the use of the towers, or by closing one of the levels."

In the course of developing the project, this architectural flexibility has permitted — efficiently and happily — a continuous evolution in the site planning for the spaces, coinciding with the evolution of the overall project and the requirements of its master planning.

From the Plaza level, from which pedestrians enter, the major features of the new library immediately are apparent — the successful resolution of the debates and controversies which contributed to the extensive, and international, public discussion of the building's design. (Courtesy of Bibliothèque Nationale de France François Mitterrand, Dominique Perrault, Architect. Photograph by Alain Goustard.)

Architectural Techniques

The construction of a building of such great dimensions (in the final analysis 360,000 square meters of floor space) over a period of 36 months involved, for the architect, choices among industrial methods, such as the outsourcing of major structural elements. To achieve this, Dominique Perrault had to undertake a study of construction methods prior to the beginning of construction, and he had to contact fabricators to test the feasibility of certain techniques and to prepare prototypes. After a fashion, the aesthetics (the repetition of modular units) coincided with the technical choices and economics of this project in an unprecedented manner.

Nine different types of concrete were used, of which four were of high performance quality. In twenty-one months, 180,000 cubic meters of concrete were poured, of which 70,000 cubic meters were structural: that is, in situ, crude, without any possibility of resetting. Two thousand tons of concrete per day were poured at the high point of the project's construction activity, by 800 personnel using twenty giant construction cranes which had towers eighteen stories high. Once the foundations and the base were completed, the construction reached a pace of nearly two stories being completed every four days.

The symmetries of the building's design helped the development of standardized techniques and the partial use of prefabrication, notably for the floor slabs. One of the most spectacular achievements was the construction of the porticos of the walkway which circles the central garden: this "cloister" is formed by 122 porticos, each 15 meters high. Each portico is composed of two columns supporting a beam of 15 meters reach and 1.76 meters span. All the concrete structural columns were poured at the same time, to obtain a uniform appearance and to avoid the necessity of making later adjustments. The beams also were poured at one time, generally during the evening, with the forms being separated the following day thanks to the use of quick-drying cement. To help in the semi-automated construction of the beams, the Bouygues company developed a special pouring form, covered in polished metal, which was portable and could be moved by rail.

Even though the basics of the building's structure are composed of concrete, this material does not dominate visually. The architect did not allow it to appear except in precise areas, such as the columns of the porticos or the front walls of the four halls which provide access to the research areas, where it still most often is blended with materials in metal or wood. The taste of Dominique Perrault for "primary, basic, essential" materials, and his sense of the play of volumes and of light, have inclined him toward the choice of glass, of metal, and of wood.

The total surface area of the glass facade of the building is 67,500 square meters, of which 78 percent are contained in the towers. Glass is amply used in the curtain walls of the towers, and in one part of the structure's base. These curtain walls furnish a good example of the technical novelties which had to be created for the library. Innovation was applied equally to the quality of the material ("extra-clear" quality, made specially by the Saint Gobain firm), to that of the framework and the positioning, and even to the development of fire protection measures.

These curtain walls are composed of double-paned laminated panels (3.6 by 1.8 meters). The inside panel, 20 millimeters thick and fire-resistant, is mounted in stainless steel frames which are fixed to the same aluminum supports (12 or 16 mm.) used for the exterior panel. A space of 70 millimeters separates the two glass panels. This space is pressurized, to avoid any risk of condensation. The air is dehydrated and filtered before being injected. Pre-assembled in a workshop,[8] 8,400 panels thus were placed or mounted in their stainless steel frames within the concrete structure. The placement of the panels on the towers was made using a remote control device, specially made for the purpose,[9] which allowed the installation of forty panels per day.

The most remarkable technical aspect of this type of building, however, lies in its resistance to fire. Tests showed that a fire would take at least one hour to spread from one level to another. It is the first time that the panels of a glass facade have played such a fire prevention role in such a large building open to the general public.

On the exterior of the library, as in its interior — dressing it up or buried in its concrete — *metal* is omnipresent, whether as steel frameworks, stainless steel, or aluminum. Fifteen thousand tons of steel were used for the reinforced concrete structure. The floor slabs for the book stacks were reinforced to a strength of 350 kilograms per square meter; this was done for the eleven stories of book stacks in the towers, and in the mezzanine for the rare books Réserve, found in the structure's base. The structure of the building also called upon steel for the tubular shear supports (27.3 centimeters in diameter), placed diagonally between the floors of the towers, beginning at the ninth story.

The dominant visual element, matte-finish laminated stainless steel, is used in panels in numerous locations in the library, on the exterior as well as in the interior (walls and coffered ceilings of the entrance halls). But the most spectacular, and doubtless the most innovative, use of steel is its use in the form of metallic weavings, a sort of "coat of mail," serving as hangings (entry to the research library, entries to the auditoria) or as "veils" (false ceilings of the reading rooms). These weavings are made from stainless steel wires which have been interlaced, braided, woven, knitted, or knotted, in multiple design motifs. They can be found on the furnishings and equipment (air conditioning outlets on the research level, light stands in the reading rooms). Above all, used either on the exterior or in the interior, they add — to the rectangular volumes — suppleness, lightness, and clarity. In addition, if they are finely made they help with sound insulation. Most importantly, they decorate the large surfaces, filtering the light, and they take part in the graphic ambiance of the structure's overall design.

But this ambiance owes much as well to *wood*, both in the interior and on the exterior of the library. It is first of all in the central garden, around which the building seems to have been constructed, that the living wood asserts itself, thanks to the broadleaf trees and tall pines which have been planted there. On the esplanade, the trees dominate: the planks of Brazilian hardwood (*ipé verdadeiro*) have taken on an ashen tint which harmonizes with the glass and the metal. Inside the public spaces, the *doussié* (afzelia, a tropical hardwood) and the *padouk* (pterocarpus, a tropical hardwood) ornament the reading rooms and meeting rooms with their warm colors.

Technical Equipment — The Physical Plant

In the development of the building a special call for proposals was made for the different physical plant technical systems (electricity, heating/ventilation, air conditioning, security). Centralized technical management is provided by autonomous sub-systems linked by communication networks. Thanks to the presence of four servers and fourteen work stations, a large amount of equipment can be administered remotely: air conditioning, escalators and elevators, security, fire safety, cutting and restoring electric power, and so on.

Nearly all of the energy planned for the functioning of the library is electric, with the exception of heating supplied by the city heating system. This is a building containing over 300,000 square meters of power-supplied space, equipped with three power panels connected using four 20,000 volt cables. Each cable is capable on its own of supplying all of the electric power needed by the building. Backup power is available from two central locations at the site containing three power sources, each capable of producing 1000 kVA.

The Danto Rogeat Entreprise company was designated chief contractor for the project's heating, ventilation, air filtering, and air conditioning. With a capacity of 16 mw cold, the cooling unit installed in the basement of the building is the most powerful in Europe. Cold water is sent through a circuit supplying the 120 air treatment centers throughout the library. The centers for the book stacks are equipped with a very precise system for air filtering. The entire system is run by regulators which are digital and programmable.

The expected temperature in the book stacks is 18 degrees +/- one degree Celsius (64 degrees Fahrenheit). The humidity varies according to the nature of the collections being stored: 55% (+/- 5%) for books, and 45% (+/- 5%) for audiovisual materials. The subterranean storage areas are heated, as they have no contact with the outside air. The works in greatest demand are stored there, as these spaces are closest to the reading rooms. Fresh air there is supplied by one air treatment center per 12 storage units.

In the towers the book stacks are two per floor, or 88 in all. Completely shielded from light, these book stacks are encircled by a protective wall of plaster panels 10 centimeters thick, insulating materials 7 centimeters thick, and metal sections covered with a thin layer of wood. An insulating space 80 centimeters wide separates the wall panels and the double-paned glass windows of the exterior. This space can be ventilated in the case of any heat excess. The air conditioning of the book stacks is provided by units installed at the summits of the towers, which produce fresh, filtered, and decontaminated air. The ceiling height in the reading rooms (14 to 15 meters) made the use of air conditioning vents located in the ceilings ineffective and costly. So an air-replacement solution was chosen instead, using "air fountains" of stainless steel, two meters high and eight meters in diameter. Produced in such a "free-cooling" center, the air is circulated at a very gentle speed (½-meter per second), to keep the environment quiet for the readers: this is in preference to a blower system, which inevitably would have been noisy. This very economical system permits the regulation of users' comfort to a height of three to four meters, the "fountains" having been placed so as to cover each 120 square meters.

It should be noted, as well, that the library is equipped with an "automated document transport system" (TAD), used both for delivering work from the book stacks to the reading rooms and for the different stages in storing and preserving documents. The system serves the entire building, using 152 service points throughout the library and eight kilometers of rails: it is composed of 450 automated carts equipped with bins which hold the documents. Delivery time for a document from the stacks to the reading rooms is to be less than 20 minutes. Traffic management for the carts is administered by a computer sub-system which is integrated with the main information system of the library.

Furnishings

The harmony of colors and the marriage of the spaces irrevocably blend the architecture and the furnishings in the perception of the interior spaces of the library. In 1993, the Bibliothèque de France assigned to Dominique Perrault the work of interior design, meaning the development of an integrated design concept for the reception areas, cloakrooms, and reading rooms, and the lighting and furnishing of the offices and reading rooms.

The architect selected commercial furniture already available on the market for the office furnishings, and designed his own furniture for the reading rooms. After a Europe-wide call for proposals, and a competition, the largest contract — that for the office furnishings — was awarded to the Swiss firm, USM Haller. All of these furnishings are made and assembled at the factory, reducing the need for on-site assembly to a minimum. The elements of any typical work station of course are modular.

Individual light fixtures are the Lifto model of the Swiss Belux company. Lightweight, easily adjusted, and quickly installed on the corner of any table, they supply an ample amount of light throughout the workspace. Cushions, and some special chairs, come from the Tecno firm. The tables and chairs of the staff restaurant, finally, along with the easy chairs, come from the Danish maker, Fritz Hansen.

The original design furnishings are primarily for the reading rooms: reading tables, chairs, lamps, open-access shelving, but also information stations, reception areas, and corridors. The firms involved competed in a call for proposals which associated the Perrault studio with the makers. The technical and functional specifications were developed from preliminary work undertaken by the architect. To harmonize with the flooring and the wall murals, the wood furnishings (reading tables, shelving, information stations) are in *doussié* wood (afzelia, a tropical hardwood).[10] Only the fixed table lamps are metal (aluminum with a cast base).

The reading tables are conceived as monolithic blocks in the shape of a "T." Most of the tables are juxtaposed in two rows. Their central upright is attached to the flooring, to provide for the "intelligence" of the table: high-power electric current, low-power current, fiber optics, a system for document delivery to the user's seat, and computer use (a unit built in to the footing of the table). This upright is connected to a cable channel in the center of the room, thus allowing some flexibility in the arrangement of reading places, and the eventual addition of other equipment for the readers.

Lamps generally are designed to light two seats. The lamp chosen is a sort of miniature stadium projector. It was developed with the Philips company, following strict standards for illumination and comfort: 750 lumens, using an optical fiber system, spread evenly to cover two readers' places.

Two 50-watt halogen bulbs are lit using low-tension current. Ultraviolet and infra-red rays (heat carriers) are filtered, to protect documents which might be in use. This type of fiber optic lamp already exists in industry, but this is the first time that it has been manufactured to operate in a series and not just as a stand-alone unit.

The open-access book shelving integrates illumination with signage. Different types of structure were designed at the request of the librarians: simple shelves for monographs, shelves equipped with slide-out tables for taking notes, cases for periodicals.

For chairs and other readers' seats, research was undertaken by the architect and the maker (Martin Stöll) for both the technology and the ergonomics involved. The seat is a leaf of *doussié* wood, separated from the body of the chair by a metallic piece. Finally, among the furnishings designed specifically for the project, some mention should be made of Richard Peduzzi's design of the furniture for the administrative council's meeting room, and the offices of the president and of the general administration.

Functional Analysis of the Spaces

Compared to the 1989 project, the functional program has evolved significantly. Before looking at this evolution, and the choices which it has entailed, it is necessary to present the final spatial arrangement and the function of those spaces.

It will be recalled that, viewed in cross-section, the new building at Tolbiac may be seen as three superimposed levels. For each of these levels there is a corresponding purpose and usage which are clearly defined.

1) Dominating the Seine for a length of 380 meters, the *esplanade level* is a plaza, occupying three hectares (equivalent to half the size of the Place de la Concorde). This public plaza, which links the different zones of the surrounding

urban neighborhood, provides access to the library via two escalators, one on the west and the other on the east of the plaza.

2) The *upper garden level* is the level intended for the general public.

It includes first of all the entrance halls (one in the west and the other in the east), then two exhibition halls (800 and 400 square meters), six small meeting rooms for fifty people each, two auditoria (for 350 and 200 people), and nine reading rooms, each oriented toward a different subject theme and two of which are on the mezzanine.

Intended primarily for study, these reading rooms offer a total capacity of 1,600 seats, and an encyclopedic and multimedia open-access collection which eventually will contain 320,000 volumes. Open to the public since December 1996, they are accessible from Tuesday through Sunday, to anyone 18 years or older or holding a baccalaureate degree. There is a charge for access: users have a choice between paying a daily fee of 20 francs (about U.S. $3.50) or an annual fee of 200 francs (about U.S. $35). Half-price tickets are available for students.

In addition to cultural services, this level also offers the conveniences of a restaurant and a bookstore.

3) *At the garden level,* one finds the areas reserved for research. Designed to be open six days out of seven (from Monday through Saturday), it includes twelve reading rooms as well as study carrels on the mezzanine. Opening in 1998, this level, with its 2,100 seats of which 1,800 may be reserved, eventually will offer more than 400,000 volumes in open access. It is only in these spaces that the patrimonial collections will be available, that is, 10 million printed volumes, about 350,000 periodicals titles, and one million sound recordings.

This level will only be accessible through payment of a daily fee of 30 francs (about U.S. $5) or of an annual fee of 300 francs (about U.S. $50), payable at the desks positioned in front of the access halls at the upper garden level.

Throughout the building, the vertical structure of the 21 reading rooms is determined by *the general thematic groupings* of *the departments.* Thus one finds, from top to bottom, the following departments:

D1: Department of philosophy, history, and the sciences of humankind and of society;
D2: Department of law, economics, and political science;
D3: Department of science and technology;
D4: Department of the arts and literature;
D5: Audiovisual department.

Each level likewise offers reference services. But the general public and research levels also have their own unique features: a newspaper room at the upper garden level, the Réserve for rare books at the lower garden level. In addition, at the research level, the audiovisual department will accommodate a part of the services and collections of the Institut National de l'Audiovisuel (INA), which in France is charged with preserving radio and television archives.

The ease of working in the library is reinforced by the simple structure of the

The lower-level "research" rooms — reserved for scholars from all over the world, who enjoy the wonderful light and the beautiful garden to look out upon. (Courtesy of Bibliothèque Nationale de France François Mitterrand, Dominique Perrault, Architect. Photograph by Alain Goustard.)

circulation patterns provided within the building. Proceeding from the center to the periphery, the architecture organizes concentric patterns centering on the garden:

— corridors which give access to the different spaces (around the garden);
— public rooms (exhibitions, auditoria, restaurant, reading rooms);
— professional spaces, for book shelving work (50 percent of the shelving capacity will be located in the base), for offices and for conservation services;
— a technical workshop serving all of the installations of the library.

Within their 76-meter height, the towers are divided into 18 identical levels. The first seven levels house one part of the offices of the library. The following 11 levels house book stacks. The only exception to this symmetry is the presence on one of the towers of a terrace used for meetings.

At once a collection of books and a center for searching, retrieving and using information in all its forms, the BFM provides technology as a means to an end: This is one place, in central Paris, where readers can obtain information nearly regardless of, as the French say, its "support"— whether the information is "digital" or "non-," a reader now may find it at the new BFM. (Courtesy of Bibliothèque Nationale de France François Mitterrand, Dominique Perrault, Architect. Photograph by Alain Goustard.)

The Evolution of the Initial Program

Compared to the initial proposals, what have been the most significant changes in the project?

The first and one of the most important changes has been the increase in the space to be used for book stacks. Initially the project foresaw only the transfer of collections of printed works which have appeared since 1945, about three million volumes. When this split in the collections — proposed by the Cahart/Melot Report — was hotly contested, notably by the university community, backed up by the press, a decision finally was made to move the entire print collection, or 10 million volumes. The architect therefore revised his plans, from 1990 on, to design book stacks in the building's base.

The second notable evolution concerned the design of the public spaces.

The great prize of the architecture that surrounds and presents the BFM's information resources to readers is its garden. Architect Dominique Perrault filled the vistas of the library's great glass courtyard walls with light filtered gently through leaves and branches. Few settings are more congenial to reading and thought. (Courtesy of Bibliothèque Nationale de France François Mitterrand, Dominique Perrault, Architect. Photograph by Alain Goustard.)

Thus in 1989, as described earlier here, the original project specifications anticipated spaces for conferences and exhibitions, and four large libraries (news,
study, images and sound, research), combined in a single continuous space, following a model largely inspired by the French "bibliothèques municipales."

The final specifications called for, on the contrary, the option of having dis-
continuous spaces, firmly separating the upper from the lower garden, that is, the
"general public" zone from the space reserved to accredited researchers. It gave
a larger place to multimedia usage, and it proposed a more homogeneous overall conception for the library. A national library, it would organize its offering
around two complementary poles: a study library, largely open to the public, on
one level; a research library on a second level.

The choice of a thematic organization for the reading rooms also constituted
one of the major choices determining the course of the project. It must be emphasized that the classification of reading rooms by disciplines marked a departure
from the tradition of the Bibliothèque Nationale (departments classified by types
of documents). This classification by themes ensured the scientific coherence of
the upper and lower garden levels. It also appeared to be more suitable than the
organization scheme proposed in the original specifications.

Whether one speaks of conservation areas or public spaces, these modifications resulted directly from the balance sought between the initial program
and the challenges of maintaining the collections and the functions of a national
library.

All of these questions of course were at the center of the vigorous polemics
which rocked the universities and the press, notably between 1989 and 1993,
whether one thinks of the juxtaposition of two audiences ("cultural fortress or
cultural supermarket?"), or of the storage of books in the towers and the resulting preservation problems ("solar ovens shaped like open books," "Bradburyan
book-burners," wrote Marc Fumaroli), or the duality of the two organizations
(Bibliothèque Nationale and Bibliothèque de France).

These polemics have been resolved. The January 1994 fusion of the two organizations into one, the Bibliothèque Nationale de France, the combination of the
two teams, the adoption of a design clearly separating on the one hand a group
of cultural services accessible to the general public, and on the other the patrimonial collection available only to researchers, today generally is agreed.

All of these measures allowed the resolution of the initial contradictions
without compromising the fundamental ideas of the project, all while using a
unique project management approach. Responsible for both ongoing library
operations and the construction project, the Bibliothèque Nationale de France
put an organization into place, a unit for following the general planning work,
to consolidate project management for computerization and information and to
develop a scenario for opening the library in two grand phases: the upper garden at the end of 1996, the lower garden in 1998.

One will note in passing that the essence of the controversies often was the
architecture and the development plan; or at least the rest — the technical program,
that is — received less attention. They include, however, fundamental aspects of

the project. A library, and certainly a new 21st-century library, has to define itself as much by its services as by its architecture.

Technical Programs and Services Rendered

Without entering into the utopia of a "push-button" library, for which the entire collection would be accessible in real time on the networks, the Bibliothèque Nationale de France has put into place six grand technical programs which realize the initial ambitions of the project for its services:

1) The various catalogs will be combined into a single one. This union catalog of all of the printed and audiovisual works will include eight million bibliographic records. As a precondition of this undertaking, a retrospective conversion of older records has taken five years of work: it is one of the grand technical tasks of the project. It will permit access to a catalog describing all of the public documents in France, from the beginning to our day. Readers will be able to search the entire print and audiovisual collection of the Bibliothèque de France by author, by subject, by title, and by numerous other access criteria. They will have a work tool of unprecedented power, which will offer them a great wealth of functionality (navigation, sorting of results, downloading, and so on).

2) The Bibliothèque Nationale de France is in the process of installing a fully integrated information system. Through the Cap Gemini corporation for software integration, and through a consortium headed by the Bull corporation for the hardware, the new information system will assemble all of the different applications used by the library:

- a) resource management: accounting, personnel, office systems, meetings and exhibitions;
- b) physical plant management: storage, conservation, building and equipment;
- c) internal bibliographic services: receiving (copyright deposit, acquisitions, gifts, exchanges), cataloging, digitization;
- d) public services: ticket sales, readers' check-in and accreditation, access control, general information services, interlibrary lending and document delivery, long-distance document consultation.

The new system will include 3000 client-server work stations, with 14 central servers and 47 routers, and is planned for introduction in three successive versions, from 1998 through 1999.

Among the services provided to the readers are the long-distance reservation of readers' seats and documents, catalog consultation integrated with document paging, direct access to digitized collections, and even a very good possibility of using the reader's own personal computer to access the system.

3) A program for the modernization and extension of the conservation workshops is associated with the creation, within the Paris region (at Marne la Vallée),

of a new center for the treatment of the collections. On a space of 13,000 square meters, this will include vast storage spaces for the conservation of a "security collection," a specialized technical laboratory, and new workshops for restoration, photography, and treatment of audiovisual documents. As a project for cooperative research with French firms,[11] the implementation of new techniques for mass deacidification is planned, with an objective of treating 300,000 documents per year. At the same time, in a joint project with the *Deutsche Bibliothek*, the introduction of paper-splitting techniques is anticipated.

4) A vast digitized collection is in the process of being assembled. Composed primarily of patrimonial documents, it will include 100,000 works, 300,000 images, and the equivalent of 1000 hours of sound recordings. The personal computer work stations spread throughout the library for catalog consultation, CD ROM networks, and high performance work stations all will provide access to these digitized collections. Equipped with a very complete collection of software, the "postes de lecteur assistée par ordinateurs/PLAO" work stations will permit complex work with text and images.

5) Founded on the complementarity of the collections, a program of scientific partnership with other libraries in France (the *pôles associés*) permits the realization of a true network concept. Forty cooperation agreements have been signed with cities and universities; others are being prepared. At the same time, international cooperation is being reinforced with other great libraries around the world.

6) Finally, the *Catalogue Collectif de France*, the union catalog of libraries in France, ought to permit the 1998 achievement of a digitized network of about 5000 libraries, then in 1999 the identification of 13 million documents spread throughout the country and held in *bibliothèques municipales* or in university libraries.

But without detracting from the promise of all of these projects, the Bibliothèque Nationale de France already offers long-distance services today: book and seat reservations via Minitel, Web[12] access to the catalogs, a "visite virtuelle" to the new building, and "virtual" exhibitions on the Internet ("1000 Enluminures," the exhibition "Creating French Culture" mounted in cooperation with the Library of Congress, the exhibition "Tous les Savoirs du Monde"). The library also offers a range of digital products (databases online or on CD ROM, CD Photos associated with exhibitions) which complement a series of printed products.

A Project in Process

The achievement of the technical programs associated with the launch of the new library at Tolbiac is not yet completed, yet already the historic location on the Rue de Richelieu is being redefined. Thus after the 1998 move of the print and audiovisual collections, the specialized collections (theater arts and cinema, manuscripts, prints, music, maps and drawings, money and medallions) will be installed in better conditions. A National Institute for History and Art, permitting a centralization of different research services, will be created in conjunction

The site of the BFM — "four open books and a garden." (Courtesy of Bibliothèque Nationale de France François Mitterrand, Dominique Perrault, Architect. Photograph by Alain Goustard.)

with various universities and museums. Certain specialized libraries will move into the renovated location. One among these, the Bibliothèque d'Art et d'Archéologie, founded by Jacques Doucet, already has been installed there since 1993.

With the completion of the building at Tolbiac in March 1995, then the opening to the general public in December 1996, several important steps have been achieved. The next step is the opening to researchers of the lower garden level, planned for 1998. Without any doubt the public will be the best judge of the level of innovation and the services of the Bibliothèque Nationale de France. Its degree of novelty, and its offering of services, will be appreciated by the public most in their national context. The opening to the general public, the development of scientific and technical collections, the access to audiovisual collections until now not readily available, all will radically change the accommodation of the reader and most probably the overall image of the Bibliothèque Nationale in the eyes of the French.

From the point of view of the researchers, the innovation is even greater in its international context. The access from outside the library to its databases, the furnishing of digital documents, and also the increase in foreign acquisitions, all will count among the criteria of appreciation.

Of course it will remain to the Bibliothèque Nationale de France to achieve real success in this growth. These numerous projects translate themselves in all areas into a change of scale, one which will demand significant means to achieve them. As one example of an effort on the giant scale of the project, nearly 1000 new employees have been hired since the beginning of the work, and for operations a budget of more than one billion francs (about U.S. $1.8 million) will be necessary every year. In this period of strong economic tensions, and of reductions in public spending, these questions logically are being much discussed. After a decade of construction and of the mounting of projects, the next decade ought to be one of management, of operations, and of organization.

In December 1996, the opening exhibition, entitled *Tous les Savoirs du Monde: encyclopédies et bibliothèques*—"All of the Knowledge in the World: encyclopedias and libraries"—filled the need for a demonstration to be made to French and foreign researchers. The objective for the Bibliothèque Nationale de France for the 21st century is in fact to assemble the sources of knowledge, whatever their "media" might be, to organize them, and to encourage their use by enlarging them and providing long-distance access to them, all with the aid of electronic and digital techniques.

In this manner the Bibliothèque Nationale de France renews itself, not only with encyclopedism but also with the spirit of the Encyclopedists of the 18th century, subscribing to a long cultural tradition in its "European" dimension.

Begun under the sign of a division, the Bibliothèque Nationale de France is pursuing on the contrary a continuity, which is a Bibliothèque Nationale transformed.

References

1. Letter of François Mitterrand, President of the Republic, to Michel Rocard, Prime Minister, August 1989.

2. Cf. Serge Goldberg. "Beginnings Remembered," in *Bibliothèque Nationale de France 1989–1995: Dominique Perrault, architecte*, p. 40. Serge Goldberg was the first director general of the Bibliothèque de France.

3. "Décret No. 89-777 du 13 octobre 1989 portant création de l'établissement public de la Bibliothèque nationale de France," *Journal officiel de la République française*, 24 octobre, 1989, pp. 317–318.

4. "Rapport du groupe de travail sur la mise en service de la Bibliothèque de France à Tolbiac, présidé par M. Philippe Bélaval, ..., remis le 30 juin 1993 à M. Jacques Toubon, ministre de la culture et de la francophonie."

5. "Décret No. 94-3 du 3 janvier 1994 portant création de la Bibliothèque nationale de France," *Journal officiel de la République française*, 4 janvier 1994, pp. 149–152.

6. Peter Buchanan. "Place and Projection," in *Bibliothèque nationale de France 1989–1995, op. cit.*, pp. 28–31.

7. Richard Rogers. Interview, in: *Bibliothèque nationale de France 1989–1995, op. cit.*, p. 42.

8. Société Rinaldi at Colmar.

9. Pal-Héli, designed by Rinaldi Structal.
10. Designed by a group of companies, Dennery/Bel/Champs.
11. Société SEPAREX (Nancy).
12. www.bnf.fr

Bibliography

Numerous articles have appeared about the Bibliothèque Nationale de France, most of them in French. Considering the many changes which have taken place in the project, up to 1996, a large part of this literature today is out of date or incomplete. We therefore propose a selection of the most recent or the most comprehensive documents, with several titles in English. Many of these references contain more complete bibliographies which will permit researchers to go further if they wish to.

Bibliothèque Nationale de France, 1989–1995: Dominique Perrault, architecte. Zurich: Artemis/ Arc en Rêve, Centre d'architecture, 1995. (Photographs, and text both in English and in French; printed on the occasion of the opening in 1995.)

The Bibliothèque Nationale de France into the Twenty-First Century. Paris: BNF, 1996. (Published by the library, an illustrated booklet in English introducing the history, collections, and main features of the BNF.)

Bibliothèque Nationale de France. Premiers Volumes. Paris: Institut Français d'Architecture: Éditions Carte Segrete, 1989. (Documents and pictures of the leading entries, published on the occasion of the architectural competition.)

Blasselle, Bruno. *La Bibliothèque Nationale.* 2ème éd. Paris: Presses Universitaires de France, 1989. (Que sais-je?)

_____, et Melet-Sanson, Jacqueline. *La Bibliothèque Nationale, Mémoire de l'Avenir.* 2ème éd. Paris: Gallimard, 1996.

Cahart, P. Melot, M. *Propositions pour une Grande Bibliothèque: Rapport au Premier Ministre.* Paris: La Documentation Française, 1989. (The first report, ordered by the President of France, which set the main guidelines for the project.)

Gattégno, Jean. *La Bibliothèque de France à mi-parcours: de la TGB à la BN bis?* Paris: Édition du Cercle de la Librairie, 1992. (The story of the project from 1988 to 1992, by the former technical director of the Bibliothèque de France, who also was responsible for national book policy in France during the 1980s.)

Grundberg, Gérald et Ygouf, Yann. "L'Offre audiovisuelle de la Bibliothèque Nationale de France," *Bulletin des Bibliothèques de France,* 1997, 3, pp. 8–15.

Leroy, Jacqueline. "Paris, Bibliothèque de France," in *Nouvelles Alexandries,* ed. Michel Melot. Paris: le Cercle de la Librairie, 1996. (Latest published summary of the Tolbiac project.)

Perrault, Dominique. "Bibliothèque Nationale de France 1989–1995," *Architecture d'Aujour-d'hui,* September 1995.

Renoult, Daniel. "The Digitizing Program of the French National Library," Proceedings of the International Symposium on Digital Libraries. *Journal of Processing and Management,* vol. 38, no. 11, February 1996, pp. 981–996.

_____. "L'Informatique au Service du Public: de la Bibliothèque Nationale à la Bibliothèque de France," *Bulletin d'informations de l'Association des Bibliothécaires Français,* no. 174, 1er trimestre 1997, pp. 85–90. (A brief history of information systems in the BNF, from the early 1980s to 1996, with a description of the new system.)

Conclusion:
Rational Space

In his effort to explain the existence of the masterpieces of art and invention that have been precursors to new movements and industries, Kubler identifies what he calls "prime objects":

> Prime objects and replications denote principle inventions, and the entire system of replicas, reproductions, copies, reductions, transfers, and derivations, floating in the wake of an important work of art. The replica-mass resembles certain habits of popular speech, as when a phrase spoken upon the stage or in a film, and repeated in millions of utterances, becomes a part of the language of a generation and finally a dated cliché [39].

Kubler observes that a prime object may differ from the standard only in a certain trait, the way a biological mutation might differ from its species only by the presence of a mere gene. In the case of a prime object, however, as with a genetic mutation, the slight difference may be highly consequential: "The mutant gene may be infinitesimally small but the behavioral differences which it occasions can be very great indeed" (40).

> Our interest therefore centers upon minute portions of things rather than upon the whole mosaic of traits that constitutes any object. The effect of the mutant fraction, or prime trait, is dynamic in provoking change while that of the whole object is simply exemplary, exciting feelings of approval or dislike more than any active study of new possibilities [40–41].

Then Kubler makes a salient observation: "The precursor shapes a new civilization; the rebel defines the edges of a disintegrating one" (91).

Are the new libraries in these chapters "precursors" or "rebels"? Is any one of them a new prime object that other libraries will emulate in future decades? Or are they all heralds of disintegrating librarianship? Every design team in this book wanted to build a different kind of library in some way. Not just bigger, grander, more efficient or somehow better, but a different species of library. The form of these libraries has remained basically the same because their function has remained the same, just the way the functions of art remain the same across stylistic changes. The libraries in this book are, however, different in content and scope from their predecessors. Is that difference enough to constitute a successful adaptation to what promises to be a new type of civilization, an information-based society? Or is it a final thunderclap in a sequence of replications of an earlier prime object — a library — now turning to cliché?

Libraries have in fact changed greatly since the Carnegie libraries. And people are learning to see libraries as flexible, changing institutions; not altering their missions, but adding to them by providing new services and exploiting new technologies. As Buckland said, "Any significant change in the technology of text-bearing objects or of handling them could have very profound consequences, not on the purpose and mission of library services, but on the means for achieving them" (72).

The Technological Challenge

The chapters clearly indicate that much more is involved in predicting the future of libraries than simply answering the questions, "Will technology make libraries unnecessary or obsolete?" and "What effect will technology have on library design?" While the new technology is certainly having a major impact on the way we think about libraries, the building of a new library involves many other issues, such as a sense of place, partnering, funding, flexibility, mission, and others, some of them quite specific to a certain library or a particular site. The authors of the chapters in this book talk about much more than the Internet and the World Wide Web.

Information technology is still only communication — the transfer of precise and specific messages. Nor has the process of gathering knowledge and information changed: answers are requested and delivered, which the information seeker must then fashion into findings, conclusions, learning, and wisdom. Information technology does not replace face-to-face instruction or counseling; it merely facilitates these human interactions.

Contrary to what some people are saying in their praise of the new technology, time and space have not disappeared. Even many librarians think that information technology is a substitute for place, that is, a substitute for space. Instead, it is a substitute only for document delivery. As Gross and Borgman observe, "Cyberspace is just another name for interlibrary loan" (902). Time and space do not disappear. That's an absurd notion, an illusion. Nor do such things disappear as gender, ethnicity, age, and other individual characteristics that contribute to the formation of our thoughts, personalities, communication patterns, and personal identities, no matter what computer manufacturers might otherwise suggest in their advertisements. Online "communities" are not real communities; they are only new extensions of real communities, uni-dimensional layers more like the illusory community of reading books and watching movies than the real thing. That they will affect our lives and thoughts is indisputable, like any other form of media. But people will not be hermitized by their computers and the informatization of all text, should it ever actually be realized. For most people, productivity and creativity will still thrive on mobility of the geographical variety and face-to-face interaction.

The Sense of Place

Despite the construction of several major new U.S. public libraries, and major new ones abroad as well, and an even larger batch of major academic library building projects here and abroad (Wiley, 110; Michalak, 95), Neal says library construction will decrease sharply (76).

In fact, just the opposite may occur, as the contributors to this book seem to be telling us. Information technology and spectacular new buildings have centered libraries more in the public spotlight now than ever before, and that's right where we have always wanted to be so we can celebrate and enlarge our effectiveness. That's the lesson of San Antonio Public Library and of others in this study. But having a place in the spotlight is also a very conspicuous position. That's the lesson from San Francisco.

Even the Leavey Library at USC, one of the more digital libraries in the United States, is still very much a place. Calling it a "'think tank' for new modes of teaching," Commings states, "Packed with modern electronics, *it's a place* where faculty and librarians will teach students how to navigate both the traditional world of print and the burgeoning world of digital information" (18; emphasis added). Chris Ferguson, head of the Leavey, agrees: "It will be an intellectual *center—a place* where students and teachers will come to exchange ideas — and I very much want the Leavey to be *a center for social life as well*" (quoted in Commings, 19; emphasis added). The Shanghai Library, the GMU library, even the BNF, and others share the vision of their new facilities as information agorae, the new Academies. Michalak concurs: "Collaborative study and research will also find a place within the library and will be dependent, at least to some degree, on library information services to facilitate that process" (99).

There will also be a continuing importance of the library as a place not only for its users, and not only for a sense of society, but for librarians. To continue doing what they now do, such as reference consultation, instruction, collection development, and to do what they will start doing soon, librarians need a space where they can work and consult with their associates and users freely and in real, face-to-face time. According to Neal, the new library processes will include retrospective digitization of the type being undertaken in Shanghai and Paris:

> The retrospective digitizing of library collections, particularly unique
> materials, will evolve as a central activity in academic libraries. Newly
> formed digital knowledge centers will manage the operations and partner
> with academic departments, publishers, and other libraries [Neal, 75].

Other tasks will include making customized collections and databases, electronic publishing, preserving information and knowledge, and acting as organizers of information published by other authors and agencies:

> In the new information environment, the academic library will continue to be responsible for the preservation of recorded information; the organization of information to enable effective retrieval; and equal opportunity for access to information [Neal, 76].

These tasks will require places in which to do the work.

Neal, Michalak, and Commings are talking about academic libraries, but the same can be true for public libraries as well. The Benton study on public libraries found that 65 percent of a general public sample believed that maintaining and building public library facilities was *very* important, and another 25 percent responded that it was moderately important, for a total of 90 percent. And 70 percent of the Benton study respondents felt that providing space for community groups and public activities was very or moderately important, a high total for an activity that is not even among the major activities of many public libraries (*Buildings*, 27).

For a number of libraries in this study, however, it is a major function. For instance, the Shanghai Library was specifically designed as a venue for many different types of public gatherings. And the popularity of the San Antonio Public Library was so overwhelming that an events coordinator position was created to handle the demand. Commenting on the public perception of the library as an important community icon, the Benton report stated, "Libraries may be drawing on decades of good will when the public displays such unequivocal support for their continuing service to communities — even with the advent of the digital age" (*Buildings*, 21).

The Benton study reports that "libraries are definitely not off Americans' radar screen and in fact are enjoying considerable public esteem," and points to the "library building boom" in the nation's big cities as evidence of this (*Buildings*, 15). Playing the cautious role, however, Estabrook and St. Lifer and Rogers ("Benton") focus on the downside of the Benton report, which also found that the public by and large, 1) does not appreciate the training and abilities of librarians, 2) tends to exclude public libraries from their vision of the digital age, and 3) may frequent libraries less as more electronic information becomes available from personal computers at home.

Yet even these cautious analysts give in to optimism and see the opportunity that surprisingly strong public sentiment presently affords libraries and the library profession. According to Estabrook, librarians "need to develop new services but ones shaped to the traditional roles the public values," and adds that such services will not require libraries

> to change radically ... or to become something new. Instead, they allow libraries to build on historic strengths, to use new information technologies to become more relevant to their communities and to extend their influence [48].

Partnering

The consensus among U.S. library leaders seems to be that libraries need to cooperate and collaborate with outside groups, agencies, and even companies to strengthen their position in the community and in society. The library leaders involved in the Benton study, for instance, formulated a visionary strategy that proposes "new life forms,"

> in which libraries team with other public service information providers to form community education and information networks open and available to all. With some communities already experimenting with collaborations and cyberspace creating myriad cyber-communities for information exchange of all kinds, libraries should create broad-based, real-time networks with public service partners that can facilitate this exchange of information [*Buildings*, 38–39].

Resembling very much Kubler's descriptions of genetic mutations and prime objects, these new life forms would "tackle the community's needs and problems" by weaving "a network of community public service information providers to enhance each other's value and their combined value to the communities they serve" (*Buildings*, 39, 40).

Networking with public service agencies to construct "a seamless web of community information" (*Buildings*, 39) is certainly an important and worthy goal. Projects like those at the Carnegie Library of Pittsburgh and others (Hubbard *et al.*) have clearly demonstrated that this type of online community information resource is in great demand, and they are teaching us how to step into that void and fill the need. In the present collection, the GMU library seems to come the closest to what the Benton report calls collaboration of service agencies, while the Shanghai consolidation of the library and ISTIS is an extreme example of merging two large formal organizations.

But collecting community information for wider dissemination is not the only goal of collaboration by any means; and other public service agencies are not the only potential partners possessing information and knowledge that would be valuable to our users, whether we be public, academic, or special libraries. Out there in our communities are also professional associations, research centers, hospitals, ethnic groups, and even corporations that gather information that would be of great value to sectors of our immediate user group and to potential distant user groups as well, if the information were better known and more accessible.

The purpose of partnering is not simply to make political allies, nor to obtain needed funding, nor to enlarge the user base, nor even to assure survival of the library as a social institution. Even though these are important objectives of collaboration, the real purpose should be, as Estabrook and the contributors to this volume attest, to "*build* on the historic strengths" of libraries that have already shaped "the traditional roles, *the public values*" (48; emphasis added). In other words, although the present study implies that library construction will not suddenly cease, a library does not need to construct a new facility to build itself into a new future. Each library must study its mission, analyze its existing and potential audiences, and then decide how best to "build" itself for the future, just as the libraries in this book decided how best to design and build their new physical facilities.

If anything, libraries are poised to become more important in society, not less. And that does not mean to become electronic and wall-less, nor does it mean simply to accommodate new technologies and absorb them into our standard procedures. It means to create a new entity, as did the BNF and some of the other libraries in the foregoing chapters. It means becoming a more active supplier of knowledge and information regardless of where those commodities originate.

Digitization

Making libraries more important in society undoubtedly also means getting higher up on what Kessler and the French call the publication chain that proceeds "from author to reader by way of editors, publishers, printers, distributors, and all the others who may be involved — in which the ends are satisfied simply by getting the information to the user" (see chapter 12). Librarians routinely uncover huge caches of information and knowledge in the possession of community groups and agencies, archives, local history centers, and many others. This information could be of great value to the right users, but it

> never reaches commercial publication because the audiences are too few or too widely dispersed for the information to be marketable through conventional publication. Using Internet and World Wide Web (WWW) technology, however, libraries can gather this information and make it available worldwide through local online databases created by the libraries themselves [Webb and Zhang, 146].

Publishing is the process that brings new knowledge and information from the writer/researcher to the appropriate audience. Conventional publishers are only middlemen between the knowledge/information producers and those who make use of those commodities, and libraries are even lower on the chain. But the Internet and WWW are reinventing the publishing industry, or at least providing an alternate and very accessible publication mechanism by making local online information resources very easy to create and manage. It is a unique opportunity for libraries to become primary links in the information delivery chain, in a way that was never possible in the dependent relationship we customarily have had with the publishing industry.

Information delivery by libraries will require strong partnerships between libraries and with other important information providers. The quality of the new information products will be assured by judicious partnering with outside subject experts and specialists, and the information will be distributed through the close cooperation between libraries and their partners' affiliates.

Information is the new raw material, the new wealth of nations, as Singapore's

Library 2000 put it (iii). Education and information delivery are no longer public services; they have taken on the proportions of an industry, and that's what is throwing librarians off-balance. But although we are unaccustomed to an industrial pace, we are still at the center of information and education. No one is actively trying to subvert or dethrone us, although our user groups are attractive markets to for-profit information providers, and the new industry trends could easily by-pass and outdistance libraries. But with a concerted effort, we can help assemble the information delivery mosaic of the next decade and century, influence its structure, and even be a major provider of original information resources, society's new precious raw materials. Quoting Andrew Carnegie, Librarian of Congress James Billington says, "Unlike private commercial data banks, libraries are uniquely capable, as Carnegie pointed out, of opening the 'chief treasures of the world' to all who are literate, regardless of income" (709).

As Neal implied, libraries literally sit on mountains of information in the form of our collections and our familiarity with the sources of hidden or little-known information and knowledge; we must mine them and make them negotiable; our task is to turn them into liquid assets. According to Billington, "We must move from being a passive storehouse of information to an active disseminator of it" (quoted in Lamolinara, 31). Here Billington was speaking specifically of the Library of Congress, but he might just as well have been speaking of libraries in general. Libraries have no competition for what they can provide. They simply have to step into the void and fill the need.

The tools to do so are at hand in the form of the new publishing technologies — the Internet, the World Wide Web, and the others on the horizon. And in some quarters, there seems to be the will to step into the new role and energize the stored collections, tap the unpublished resources, and informatize them. Paris, Beijing, Shanghai, and others in this collection of case studies are positioning themselves to go beyond a sense of place and actually broadcast culture. Who better to assume that enormous role than libraries? If only they will.

The closest partnerships of the future will probably be between libraries themselves in the form of cooperative electronic collection development and resource sharing. In his discussion of the need to control spiraling print collections, Geoffrey Freeman stated in chapter 10 that "as institutions increasingly develop specialties and share resources, the issue of identifying and assessing core collections becomes even more critical." And as libraries begin to convert portions of their collections or electronically publish new information on their own, resource sharing will become even more important to assure minimum duplication in the digitization process. Paul Zarins states that it would be wise for libraries "to maintain the local expertise and resources for particular areas of emphasis" (91), and he stresses the increasing importance of sophisticated networking in this intensified brand of library cooperation. Ann Kenney states,

> Greater collaboration between libraries is inevitable. A lot of libraries are
> hoping that if they develop digital libraries, they won't have to build new
> buildings. But I don't think that's where the payoff is going to come. It's

going to come from resource sharing, which will not only increase access
to information but eliminate much of the redundancy of collections
[quoted in Chepesiuk, "Future," 48].

In addition to cooperative resource sharing, collaborative conversion or electronic publishing projects involving libraries with similar subject interests and
collection strengths are likely to be a growing part of future library partnerships,
and will involve a great deal of international library cooperation as well.

Funds and Economies

Funding new libraries — a major anxiety for library administrators even in
Andrew Carnegie's day — is likely to become even more disturbing in the 21st century. It is very clear that costs will escalate as technology evolves, as for-profit
information providers enhance their services and products, and as user needs and
expectations rise accordingly. In the 21st century, fundraising may be the fastest
growing specialty in librarianship, and development officers may even be more
sought-after than systems librarians and server administrators.

Price tags for the new buildings described in this collection had a wide range,
but different chapters have described various ways to raise the money. Of course,
wealthy benefactors, such as the PKU Library's Hong Kong tycoon and IUPUI's
Lilly Endowment, are the most desirable sources, but they are also hard targets
to hit. Usually donors like this are already inclined or beholden toward certain
institutions, so it is worth a fundraiser's time to scour patron files, donor records,
and, for academic libraries, rolls of graduates or possible recipients of honorary
degrees and other recognitions for potential benefactors. The successful fundraising campaigns at Seton Hall and IUPUI demonstrate that high-profile building
projects can attract substantial support from business and industry. And Anita
Taler's description of the Walsh Library's case statement, which is a fundamental development tool, is good instruction for any library.

Public libraries have their bond elections, but as this study shows, they are
no sure thing, and even if voters approve the bonds, the money raised still can
fall short. San Antonio's Central Library Enrichment Campaign was a well-
orchestrated response to such a situation, and the Phoenix Public Library strategy of designing economies into its new building is another. Furthermore, the
Phoenix plan for future expansion of the new library on all floors is a model for
long-range economy that all libraries should consider.

For some libraries, federal construction funds of one type or another may
or may not be available in the next century, but the intense competition and the
exacting federal proposal guidelines can wither even seasoned grant writers. And
although partnering with other agencies and private firms has been discussed
only as a means to raise equipment and operational funds for specific library
projects, it may also hold some promise for construction funding as well.

The Walsh Library chapter demonstrates the potential of the design/build method for achieving economy in new library construction projects. And the CSUMB library suggests that in appropriate instances, facility renovation, even of non-library buildings, is at least worth considering as a means to stretch the available funding.

Flexibility

The chapters in this study reveal that a lot of cross-pollination and idea-grafting has occurred among the libraries. Yet each library is unique, different in some way from the others. And taken together, they are as different from the libraries of the mid–20th century as those facilities were from the Carnegie libraries. This implies that there will be *no such thing* as the 21st-century library. Libraries of the next century will evolve through successive versions, just as those of this century have. And even then, each will be as distinct as libraries are now; homogeneity will exist only on a level above the particular, the level of mission; there will still be no formula for positioning and symbolizing a commodity as precious and fertile as knowledge, unless people cease to revere it.

That means that libraries will need to be flexible and that they must learn from each other, as the chapters in this study have shown. Perhaps the GMU library is the ultimate example of flexibility. Its new Johnson Center Library has flexed itself into a new social milieu, a new popular culture, its mission and myths still intact like the sails of a clipper ship emerging from a gale. In contrast, the KCC library was constrained by the pre-determined footprint of the building, but worked with the flexibilities within that circumscribed interior space as much as possible to achieve its objectives. The chapter on the new CSUMB library shows that information technology can supply a kind of virtual flexibility even when architecture cannot. And the IUPUI chapter suggests that a physical library and a digital library provide complementary flexibility to each other. Together, the chapters in this study show that libraries will continue to have walls, but will use digital technology to reach beyond them. It is the information within libraries that is, always has been, and always will be without walls, virtual.

Predictive Space

It will no doubt still be necessary for libraries of the 21st century to reconfirm regularly their mission and essential components because they will be called upon to be even more flexible in their space utilization, technology integration, management style, and responsiveness to user needs. For the future of libraries is not without challenge and uncertainty, like any form of evolution. The Benton study reported that "ambivalence is just below the surface" of the public's positive view of libraries (*Buildings*, 31).

According to the Benton report, the 18- to 26-year-old respondents are the least convinced of the need for new library buildings; and those who have home computers are not so sure, either. We may lose our place in society if we allow our users to get away from us. Some respondents in the Benton study even believed the library of the future will be like a museum.

This is hardly a cheery thought. But on further consideration, it reveals why information and knowledge are so important, and why their presence in library collections has made libraries objects of public esteem and even reverence. Like museums, libraries appear to form a chain of human understanding and knowledge from past precedents to present conditions. But libraries also offer real insight into the future, at least to the extent that the knowledge obtained from the library's resources can help solve problems, avoid misfortune, and improve personal or even global circumstances. On the other hand, most people see museums as repositories of curiosities, historical artifacts, or aesthetic objects. Museums provide understanding of historical precedents, but offer little insight into applying that understanding to personal betterment.

The significance of this subtle difference is profound. It means that the uncertainty as well as the promise of the future of libraries lies in whether or not the library can continue to give its users a vision of the future. The future can only be glimpsed, and only by looking at the most current information, which must be further informed by interpretive ability: probability factors, the educated speculation, and the expert opinion. This interpretive ability, in turn, requires access to, and a vast familiarity with, past events and their causes and consequences.

Libraries can fulfill this past-to-present-to-future passage by performing the same functions they always have, only intensifying them. We still cannot predict the future, but we are closer now than ever before to doing just that. At least we have amassed enough knowledge to greatly increase our ability to predict the probable outcome of certain societal events and personal actions. As Jean Favier said, "Do you know of any period in the past like ours, in which, if you wish to read a great work of world literature, you can find it, at a good price, in a good translation, at your neighborhood bookstore?" or for that matter at the local library? (quoted in Muratori-Philip, 11; trans. TDW).

And though it may be a popular myth, the common belief is that the more knowledge and information society possesses, the more certain our answers to problems will become. Society still needs and looks for its oracles, predictive spaces where answers to pressing questions can be obtained. But instead of oracles, modern society has learned to depend on human learning, experts, education, and a good dose of rationalism. Much of the learning has been gathered in the physical space of libraries. Now we can also find our answers in virtual space. But both are rational, predictive spaces, and libraries will continue to develop combinations of physical and virtual environments, and into them put books and Webpages, online resources and buildings. This is the cognitive, and I will add, rational and predictive space Barlow urged librarians to create (see Chepesiuk, "Librarians," 51).

Mission and Myth

Civilization's respect for knowledge and information is not directed toward the origins or any mystic qualities of those commodities, but toward their extreme practical value when applied to solving problems, or for self-betterment. Libraries and librarians have been the beneficiaries of that same respect because their mission is to accumulate knowledge and deliver information. And libraries have performed their mission so well that the public's high expectations for them have assumed the proportions of popular myth. This has brought libraries reverence, and placed them in a social position as close to that of an oracle as a modern institution can be. But the library's mission and the public's mythic expectations are closely and delicately connected. They are fuel for each other. Losing sight of either the mission or the expectations, allowing either to diminish, will seriously disrupt the library as a social institution.

In their public opinion survey, George D'Elia and Eleanor Jo Rodgers found that the public believed the educational role of the public library to be its most "important" service, and held its role as a provider of popular reading comparatively low (27). Yet D'Elia and Rodgers admitted that this finding was not supported by the high usage statistics consistently recorded for popular, non-educational reading materials in most public libraries. D'Elia and Rodgers accounted for the discrepancy between the findings of their survey and the popular usage statistics by stating that demand for library services

> is manifested both in terms of what is most used and in terms of what is most important. The use/importance dichotomy is not necessarily contradictory. It would appear to be good management practice to attend to both of these manifestations of user demand [27].

The "importance" measure represents no less than the public's fondest expectations and even the myths of libraries, and it is what symbolic librarianship is all about.

The chapters in this book show that, overall, library missions, symbols, and myths will remain consistent in content, but will gather more strength and credibility through the exploitation of new technologies. Despite any trend toward zero-growth among an increasing number of libraries, large comprehensive libraries will continue to build large book collections, much as they do now, as long as publishers continue to produce books. Smaller libraries may be more adept at providing information than knowledge; they will see a larger degree of change by adopting new technologies to make up for their smallness, and because they are by their nature more able to adapt more quickly. Or in Freeman's terms from chapter 10, "Smaller institutions are less burdened by materials and are more free to concentrate on accessing and dispersing information than on acquiring it."

The BNF provides a clear example of symbolic librarianship and the very important expectations and myths that attach themselves to collections of knowledge and information materials. And the BNF decision to extend its services by initiating public access and by the digitization project demonstrates a new recognition and acceptance of the connection between a library's mission and the growing expectations of the general public.

The BNF and the other libraries in this study, taken together with their special circumstances and adaptations of library strengths and values, provide a future glimpse, a prediction, of a new type of library. The fact that Daniel Renoult does not talk much about the technology at the BNF speaks very loudly nevertheless. Technology will not be the force for major change some have thought it would be. Instead, the major force for change will be the library-user connections on the practical as well as the symbolic levels; the technology will simply be the vehicle for change. Kessler calls the new BNF a civic monument as well as an information system. The same might be said of every 21st-century library. As technology appears to diminish the need for a locus of knowledge, the need for a monument to knowledge becomes even more intense.

Of course, every library is not the BNF or the Library of Congress. But all libraries share the halo effect of the good that libraries do for society. Those public attitudes have achieved mythic stature, and they must be adapted to a new abundance of information, accessible through electronic channels that libraries so far do not control as well as they do print resources. And as society's attitudes adapt to the new information and knowledge resources, librarians must adapt as well, and learn to control the new resources and technologies as precisely as they now control print resources, and then take them into their libraries. These adaptations will be continuous, and will be reflected in new library facilities of the next century.

Will there be all-digital libraries in the 21st century? No doubt they will certainly proliferate. But they will not eliminate physical libraries. Will libraries become museums of old books? A few of them probably will suffer that fate. But the rest will take the knowledge and information of their collections and their expertise beyond their walls to provide a new type of service in support of their still vital missions.

Works Cited*

Adler, Jerry. "Where the Books Are: Both Britain and France Build Massive Monuments to Culture." *Newsweek* 130.2 (14 July 1997): 72–73.

Allen, Frank R., and Sarah Barbara Watstein. "The Value of Place." *C&RL News* 57.6 (June 1996): 372–373+.

"Beijing 1996: An Overview." *IFLA Journal* 22 (Nov. 1996): 303–310.

Billington, James H. "Library of Congress to Open Collections to Local Libraries in Electronic Access Plans." *American Libraries* 22.8 (Sept. 1991): 706–709.

Buckland, Michael. *Redesigning Libraries: A Manifesto*. Chicago: American Library Association, 1992.

Buildings, Books, and Bytes: Libraries and Communities in the Digital Age. A Report on the Public's Opinion of Library Leaders' Visions for the Future. Washington, D.C.: Benton Foundation, 1996.

Chang, Min-min, and Donald Wassink. "Electronic Versus Print Information: A Case Study at the Hong Kong University of Science and Technology Library." 62nd International Federation of Library Associations and Institutions General Conference. Beijing, 25–31 Aug. 1996.

Chepesiuk, Ron. "The Future Is Here: America's Libraries Go Digital." *American Libraries* 27.1 (Jan. 1997): 47–49.

_____. "Librarians as Cyberspace Guerrillas." *American Libraries* 27.8 (Sept. 1996): 49–51.

Commings, Karen. "Inside the University of Southern California's 'Cybrary.'" *Computers in Libraries* 14.10 (Nov./Dec. 1994): 18–19.

Crawford, Walt, and Michael Gorman. *Future Libraries: Dreams, Madness, and Reality*. Chicago: American Library Association, 1995.

Davis, Mary Ellen. "George Mason Creates New Center of Learning." *C&RL News* 57.5 (May 1996): 277–278.

D'Elia, George, and Eleanor Jo Rodgers. "Public Opinion About the Roles of the Public Library in the Community: The Results of a Recent Gallup Poll." *Public Libraries* 33.1 (Jan., Feb. 1994): 23–28.

Estabrook, Leigh S. "Polarized Perceptions." *Library Journal* 122.2 (1 Feb. 1997): 46–48.

"Fact Sheet: The Hong Kong University of Science and Technology." Brochure. October 1988.

"Global Entrepot Becomes a Higher-Education Boom Town." *Chronicle of Higher Education* 39.25 (24 Feb. 1993): C4–5+.

Gross, Robert A., and Christine L. Borgman. "The Incredible Vanishing Library." *American Libraries* 26.9 (Oct. 1995): 900–904.

Hafner, Katie. "Wiring the Ivory Tower." *Newsweek* 125.5 (30 Jan. 1995): 62–63+.

Hertling, James. "Jitters in Hong Kong: Despite Assurances, Universities Worry About Their Fate Under Chinese Rule." *Chronicle of Higher Education* 41.36 (19 May 1995): A42–43+.

Hubbard, Bette Ann, *et al.* "Newest Members of the Net Set: Pittsburgh's Carnegie Cashes in on Community Info." *Library Journal* 121.2 (1 Feb. 1996): 44–46.

Kaser, David. "Current Issues in Building Planning." *College and Research Libraries* 50.3 (May 1989): 297–304.

Several of the earlier chapters also include bibliographies and references.

Kessler, Jack. "The Bib[liothèque]. de France at Berkeley." 4 parts. 14 Apr.–7 May 1992: n.pag. Internet posting. *FYI France* <http://www.fyifrance.com>.

Koopman, Ann, and Sharon Hay. "Large-Scale Applications of a Web Browser." *C&RL News* 57.1 (Jan. 1996): 12–15.

Kubler, George. *The Shape of Time: Remarks on the History of Things.* New Haven: Yale UP, 1962.

Lamolinara, Guy. "Metamorphosis of a National Treasure: Technowizards at the Library of Congress Bring the Metalibrary One Click Closer." *American Libraries* 27.3 (Mar. 1996): 31–33.

Library 2000: Investing in a Learning Nation. Report of the Library 2000 Review Committee. Singapore: SNP, 1994.

McKinzie, Steve. "Finding Common Ground: Creating a Future Library." *C&RL News* 57.6 (June 1996): 365–367.

Marzynski, Marian. *Design Wars.* Videotape. Boston: WGBH Educational Foundation, 1989.

Michalak, Sarah. "Planning Academic Library Facilities: The Library Will Have Walls." *Journal of Library Administration* 20.2 (1994): 93–113.

Moinet, Jean-Philippe. "Bibliothèque 'Mitterrand': Les Écrivains Réagissent." *Le Figaro* 11 Dec. 1996: 11.

Morton, Roger. "Walsh Library: A Design/Build Success Story." *School and College* 34.2 (Feb. 1995): 25–27.

Muratori-Philip, Anne. "Jean Favier: l'Homme Maîtrise tous les progrès." *Le Figaro* 11 Dec. 1996: 11.

Museum Division, Arizona Department of Library, Archives, and Public Records. *Arizona Hall of Fame Museum.* Brochure.

Neal, James G. "Academic Libraries: 2000 and Beyond." *Library Journal* 121:12 (July 1996): 74–76.

Nelson, Milo. "The New British Library: Thirty-One Years in the Making." *Computers in Libraries* 13.9 (Oct. 1993): 11–12.

Nelson, Nancy Mellon. "Britain's New National Library." Editorial. *Computers in Libraries* 13.9 (Oct. 1993): 4.

Rouart, Jean-Marie. "Le Défi à l'Histoire et au Bon Sens." *Le Figaro* 11 Dec. 1996: 2.

St. Lifer, Evan, and Michael Rogers. "Benton Study: Libraries Need to Work on Message to Public." *Library Journal* 121.14 (1 Sept. 1996): 112.

_____. "Online Services Cutting Deals with Libraries for Local Content." *Library Journal* 121.15 (15 Sept. 1996): 12–13.

Salomon, Serge. "La Bibliothèque Nationale de France: Une Nouvelle Bibliothèque. Un Nouveau Système d'Information." 62nd International Federation of Library Associations and Institutions General Conference. Beijing, 25–31 Aug. 1996.

Webb, T.D. "After Document Delivery, What?" *Information Imagineering: Meeting at the Interface.* Ed. Milton Wolf, Pat Ensor, and Mary Augusta Thomas. Chicago: American Library Association, 1998.

_____. *Public Library Organization and Structure.* Jefferson, NC: McFarland, 1989.

_____, and Bin Zhang. "Information Dropshipping." *Library Hi Tech* Issue 57–58, 15:1–2 (1997): 145–149.

Wiley, Peter Booth. "Beyond the Blueprint." *Library Journal* 122.3 (15 Feb. 1997): 110–112.

Woodward, Jeannette A. "Auto Aces or Accident Victims: Librarians on the Info Superhighway." *American Libraries* 26.10 (Nov. 1995): 1016–1018.

Zarins, Paul. "International and Foreign Information Services in the Expanding Global Community." *Journal of Library Administration* 20.3/4 (1995): 81–96.

Index